The Bellstone

THE
BELLSTONE

The Greek Sponge Divers of the Aegean

One American's Journey Home

⚱

MICHAEL N. KALAFATAS

Brandeis University Press
Published by University Press of New England
Hanover and London

BRANDEIS UNIVERSITY PRESS

Published by University Press of New England, 37 Lafayette St., Lebanon, NH 03766

© 2003 by Brandeis University Press

Printed in the United States of America

5 4 3 2 1

Includes the epic poem "Winter Dream" by Metrophanes I. Kalafatas written in 1903 and published in Greek by Anchor Press, Boston, 1919. The poem appears in full both in its English rendering by the poet Olga Broumas, published here for the first time, and in the original Greek, in chapters 11 and 12.

"Harlem (2)" on page 161. Reprinted by permission of Harold Ober Associates Incorporated. From THE COLLECTED POEMS OF LANGSTON HUGHES by Langston Hughes, copyright © 1994 by The Estate of Langston Hughes. Used by permission of Alfred A. Knopf, a division of Random House, Inc.

Title page illustration: Courtesy Demetra Bowers, from a holograph copy of the poem by Metrophanes Kalafatas.

Library of Congress Cataloging-in-Publication Data

Kalafatas, Michael N.
  The bellstone : the Greek sponge divers of the Aegean / Michael N. Kalafatas.
    p. cm.
  Includes bibliographical references.
    ISBN 1–58465–272–1
    1. Sponge divers—Greece—Dodekanesos—History. 2. Sponge fisheries—Greece—Dodekanesos—History. 3. Sponge divers—Greece—Dodekanesos—Poetry. I. Title.
    HD8039.S55552 G763 2003
    331.7'6397—dc21   2002153371

For Joan,
for the children, and
for those so loved now gone

And don't forget
All through the night
The dead are also helping

—Yannis Ritsos, from
"18 Thin Little Songs of the Bitter Homeland"

The poem is like an old jewel buried in the sand. And now
the time has come for it to be an ornament in the spirits and
hearts of the people.

—Writer Irene Voyatzi-Charalambi
introducing "Winter Dream" at the Symi Arts Festival, 1996

Contents

Genealogy of the Kalafatas Family of Symi • xi

Chronology • xiii

Prologue • 1

1. Hit by the Machine • 9

2. Protest • 32

3. Penelope's Revenge • 53

4. The Poetics of Manhood • 69

5. Swallowing the Wind • 95

6. The Sponge Wars—Tarpon Springs, Florida • 121

7. Sea Fever • 162

8. Pearling in Australia • 195

9. *Mousmoulo* • 217

10. The Purloined Letter • 222

11. "Winter Dream" • 227

12. *Kheimerinos Oneiros* • 253

Epilogue: *Windflower* • 277

Bibliography. • 279

Acknowledgments • 283

Illustrations follow page 144.

Genealogy of the Kalafatas Family of Symi

Only names that appear in the book are included below, with the exception of several names added to help illustrate island naming tradition. A full listing of Kalafatas family names would be the size of the Rhodes-Symi telephone book.

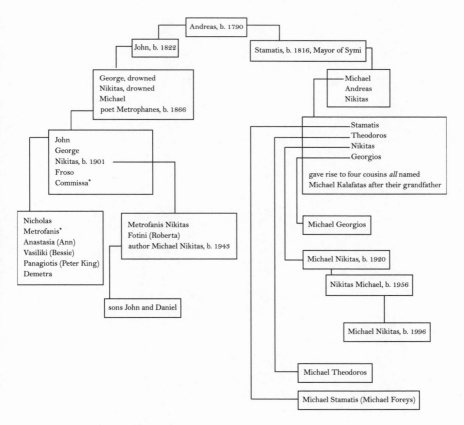

Andreas, b. 1790

John, b. 1822

Stamatis, b. 1816, Mayor of Symi

George, drowned
Nikitas, drowned
Michael
poet Metrophanes, b. 1866

Michael
Andreas
Nikitas

John
George
Nikitas, b. 1901
Froso
Commissa*

Stamatis
Theodoros
Nikitas
Georgios

gave rise to four cousins *all* named
Michael Kalafatas after their grandfather

Nicholas
Metrofanis*
Anastasia (Ann)
Vasiliki (Bessie)
Panagiotis (Peter King)
Demetra

Metrofanis Nikitas
Fotini (Roberta)
author Michael Nikitas, b. 1943

Michael Georgios

Michael Nikitas, b. 1920

Nikitas Michael, b. 1956

sons John and Daniel

Michael Nikitas, b. 1996

Michael Theodoros

Michael Stamatis (Michael Foreys)

*Died in childhood

Chronology

B.C.

1180   Traditional date for Fall of Troy (July 4).

480   Aeschylus wins Athens drama festival.

334–323   Conquests of Alexander the Great.

A.D.

95   St. John writes the book of the Apocalypse on Patmos.

410–1453   The Age of Byzantium.

1309   Crusader Knights of St. John take control of Rhodes.

1453   Fall of Constantinople to Ottoman Turks. Period of
              Tourkokratia begins when Greece was under the rule of the
              Ottoman Empire, 1453–1821.

1522   Suleiman the Magnificent defeats Crusader Knights of St.
              John on Rhodes. Dodecanese islands come under Ottoman
              rule.

1566   Suleiman dies, leaving Constantinople Europe's largest city.

1821–1829   Greek War of Independence. Dodecanese remain under
              Ottoman control.

1863   Deep-diving equipment introduced into the sponge fishing
              islands of the Aegean.

1876–1909   Reign of Sultan Abdul Hamid II, "Bloody Abdul."

1904   Poet Metrophanes I. Kalafatas dies.

1905   500 Greek spongers arrive at Tarpon Springs, Florida.

1912   Italians seize Dodecanese from Turkey.

1914–1918   World War I. In 1917 Greece joins Allies.

1919   Allies encourage Greeks to retake Smyrna. The war with
              Turkey that ensues is disastrous for the Greeks.

1940–1941   Italians and Germans invade Greece.

1944   Greek and British troops liberate Greece.

1947   Dodecanese "retroceded" to Greek administration.

1948   Dodecanese officially reunited with Greece.

1944–1949   Civil war in the north of Greece between Communist and U.S.-backed pro-government forces.

Late 1950s   Cultured pearl industry begins to be developed in Australia. Paspaley family, originally of Kastellorizo, will become the industry leaders.

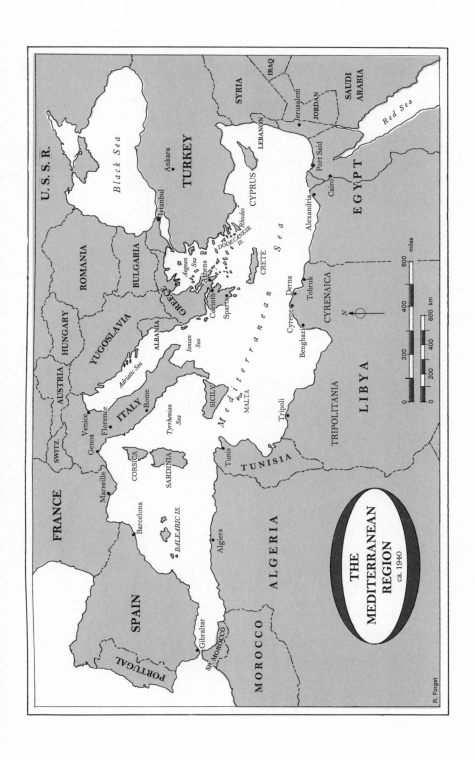

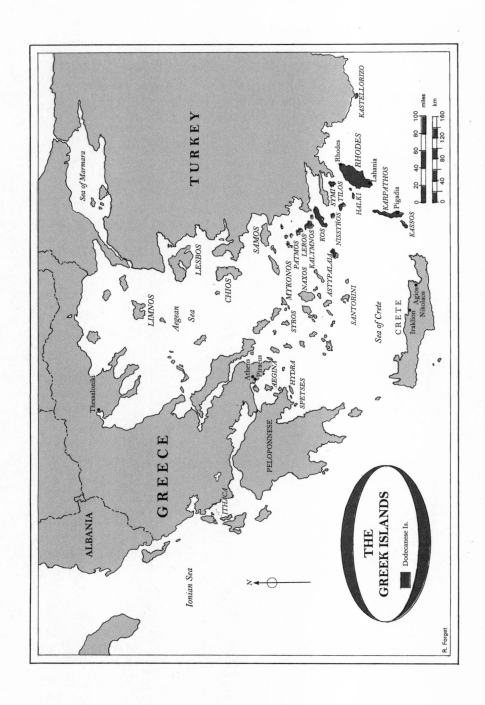

THE
GREEK ISLANDS

■ Dodecanese Is.

ALBANIA

GREECE

TURKEY

Sea of Marmara

Ionian Sea

ITHACA

PELOPONNESE

Thessaloniki

Athens
Piraeus
AEGINA
HYDRA
SPETSES

Aegean
Sea

LIMNOS

LESBOS

CHIOS

SAMOS

SYROS
MYKONOS
PATMOS
NAXOS
LEROS
KALIMNOS
ASTYPALAIA
KOS
NISSYROS
SANTORINI
SYMI
TILOS
HALKI

Rhodes
RHODES
Lahania

KARPATHOS
Pigadia

KASTELLORIZO

KASSOS

Sea of Crete

CRETE
Iraklion Agios
Nikolaos
Chania

N

miles
km
0 20 40 60 80 100
0 40 80 120 160

R. Forget

PROLOGUE

One time the people tried to break the gear
  before its strength gained on the land,
before its atrocities prevailed,
  its wings spread like today.

The crowd had gathered of one mind,
  men, women, children in agreement,
swarming the shore like angry bees,
  roads full of men and boys.
A roar was heard in the cafes,
  let's break the gear in storage!

They were unyielding, very wild,
  railing against the gear like rabid wolves.
And then the throng descended,
  and in five minutes
destroyed breathing tubes and suits.

—"Winter Dream"

DISCOVERY

"The ideal traveler is a passionate pilgrim," Paul Theroux has written. As was I in the eastern Aegean in the summer of 1997. A beautiful old poem, written by my grandfather almost a century earlier, had taken me on a remarkable personal odyssey from my home outside Boston to the Dodecanese islands of Greece.

My grandfather had been a school principal and poet on the island of Rhodes. In 1903 he wrote a long, stunning poem about the plight of the valiant young sponge divers of these islands. By marriageable age, one-third of the young men of these sponge-fishing islands lay dead or paralyzed for life from "the bends," or what physicians today call decompression disease. Alas, within four months of writing the poem, at age thirty-eight, the poet himself died, too young, on the operating table following surgery for mastoiditis.

Gradually, in a story utterly American, all his children emigrated to the United States, my father among them. They brought with them the poem as their sole possession. My father would speak of it lovingly as I, uninterested, would back-pedal out the kitchen door with my baseball glove in hand, headed for the outfield, so desirous of being an American.

In 1994, I took the poem to Olga Broumas, the poet-in-residence at Brandeis University where I work. Olga is a distinguished poet, with more than ten published volumes of poetry, and one of the major translators of Odysseus Elytis, the great Greek Nobel laureate poet. She was born in Greece on the island of Syros. Olga read my grandfather's poem and said to me, "You should know that this poem is deeply beautiful; in fact, it is national treasure of Greece."

Immediately I began to read all I could lay my hands on in English about the sponge-fishing islands of Greece. I took up the study of Greek, a subject I had fervently avoided as a child. I traveled to Tarpon Springs, Florida, where for a century there had been a flourishing sponge industry run by daring Greek divers from the Dodecanese. I conducted oral history interviews in Tarpon with sponge merchants and sponge divers. I made new friends over the Internet, like the anthropologist Russ Bernard at the University of Florida, who has written about the sponge-fishing islands of Greece and went to sea with the divers, and Tom Buttolph, a physician-diver-researcher at the Naval Medical Research labs in Bethesda, Maryland, who studies decompression disease for the Navy.

ODYSSEY

But, still, I wanted to follow the story back to the Dodecanese, back to a place where everyone knew my name. Using the magic of an old Dodecanese name, I wanted to ask, in Greek, what I desperately wanted to know: Why had so many divers died or been paralyzed long after knowledge of proper deep-diving technique had become widely available? I, whose emigrant father had led the Greek contingent in marches in behalf of Sacco and Vanzetti, wanted to know more about the protests, about the men and women portrayed in my grandfather's poem who had carried on a dramatic fight to ban the use of deep-diving equipment. And most of all, I wanted to know why my grandfather, who had taken up pen against the powers-that-be, uttered as his last words: "They have killed me."

And so, on the occasion of my thirtieth anniversary of employment at Brandeis, I was graciously granted a six-week sabbatical by the University to follow the story to the Aegean. Fortuitously, my wife, Joan Furber Kalafatas, was leaving one job and not due to start her new job for six weeks, so we were able to travel together.

Over the next six weeks—amazed—I watched people weep at my grandfather's words nearly a century after he wrote them. I met with old-time divers and with the widows and children of divers who had perished in the sea. I palpated nitrogen bubbles still lodged in a diver's leg twenty-five years after he had been "hit by the machine," as divers intriguingly call the bends, and saw the broad black streak across his chest from the negative tissue it created.

Everywhere people stopped what they were doing to listen to the sad, beautiful Greek cadences of the poem. Instantly, there was a party wherever I went and people eager to tell their own stories of what had happened to them or to their loved ones that one, unforgettable, horrifying day in the deep off the coast of Alexandria, Benghazi, Tripoli, Crete, Cyprus, or Corsica. Always the place names themselves dripped of poetry.

They loved the poem and they loved my odyssey, my return to these islands to follow the story of my grandfather's poem. In my spanking-new Greek I was interviewed on Patmos for the top morning television news show in Greece, with portions of the poem read by Christos Stergiou, a junior at Brandeis and my ever-patient Greek tutor. The journalist who interviewed me promised a related article, with photos, in the Sunday edition of *Eleftherotypia*, the largest circulation newspaper in Greece. Three historical journals in the islands asked if they could publish the poem with an essay from me about the poem. On Kalymnos a crew from Greek national television that was shooting a documentary on the history of the sponge-fishing industry eagerly took a copy of the poem.

Time and again, when checked, all references and allusions in the poem proved to be utter fact: the heroic characters, the violent protests, the imprisonment, twice, of the president of the senate of Symi, Stamatis Kalafatas, by Ottoman Turks who then controlled the islands. I was even given the seeds, which my grandfather describes, that were crushed and applied as liniment to horrible rashes that would break out when divers brushed against certain undersea growth.

Long ago, in a more innocent time, before the arrival of the deep-diving equipment, young men in pursuit of sponges would descend to the bottom of the sea on just a single breath of air, using as a weight and rudder a beautiful, flat, marble diving stone. On the island of Symi where my grandfather was born, it was called a "bellstone," after its shape. As I retell this story, my grandfather's poem is *my* bellstone, guiding me to some rapturous place beneath the sea, I know not where.

Eli Wiesel, quoting Gershom Scholem, says that there is magic in retelling stories. I do not fully understand why, but the magic of retelling this story has been passed to me. It is the story of a man I never knew, my grandfather, and a place I never lived in, the Dodecanese, but somehow his story and this story have become my story.

THE GOLDEN FLEECE OF THE SEA

The natural sponge, as we see it on store counters, is the cleaned
skeleton of an animal that grows in the sea, attached to the sea-bottom.
The skeleton is a network of fibers made up of *spongin*, a substance
similar to that found in our own hair and fingernails and the hoofs of
animals. A dark, slimy mass of cells envelops the sponge, which must
be thoroughly cleaned and washed until only "the golden fleece" remains.

Like black, curly haired heads, sponges were tossed up by the surf
onto the beaches of the Aegean and the Mediterranean. The ancient
Greeks, always curious, cleaned them and found them useful in everyday life. While the Egyptians and Phoenicians were actually the first
to discover and use sponges—their writings make reference to a
sponge industry—it was the Greeks who turned the fetching, cleaning, and trading of sponges into high art and a source of prosperity
in the Old World and the New.

"Sea and Greek interpenetrate," the Greek saying goes. From ancient times young men of the Dodecanese have penetrated the sea in
search of natural sponges—the golden fleece of the sea. The superior
skill gained by the ancient divers is the reason that diving was introduced into the Olympic games.

Because of the wide diversity of uses for the natural sponge, a far-
flung commerce in sponges sprang up in classical times and has continued into the present. Always it has involved the Dodecanese. Pliny
reported that the finest sponges could be fished from waters off the
island of Rhodes—the island where my grandfather wrote his poem.

ITS MANY USES

The sea sponge appears in our most beloved common texts: in the
Iliad, the *Odyssey,* and the Bible. Homer tells us that Hephaestus used
a sponge to wash off the smithy's grime. When Penelope's maidens
cleaned the dining table of her suitors, they used sea sponges. Ancient
scribes used sponges to erase ink if they erred while writing upon

papyrus. Greek warriors used sponges to clean their helmets and shields and to pad their armor; Roman soldiers carried them as soft, compressible drinking containers. In the Gospel according to St. John, Roman soldiers—as they mocked Jesus' thirst—pressed a vinegar-soaked sponge into his mouth as he hung from the cross at Golgotha. Sponges were used for bathing and medicinal purposes, and as paint brushes and mops. Mothers used small pieces of sponge soaked in honey to pacify their babies. Early Christians cleaned the dead with sponges; and in the Middle Ages the Roman Catholic Church used only "Liturgical Sponges" to wash the High Altar. Foreshadowing the catastrophe to come two thousand years later, Aristotle noted that sponges fished from the deeper fields were more luxurious than those taken from shallow waters.

Today, as always, natural sponges remain in high demand and short supply: demand exceeds supply eight to one. They have virtually disappeared from household use, replaced by cheaper synthetic sponges. But natural sponges are far more absorbent and hold up better under heavy wear than synthetic sponges; and so they are still in use in the paint, wall-covering, cosmetics, ceramics, shoe-finishing, printing, auto, and window-washing industries, and in medicine and the arts. Because they can withstand high heat—and will not burn—they are used to clean big guns on naval ships and to cushion instrument panels on rockets. A new boom has come with decorative wall painting; discount hardware stores stock natural sponges in vast supply for do-it-yourselfers.

THE POEM

"Winter Dream" is twenty-two pages long. It opens in 1902, with my grandfather sailing his swift *skaphos* back to his "homeland" Symi from Rhodes.

Prologue

I, the composer of this poem, Metrophanes I. Kalafatas, having arrived by sea to Lahanas of Rhodes, returning to my homeland

Symi in my small boat around the twentieth of April of the year 1902, found myself outside the cafe of Xenophon A. Lourtesi. Well-docked, and fatigued from seafaring, I sat for a small rest upon the stern. I also had in view my compatriots traversing the promontory on the shore.

Watching all this time, I saw many of them whisper, both on the street and in the cafe. These whispers communicated certain common concerns which, I surmised after listening, praised God. I approached some friends and, with great surprise, learned the reason for their praises. I heard that these whispers rose from certain news announcing the abolition of the deep sea diving gear—the helmet, body suit, and tank. And so my soul overflowed with joy, hearing this information from my friends.

And when, after precise inquiry and with a boiling wish to have the news confirmed, I was unable to discover its foundation and source, I felt an ineffable sorrow in my deepest innerfold and tasted indescribable bitterness; and I remained, all that day as well as the next, sorrowful, grim and thoughtful.

Suffering this position and troubled by thoughts until nightfall, I plunged into sleep wherein a woman appeared to me in dream who clarified all I desired so passionately to know.

> *Disturbed, weeping and whispering,*
> *she starts to speak:*
> *I'm neither lost nor passing by,*
> *I am your mother Symi.*
> *I know your joy in serving your land,*
> *how you detest connivance.*
> *I see you praise me in your poems,*
> *call me the Muses' mother,*
> *so I appear with a message*
> *by which your questions will be solved.*
> *My message concerns serving your land,*
> *the common life of divers.*
> *Be careful, listen well*
> *to what I say and make it known.*
> *The diving gear is old and soon will cease,*
> *the divers will again be strong,*

the time has come, the end is near,
the diving stone will rule once more.
The diving gear has weakened,
the naked dive will bloom again,
our forefathers' art will flower.
Long live the first technique!

—"Winter Dream"

STYLE

Written in fifteen-meter rhymed verse, the poem is in the tradition of "political verse" in Greek folk poetry; and, like a folk dance, it periodically circles back on itself. It includes clever rhyming in Greek, much word play, and beautiful passages, such as this elegant elegy to Michael Petrides:

The hungry he did not ignore
nor did he miss the thirsty—
in short, to any need he came across
he never answered "no."
He dressed the nude, consoled the ill,
gathered and almed the stranger,
he helped to wed the young and poor,
the girls orphaned of fathers,
was firm in friendship to all good,
and fiercely loathed the stingy.
He lent himself to God each day and then,
his soul was the Creator's.

—"Winter Dream"

one

HIT BY THE MACHINE

THE FIRST TECHNIQUE—NAKED DIVING

Until the 1860s, Greek sponge divers used the ancient and proud technique—what my grandfather called "the first technique"—of "naked diving." Today we know it as *breath-hold diving* and primarily the province of underwater daredevils who, as sport, compete to see who can go the deepest on just a single breath of air and survive the terrifying ascent back to air. In the Mediterranean alone, more than fifty "free divers" die each year of misjudgment when they fail to reach the surface in time. But for the Greek sponge divers, for millennia, naked diving was a means to a living. Wearing only a net bag slung round his waist and holding a flat marble stone fifteen kilograms in weight, a Greek diver would shoot down an inclined plane jutting from the side of the boat into the water and plummet to a depth of up to seventy meters, using the stone as a rudder to steer his descent. Called a bellstone on the island of Symi and a trigger stone on the island of Kalymnos because of its function—it triggered the dive—the diving stone was a prized possession handed down from father to son. The stone had a hole in one rounded end where a line was attached to the boat. On the bottom, if successful, a naked diver could gather one or two sponges in his net bag before tugging on the line, signaling he had to be pulled back to air. "Like a sea bird"—in my grandfather's words—he would plunge and rise up, again and again, through a twelve-hour work day, taking neither food nor water, apart from a bit of bread and coffee at daybreak.

A skilled *gymnos*, a naked diver, could hold his breath for three minutes or more on a dive and spend up to a minute-and-a-half in actual working time on the bottom. At the maritime museum of Kalymnos, I was shown a newspaper article on the legendary feat of Stathis Hatzis, a diver from Symi, who, in 1913 rescued the lost anchor of the *Regina Margherita*, an Italian ship on its maiden voyage. The captain was determined to recover the anchor, since a lost anchor on a maiden voyage was believed to be a terrible omen. On his third try, Hatzis dove to eighty-eight meters' depth on a single breath of air and tied a rope around the anchor. Italian records show the dive at three minutes and thirty-five seconds. Afterward, an Italian physician examined the diver and described his chest, when inflated, as looking like a "timpani."

Given their primitive, if heroic, technique, the naked divers could never become highly productive. Few sponge-fishing families amassed great wealth. But with the price of natural sponge always high, a steady income was possible, and the sponge-fishing islands prospered moderately into the early nineteenth century. While there was the constant danger of ruptured ear drums, drowning, and shark attacks, naked diving was not a highly lethal trade. High fatality rates would come only with deep-diving equipment and breathing of compressed air at depth.

Not surprisingly, the simple life of the naked divers is reflected in the language that they used to describe themselves. When the naked divers went to sea—captain and divers alike—they referred to themselves as *syndrophi*, a word similar in meaning to comrades. But in Greek *syndrophi* has an almost holy connotation; it means "those who eat together"—literally, "those who suckle at the same breast." Today, *syndrophi* is the term Greek socialists use to describe themselves. At the end of each sponge-fishing season—which lasted from April until October and took naked divers under sail as far as North Africa—the *syndrophi* divided their catch into equal shares regardless of who had taken more sponge. In the late nineteenth century, the language and the life of the sponge divers were to change dramatically. They would be comrades no more.

Psarofagomenos

Poseidon has struck
their well-rigged ship on the open sea with gale winds
and crushing walls of waves, and only a few escape, swimming,
struggling out of the frothing surf to reach shore,
their bodies crusted with salt but buoyed with joy
as they plant their feet on solid ground again,
spared a deadly fate.

—Homer, *Odyssey* (trans. by Robert Fagles)

The Greeks have always loved canny leaders—like Odysseus—whom the gods both challenge and watch over.

Antonios Angelides, eighty-six, of Symi, still has the charm and charisma of an island leader. Years ago, he was on a ship that went down in a storm off the coast of the island of Kos, at a site feared by Greek mariners from antiquity, where three seas converge. Forty drowned, including captain and crew, and only two survived. Angelides was one of them. He jumped free of the ship and swam through "the frothing surf" as the ship swirled and vanished into a vortex. He swam on for hours—surviving fifty-foot waves—until rescued.

Angelides is a scion of a first family of Symi and a third-generation sponge merchant. For nine years he was the mayor of Symi. The one great road that arcs the island the people of Symi owe to Angelides. He charmed the government in Athens into building it, and he was right: Today, the Greek army uses the road to move men swiftly around the island outpost of Symi, just four miles from the Turkish coast.

On the morning I left the island, I happened to follow behind as Angelides—smiling broadly under a great straw sun hat—strode the promontory of the shore. The harbor was lined with gaily colored *kaikia* that bobbed and glinted in the Aegean sun. Angelides—the old charisma still with him—tossed greetings, like bouquets, to men who fussed with their boats or sipped their sweet, thick Greek coffee at outdoor cafes.

It was Angelides who told me the story of a man nicknamed Psarofagomenos; it is a true story of man and the sea. Angelides had bought Psarofagomenos coffee many times in the *kafenia* of Symi and knew the old man's story to be true. In his youth the man had been a *gymnos,* a naked diver. One day, with his diving stone grasped firmly in his hands, the man dove into the sea, plummeted down, and straight into the mouth of a waiting shark. The shark bit—and bit again and again—but it could not eat the diver because the diving stone was jammed into the shark's mouth. The shark finally spit out both the man and the diving stone.

The diver lived to tell the tale many times over in the *kafenia* of Symi—his partly crushed skull and the shark's teeth-marks a stark reminder of the danger that lies beneath the sea. Ever after, the man was called only by his nickname, Psarofagomenos: He who was eaten by a fish.

SATAN'S MACHINE

The murderous gear wounds my liver.
I hate it, the disgusting thing,
*   as much as the devil's legions,*
*   as much as the head of Gorgon and Medusa,*
*   the venomous viper's hiss.*

—"Winter Dream"

In 1863 the Industrial Revolution arrived in the Dodecanese islands and brought with it swift and huge prosperity won at a terrible price. The deep-sea diving suit was introduced into the sponge-fishing industry, and first on the island of Symi, the island where my grandfather was born and raised and the island he considered his *patrida,* his homeland. Ironically, "Satan's Machine," as the divers swiftly came to call it, was introduced at a place of incomparable beauty. *Traveler Magazine* calls Symi harbor "The most beautiful harbor in all of Greece."

Augustus Siebe had invented the first practical underwater diving suit in England in 1819. Siebe revolutionized underwater diving by making use of a hard-hat helmet attached to a sealed diving suit, into which compressed air was fed from above by means of a hose. The system allowed the diver to see, to remain underwater—it seemed— indefinitely, and to descend to previously unobtainable depths. By 1835 the new diving suit was in use throughout the world, primarily in salvage work. Rapidly, it came into use in canal construction and bridge building as well.

His employer gave Fotis Mastoridis, a Symiot who had worked for a British company in the East Indies clearing shipwrecks, a complete diving suit and a hand-cranked air compressor as a gift when he left. He realized the diving suit's immense potential for boosting sponge-fishing production and proposed its use upon his return to Symi in 1863. Reportedly, the naked divers balked, out of fear, at using the new diving suit, and so Mastoridis dressed his wife, Eugenia—three months pregnant—in the suit and lowered her into Symi harbor. Mastoridis, so the story goes, was trying to shame the men into using the suit, pointing out that the suit was already being used by the women pearl divers of Japan and the Philippines. The naked divers called the new diving suit a *skafandro*, "a man who is a boat." The grandson of Mastoridis told me that the naked divers never really feared using the suit; they resisted only because they did not want to give up their proud, beautiful, and ancient craft of naked diving.

When the suit was introduced into the sponge industry, it increased the diver's productivity by a hundredfold. Soon many suits were on order for use on Symi, Kalymnos, and throughout the sponge fishing islands of the Aegean. The French and British were the early suppliers.

When I first heard of "Winter Dream" and the "catastrophe," it was from my father, who told me, "They were using old, patched French diving suits." My cousin, Michael Nikitas Kalafatas of Rhodes, sold diving suits on Symi years ago. Proudly, however, he recalled how— with high enthusiasm—he would open each new shipment of Gorman diving suits: "British-made and the best in the world, four to a wooden crate."

It was Symiot ingenuity that adapted the hand-driven air compressor to make it possible for Aegean divers to dive far deeper than the manufacturer had ever intended. The Symiots were after the "luxurious" sponges Aristotle described, which were to be found in deeper fields. In the last decades of the nineteenth century, the number of boats using the deep-sea diving suit soared as the number with naked divers plummeted.

The naked divers could not compete except in fishing for sponges on uneven bottoms, among crevices, overhanging ledges, or among sharp rocks that made "machine-diving" dangerous because of the likelihood of damage to the diving suit or the air hose. Many of the finest cave sponges of the Aegean continued to be gathered by naked divers.

PHYSIOLOGY OF THE BENDS

The new diving suit brought not only a dramatic change in productivity but also a fundamental change in the physiology of diving. The naked diver took one, long, all-engulfing breath of sea air *at one atmosphere* before he plunged to the bottom. Using the Siebe-designed suit, the diver was now breathing *compressed* air, in effect multiples of air, at depth. Since normal air is 78 percent nitrogen, a diver in compressed air—as Jacques Costeau pointed out—is also breathing *multiples of nitrogen*, an inert gas that does not entirely pass away in a diver's exhalations. At one atmosphere, at sea level, the nitrogen is inhaled and exhaled with no effect on the body; but in multiples, at more than one atmosphere of pressure, it goes into supersaturated solution in the blood and soft tissue of the body. When the diver rises abruptly into lesser pressure, the nitrogen quickly escapes the blood in bubbles—it "boils" or froths—similar to what happens when a bottle of warm beer is opened too quickly. In mild cases the froth gives the diver pains in the joints, but in severe cases the nitrogen bubbles can clog veins, cause nerve damage, cut off the spinal ganglia, or cause instant death by heart embolism. If a diver stays at depth too long, or ascends from depth too rapidly—or even if the interval between his dives is too brief—he risks death or paralysis from "the bends."

The first notable medical observation of the bends or "caisson disease," as it also came to be known, was made in 1870s on the sandhogs who worked in dry pressurized chambers or "caissons" to dig the pier excavations for the Brooklyn Bridge. In French *caisson* means "big box," and the big box in which the sandhogs worked was filled with compressed air. The workers often came up in tortured bodily positions that reminded their fellow workers of a feminine posture fad of the time called "the Grecian bend."

In David McCullough's book *The Great Bridge,* there is a harrowing chapter on what happened to the men stricken with this mysterious new disorder. An early victim was the chief engineer himself, Washington Roebling, who was obliged to supervise completion of the bridge from his sick room in Brooklyn Heights, overlooking the East River. For more than a decade his wife, Emily, delivered written instructions to the construction site from "The Man in the Window." Although Washington Roebling lived until 1926, he continued to suffer severely from the aftereffects of the bends, and he never set foot on the great bridge he built.

The savage pains of the bends, as McCullough points out, are caused by a stoppage of the oxygen supply in the bloodstream. Pressure, volume, and temperature trade off one against the other when it comes to gases. In the case of the deep-sea divers and the caisson workers, nitrogen gas sits dissolved harmlessly in the bloodstream at depth, to be expired safely through respiration on slow ascent. But if the ascent is too quick, the nitrogen in the bloodstream takes flight as bubbles on a brief, fantastic voyage until it lodges somewhere in the body—perhaps causing paralysis or death.

The nitrogen bubbles released by too-rapid decompression create actual mechanical blocks in the bloodstream that prevent oxygen in the red blood cells from reaching tissue. The denial of oxygen-bearing blood—called *ischemia*—is the same as what happens in a heart attack. So, as McCullough writes, "An attack of the bends might be likened to a heart attack in different parts of the body, most often the limbs and joints." The cause of caisson disease was first clinically described in August 1872 by a French physiologist, Paul Bert, who recommended that caisson workers *gradually* decompress and that divers return to the surface very slowly.

Today, the safe rate of decompression is known to be twenty

minutes for each atmosphere of pressure. In April 1872, at sixty-five feet of depth, New York caisson workers should have been spending twenty minutes in a lock, but instead they were spending two or three minutes. The speed of their exit was "disastrously swift," McCullough writes. Digging would continue down past seventy-eight feet, with Roebling stopping before reaching his goal of bedrock because the work would take another year and cost a hundred more lives to caisson disease.

As the new deep-diving suits came into wide use, casualties mounted on the sponge-fishing islands of the Dodecanese—Symi, Kalymnos, Halki, Astypalaia, Kastellorizo, and the others. Between 1866 and 1896, on the island of Kalymnos alone, three hundred young men died of the bends and six hundred more were paralyzed. Pulled to the surface, they would die there on the decks. William Travis, a British writer, describes the scene of a stricken diver: "Face blood-black, eyes shut up somewhere in swollen flesh, gasping for air, with crew men sitting on his wrists and ankles to keep them out straight and to keep them from closing up like a jackknife."

The Bends

Behold a pale horse,
and his name who sat on him was Death,
and Hell followed with him.

—Revelation 6:8

It was fitting that I heard the story of Drossos Saroukos en route to Patmos, the island of the Apocalypse. I met Drossos on the bridge of his rakish new boat, *The Kalymnos Express*. In two hours he would deliver us to Patmos, an island holy to all of Christianity. It was on Patmos that Saint John heard God's voice and dictated His words to a disciple. The words became *The Book of Revelation*—or *The Apocalypse*—the last, most disturbing book of the New Testament.

In 1974 Drossos, then twenty-three, was diving, using the *narghile* system,* in forty-five meters of water off the coast of Crete. After his first dive Drossos felt a prickly sensation, "as if bugs were crawling all over me." He went down for a second dive. His view of the sea now seemed eerie and warped. Atypical of Dodecanese divers, Drossos had been to diving school and understood the physics of diving. As a diver descends through bands of varying water temperature, the view can distort naturally, the water bending images like a fun-house mirror. But at twenty-three, Drossos was already an experienced diver, so he quickly realized what the skin sensation and the visual distortion, taken together, really meant: *He had been hit by the machine.* Hit by the bends. And so he surfaced.

Back on deck, waves of excruciating pain swept over his body, especially over his legs. His left leg, where the pain was most severe, went into a violent spasm. Within five minutes he lost all feeling in the leg, as it continued to spasm. Death might be minutes away, so he asked to be resubmerged under the sea, hoping to recompress the bubbling nitrogen wreaking havoc in his body. Perhaps, back under the sea and under pressure, the nitrogen would dissolve again into supersaturation in his bloodstream; and then his body might release the gas gradually and harmlessly through normal breathing.

---

*On the day Drossos was hit he was using the *narghile* system of diving, a variation on *skafandro* diving that affords a diver far more flexiblity of movement but still utilizes compressed air. Since he is breathing compressed air at depth, a *narghile* diver is equally subject to the bends.

The *narghile* system of diving is named after the traditional Turkish water pipe that was also smoked in the Dodecanese. In *narghile* diving the diver has greater maneuverability than with *skafandro* gear, except in swift currents. He is free of the heavy *skafandro* suit, which weighs 172 pounds including a 38-pound helmet. George Billiris, one of the leading sponge merchants of Tarpon Springs, arranged for me to try on the *skafandro* suit. I felt claustrophobic at sea level, so I cannot imagine what it is like to be enclosed in it 300 feet below. The *narghile* diver wears only a wet suit, lead belt, weights, fins, and a mask. Air is fed from above into the diver's mask through a thin, flexible hose. As Russ Bernard points out, the diver is able to move horizontally along the bottom, rather than on foot as do *skafandra* divers. But still, the diver breathes compressed air.

To recompress the gas bubbles, he knew he had to return to the depth at which he had been hit, forty-five meters. So he descended even deeper, to fifty-five meters. He stayed there for ten minutes and ascended *slowly* to forty-five meters. He then descended back down to fifty-five meters, stayed another ten minutes, and ascended slowly *again* to forty-five meters. He repeated the process two or three times. He then established a new base at forty-five meters, stayed ten minutes, and ascended slowly to thirty-five meters. Once there he descended back down to forty-five meters, stayed another ten minutes and ascended to thirty-five meters.

Dividing the sea into ten-meter bands above him, he would rest, rise, and descend several times in each band before allowing himself to move up to the next band. He was trying both to recompress the nitrogen and to give his body a chance to expel it naturally through normal breathing.

Slowly, over four hours, he made his way back to the surface; all the while alone, desperately ill, in terrible pain, and yet making fateful decisions. All the while, literally hanging between life and death—thinking of his twenty-three years, his young wife, and his four-year-old child. Throughout he had only the thinnest line of communication—a few simple messages sent by tugs on a rope—with the boat floating above on a sunbright sea.

By the time he surfaced it was seven o'clock in the evening. Like many divers, he believed that, once hit, what happened after sunset, when your metabolism settled down for the night, determined whether you lived or died: If you survived the night, you would survive. Waves of pain continued to sweep over him; nonetheless, he asked to be put ashore. All evening he walked—dragged himself—up and down the sharply steep paths of a Cretan town. At dusk the mountains of Crete are full of shadows, like Homer's "many-folded Mount Olympus." Until midnight Drossos walked the many-folded hills of the seaside town. When dawn broke over a rose-fingered sea, Drossos Saroukos, back aboard the *kaiki*, was alive. He *had* survived.

Drossos accepted, and still does, the divers' view that, if you are hit and do not dive again right away, you are finished as a diver. You will lose your nerve and reputation, and the money you receive as a diver is tied to your reputation. The next day, sick and in pain, Drossos dove twice, to twenty meters. The accident happened in September, at the end of the season. Over the remaining few weeks, he continued to dive but not to great depth.

After he told me his story, he rolled up his pant leg and showed me several large nitrogen bubbles still lodged in his leg twenty-three years after "the accident." I palpated the bubbles, but he has never shown them to a physician. "Better to leave well enough alone," he said. He then pulled up his shirt and showed me a broad black streak across his chest from the negative tissue created the day he was "hit by the machine" and lived to tell about it. He chuckled and pointed out that hair grows on the black streak though nowhere else on his chest.

Today, Drossos Saroukos and his beautiful wife, Deborah, run a thriving business ferrying passengers among the Dodecanese islands. To the British, Americans, and Australians, who have trouble pronouncing *Drossos*, he calls himself *Ross*—a Scottish name. Ross Saroukos is intelligent, handsome, engaging, and he still loves the sea. But now he is a captain and a businessman. With great pride, however, there on the bridge, he showed me his seaman papers, dating back to 1972, marked "*Ditis*," diver.

WHERE THEY DIVE

As anthropologist David Sutton has written, images of the past are always present in modern Greek life.

When Drossos Saroukos was "hit," he was diving off the south coast of Crete, not far from Frangokastello, a fourteenth-century Venetian castle of haunting legend. During the War of Independence in 1828, a small battalion of Greek soldiers was hopelessly outnumbered by Turkish forces who moved in and massacred them. Since then, in May and September, late at night when the sea is calm, a ghostly image of the gallant band of Greeks is said to appear, armed and mounted, hovering over the sea.

Visitors come to Frangokastello annually to camp and await *Fata Morgana*, the return of the restless souls. Drossos, the "returned" restless soul, was diving in September off the coast of Frangokastello, and the sea was calm.

THEIR LIFE AT SEA

We returned to our homes broken,
our limbs incapable, our mouths ruined
by the taste of rust and brine.

—George Seferis, "Mythical Story"

The caique in the distance could have been any sponge-diving boat out of Kalymnos. Its deck was heaped with gunnysacks of sponges, boxes of provisions, drums of diesel fuel; its shrouds were a ragtag of patched diving suits, drying laundry, faded bandannas: a typical Aegean working boat. Still. There was something familiar about the caique as it slowly chugged into the Bay of Lindos, guh-tonk, guh-tonk, a sound that is as much a part of Greek island life as the bray of donkeys. Sure enough, when I steered my skiff over for a closer look, the diving boat turned out to be the Pegasus, *out of Kalymnos and the captain my old friend George Lisgaris.*

—Willard Manus, "The Last of the Sponge Divers,"
Quest/80 Magazine

For six months at sea the life of the crew consisted of difficult work and long hours of boredom, as Bernard has pointed out, interrupted only by periodic disaster. The Greek *kaiki*—its design refined over millennia—was ideally suited to the rolling waters of the Aegean. In his film about the Aegean sponge fishers, *Aegean Divers: Matadors of the Deep*, Bernard—himself a trained seaman—reports that, while it might bob wildly, the Greek *kaiki* is virtually unsinkable. On this tiny, nine- or ten-meter craft, fifteen or twenty men worked, ate, and slept for six months; every space piled high with diving equipment—compressor, suits, helmets, and hoses.

For six months the men drank rusty water from storage barrels, ate a diet of mostly beans, and worked seven days a week. If lucky, they would put into port one day a month for fresh water, firm land under their feet, and a decent meal.

No longer was the diver the proud *gymnos,* 'a naked diver.' He was now called *mechanikos,* "a mechanic." The diver had become part of the machine. The heroic Greek diver, whose likeness appeared on archaic pottery, now breathed compressed air tasting of vaporized machine oil. He viewed the crystal-clear, aquamarine water through a haze of condensed oil that clouded the window of his helmet. And most telling of all, the diver called what happened to him when he suffered the bends "being hit by the machine."

NECROKAIKIA

From antiquity, light Symiot boats have been considered among the swiftest in the Mediterranean. When Jason and the Argonauts sailed to their adventures, they did so on the *Argo*—a ship built on Symi by Glaucus, famed in myth as a swimmer, shipbuilder, and sponge fisher. Although Symi is only twenty-six square miles, Homer reports that Symi sent three ships to the war against Troy—led by King Nereus, "second in handsomeness only to the great Achilles." The Ottoman Turks called Symi *Symbekir,* "the island of the lightning fast boats," and they placed Symi in charge of the postal service at sea for the entire Ottoman world. At its height the Ottoman Empire stretched from the Danube to the Nile, from Budapest to the Caspian Sea, and included most of the North African coast. Urgent diplomatic messages sent from the Sublime Porte to the far reaches of the Ottoman seas were carried on flying Symiot boats. Always, the most brilliant sailors in the Ottoman Empire were Greek.

By the late nineteenth century the well-crafted *kaikia* of the sponge fleet—many launched from the famed boatyards of Symi—had become *necrokaikia,* death boats. In "Winter Dream" the boats cry out at their humiliation. Heavy with ugly gear, rank with urine leaking from "hit" divers, and filled with the stench of liniment applied against rheumatic pain, the gaily-colored boats grieve at the misery on their decks. In verse and reply the divers imagine the boats' return to glory, if only rumor of the Sultan's ban proves true. The divers "sing" to console the *kaiki:*

If this is true, the gear will cease,
your nails turn gold and silver,
your sails to silk, your ropes to steel,
no engine nor its shame.
Flag on your mast, sign on your prow,
forget, my boat, your sorrow.
Joyful inscriptions will announce
"God give the Sultan years."
We'll write Aphrodite *at your eyes**
Seeing the words the gear will freak.

—"Winter Dream"

THE AGE OF EXCESS

The industrial revolution had created what seemed to be an ever-growing demand for soft and luxurious sponges for London, Paris, and Vienna, for Berlin, St. Petersburg, and New York. But by 1840 the sponge-fishing islands of the Aegean had fished out Greek and Turkish waters. Almost simultaneously, as Russ Bernard points out, the Dodecanese islanders of Symi and Kalymnos found vast new sponge beds off the coast of Derna, Libya. In the next several decades further searches led to the discovery of other rich new sponge beds off the coast of Benghazi and all the way west to Tunis. As Bernard notes, "There were markets for sponges and people with a long tradition of sponge fishing to supply those markets." The population of the sponge-fishing islands soared with new immigrants from other islands and from the Turkish mainland, where large Greek colonies existed until 1922. Between 1850 and 1912, the population of Kalymnos rose from 7,600 to over 23,000, and that of Symi from 8,000 to over 22,000. Sponge markets flourished, processing plants prolifer-

*Greek *kaikia* were sometimes painted with a pair of eyes—one either side of the prow, close to the water—so the vessel could "see" its way clear through the waves and frothing surf. Aphrodite, of course, was the Goddess of Love and Beauty, beguiling men and gods alike with her beauty and laughter. *Aphros* is "foam" in Greek and *ditis* is "diver"; hence, *Aphrodite*, "She who dives in the foam." Aphrodite was said to have sprung from the foam of the sea in a sea-birth. So it could be said that Aphrodite was the original naked diver.

ated, and foreign capital flowed in, encouraging merchandising and the opening of shops. Cargo transportation—always important to the Dodecanese islands of Kastellorizo, Symi, and Kassos—skyrocketed. In the summer Metrophanes himself transported goods in his swift *skaphos* between Symi and Rhodes. Each year 500 new boats were slid into the Aegean from the famed Symi boatyards to keep pace with demand. It was the Golden Age of sponge fishing.

By 1900 land values in Pothia, the port city of Kalymnos, rivaled those of the great cities of Western Europe. Between 1880 and 1890— normalized for size—Symi became the wealthiest port in all of the Mediterranean. In a single season, as William Travis points out in *Bus Stop Symi*, a merchant captain on Symi could earn an entire fortune. It was the era of the great Symiot houses—beautiful neoclassical homes built with designers from Venice, furnishings from Paris, and grand marble staircases cut from stone from distant Carrara. "Half the harbor space," Travis reports, "was reserved for caiques bringing goods from Turkish ports to satisfy the roistering all-consuming appetites of the populace." The well-traveled Symiots earned the nickname in the Dodecanese of "Sardine Juice" because they were always eating exotic foodstuffs. All along the waterfront sheep, pigs, and oxen were roasted whole—the meat free for all; many varieties of caviar were sold in stalls that lined the harbor.

"By the dozens musicians set up little three-piece bands that played under the great tamarisk tree," Travis writes. The sea seemed an inexhaustible gold mine, and the divers shared in the bounty. According to Russ Bernard, a diver could earn two and half times in six months what a man of similar education could earn in a year. With their newfound prosperity the divers forsook the old Ottoman attire: the soft, ample hat, sash, and wide baggy trousers that "wabbled" between their legs "like the stomach of a goose," as one writer described. Instead the divers wore European dress and sported gold watches with glinting fobs that dangled from velvet vests. They pulled down the brims of their hats at a rakish angle as they strutted along the promontory of the shore. They looked simply dashing. "They were treated like heroes, and they were heroes," as Kyriacos Hadzidakis reported. And they fully acted the part. Their wives also dressed in the latest Western finery—silks and satins—and slid their feet into golden plimsoles.

With their new airs, the divers expected their wives to be called *Madam*, as Metrophanes notes with disdain.

And all rested on a foundation of ever-increasing demand and increased sponge yield that came with the *skafandra*, with bigger boats and better pumps, and with the industrial organization that was now brought fully to bear on the sponge-fishing industry. Symiot and Kalymnian merchants had established an international network with representatives in London, Paris, Bordeaux, Trieste, St. Petersburg, New York, and other cities that organized the world market. Each spring in April and May, three hundred sponge boats set sail from Kalymnos alone for the six-month sponge-fishing season that took divers to sites all along the coast of North Africa, from Alexandria to Benghazi. The Symiot and Kalymnian fleets were joined at sea by large sponge-fishing fleets from Halki and Kastellorizo in the Dodecanese and from the other Aegean islands. The sponge divers dove at sites they called—and still do—by the ancient Greek names given these places two thousand years earlier in the great era of Hellenic colonization: Berenice for Benghazi, Appollonia for Marsa Susa, and Mandroucha for Paraetonium.

But with increased sponge yield came the destroying of the sponge beds as the harvesting exceeded the natural rate of regrowth. A vicious economic race had been set in motion, as Travis describes, "with the merchants demanding more sponges of the divers and the divers demanding more of themselves in order to keep pace with the growing needs of a plentiful age that supplied silks and satins, Italian marble and French furniture, family portraits and exotic foodstuffs." The known sponge beds thinned or were wiped out entirely. As Travis notes, "There was but one way, the way down. Down beyond the hundred-and-fifty-foot level, down past two hundred feet where even the Aegean daylight grows dim and faint, down to the darkness of forty fathoms that their new diving suits made possible for them. Down and down until they died. . . ."

> *Many die without justice*
> *and many walk the markets lame.*
> *Our merchants seeing them turn deaf,*
> *scramble to their cashiers*

to earn high yields on their returns.
They are the bitter enemies of their true duty.
*   With triple usury they loan,*
and seal their ears if people perish.
*   With all their powers they should try*
to cast off the gear's existence,
*   to see it as a guillotine*
and stone it down,
*   united with widows and orphans.*
But while others seek to throw it out,
*   our merchants try to shore it.*
Seeking to better their accounts
*   they shamelessly crowd graveyards.*

—"Winter Dream"

DEATH

But the diving suits were never designed for forty fathoms. They were designed for fifteen. And so, soon, a third of the young men, in the flower of youth, lay dead or paralyzed. The awful stories abound: Diving boats set sail from Kalymnos right after the joy of Greek Easter— on the morning after *Dipnos tis Agapis*, the Dinner of Love—with twenty divers on board and returned in the fall with ten. Or they left Kalymnos in the spring with ten divers and returned with *none*. Or a diving boat put in at Port Said sending back to Kalymnos, by swift *paketo*, a simple, stark message: *Send more divers!*

White Island

But many beautiful young men are lost,
*   hale and strong as lions.*
They end up beggars, impotent,
*   miserable, awful, they walk the streets.*

Happy the dead,
  who suffer no more trouble.
Happier even if buried on land,
  their funeral in order.
Many who die upon my deck
  are happy to rest in soil.
So many corpses piled with rocks,
  some thrown to sea unwilling.

—"Winter Dream"

Out in the harbor breaths of smoke
are rising from the water, sea-smoke
some call it or breath of souls

—Olga Broumas, "Mercy"

A necropolis is a city of the dead, but Aspronisi—White Island—was an island of the dead: an island entirely devoted to dead divers. The divers knew it as the likely, final, and unceremonious resting place for divers who died off the coast of Libya.

I first heard the story of White Island from Steve Katzaras, a sponge merchant from Tarpon Springs, eighty, who had been told the story decades earlier by an old man from Halki. As a young boy, the old man had watched a captain load a dead diver onto a small boat, row the body to a nearby rock island, and deposit it. The island was covered with the white bones of dead divers—a hundred skeletons fully in view. White island. White with the bones of dead divers. In 1997, sadly, I heard the story of White Island confirmed by divers throughout the Dodecanese.

The virtue of White Island was convenience. It was offshore and unmonitored—no authorities to reckon with, no reporting was necessary. A body could be dumped with a minimum of fuss. The island comprised only rocks, the white bones of dead divers, and beautiful white sea birds. With even less ceremony, dead divers were sometimes tossed to the sea in weighted burlap bags: "Arrivederci," in the sweet valediction of an old diver from Symi.

"I still get goose bumps when I think back, so many years, to the friends I left behind on White Island," Drossos Saroukos recalled. "Look!" And twenty-five years later, I could see the goose bumps running up and down his arms. He and other divers tried pressuring the captains, threatening not to dive unless the remains of dead divers were returned to their home island of Kalymnos for proper burial. "How long would it have taken?" he asked, pain upon his face. "A day or two?"

Why the cavalier treatment of the dead? And by the Greeks, of all people, who in ancient times believed that the souls of the unburied were doomed to wander in desolation forever, never to cross into the kingdom of the dead, never finding rest from their weariness. "To bury the dead was a most sacred duty," Edith Hamilton wrote, "not only to bury one's own but any stranger one might come upon." Even knowing the penalty was death, Antigone defies the State to bury her dead brother Polyneices. King Creon had ordered that no one was to touch Polyneices or say the least prayer for him: "He shall lie on the plain and the birds and the scavenging dogs can do with him whatever they like."

Today, the people of Kalymnos, "the island of the sponge fishermen," take pride that so many from the Kalymnian diaspora— from America, Australia, and elsewhere—return to the island to die or specify that their remains be returned for burial. The island of Symi, with a population of 2,500, has ninety places of worship, many built as *tamata*—acts of charity or remembrance, as for a loved one who has failed to return from the sea. In a country of little soil and little new cemetery space, the dead are still lovingly cared for. To make room for new interments, the bones of the dead are exhumed after five years, washed in wine, and kept in the church ossuary—a sacred vault for holding the bones of the dead. Relatives visit, light brightly polished silver and gold oil lamps, and pray before the boxed bones of the deceased. They pray for the soul's safe passage into paradise. The prayer is a flavoring in Orthodox Christianity of the concern for the dead that was so central in Antigone's world.

When my father returned to Greece in the 1970s, after a fifty-year absence, he found the bones of his father, Metrophanes, lovingly kept in a church ossuary, neatly bagged and tagged, seventy years after the poet's death.

"You knew my edict?" Creon asked.

"Yes," Antigone replied.

"And you transgressed the law?"

   "Your law, but not the law of Justice who dwells with the gods," Antigone said.

   "The unwritten laws of heaven are not of today nor yesterday, but from all time."

As she was led away, she spoke to the bystanders:

      . . . Behold me, what I suffer

      Because I have upheld that which is high.

But, because Time Is Money—a law of the industrial age—the bodies of divers were left behind for the birds to tear and devour, in defiance of the unwritten laws of heaven.

GLARONISI

I learned on Symi and Kalymnos of a second rock island where the bodies of dead divers were deposited near Iraklion, Crete. The island was called Glaronisi, "the island of the white seabirds." Here, I learned, the bodies of the divers were covered with stones and a wooden cross placed on each grave. I believe this second "necropolis" came into use later in the history of the *skafandra*, when the razor edge of cruelty had been slightly blunted. As I think of spare rock islands, bereft of anything living except seabirds, what comes to mind is a line from a Hebrew prayer, "Words sigh in the desolate air."

RETURN FROM HAROS'S GARDEN

My sister Roberta, Fotini, recalls that my father, Nikitas, had a vivid memory of being present, as a small child, when the bones of his father were exhumed. My grandmother lifted the skull of her beloved Metrophanes from the black earth and kissed the forehead. The anthropologist Loring Danforth, who studied death rituals in rural Greece, recorded this couplet, sung as a skull was being exhumed. It marks the departed's return from darkness to light, from Haros's garden back to the world.

> Now I have set out. Now I am about to depart,
> From the black and cobwebbed earth.

"This upward movement from dark to light," Danforth writes, "is believed to be sought by the dead themselves. Many women report dreams in which a deceased relative appears to them and asks them to perform an exhumation." One widow's husband, dead for four years, repeatedly asked in dream, "When will I be set free?" The Greek villagers called the ritual of exhumation *Xestavrono*, meaning literally to un-cross; it refers to the reversal of the process of crossing the hands of the deceased at death. Danforth concludes his treatment of the ritual by reporting that,

> ... in the world inhabited by Greek villagers, hard white bones are the purest state into which the body can ever actually be transformed. These bones, piled in heaps in ossuaries throughout Greece, testify to the fact that the limits of the material world cannot be transcended. That which has been separated so painfully by death cannot be rejoined. The opposition between life and death inherent in our mortality is real, and the contradiction between our lives and our deaths can never be resolved. What occurs at the rite of exhumation is an imperfect resurrection, at best only a partial victory over death.

In a companion note to her poem "Périsprit," Olga Broumas writes: "Though I was extremely agitated and apprehensive about witnessing my father's exhumation, the actual experience was one of relief and joy to have him back on earth and in light with us again."

Périsprit

In the hospital, in the impartial beauty of sunlight,
he tells us, *Do not weep. I don't know if I can*

come back, but if I can it will be through your joy.
Historical earth too small already to contain our dead.

In four years I will lead my mother to find the priest
walking through the garden of graves. He is ready and she

does not walk with us behind the chapel where, unearthed,
an armful of bones in a tin ossuary bathed in red wine

is set in the sun and the long night through evening
to another dawn under stars to dry.

—Olga Broumas

In the last decades of the nineteenth century, the annual death rate for Dodecanese divers approached 15 percent. Today the single most dangerous occupation in the United States is that of *fisher*, with a 1.3 percent annual fatality rate. (Tell your children to stay far from the sea.)

The following table song, "My Freshly Painted Boat," was sung on the island of Kalymnos as the fleet readied for departure:

The time to part and sail away has come,
My freshly painted fishing boat, sitting on the stocks.
They go away from Kalymnos, the branches of the vine.*
Oh stormy sea, you've burnt this heart of mine.

PLATIKA

And so the divers lit their cigars with thousand-lire notes and led a reckless life. *And why not?* So "they stole a bad hour from death," in the phrase of the anthropologist Michael Herzfeld. Since the divers might never return, they could now command 100 percent of their six-months' wages in advance of the fleet's ever setting sail. The *platika*—literally "on the plate"—or prepayment system added to, some say created, the pressure to dive with a dangerous disregard for safety. Because so much money had changed hands already, divers were under enormous pressure to harvest enough sponge to match the high *platika* they had received. It was a pressure both self-imposed as a matter of honor, and imposed by the captain who had paid their *platika*, often with money borrowed at usurious rates. No longer were captain and men *syndrophi*—comrades. Instead the captain referred to his men as *anthropi mou*, "my men." The captain now owned his men. Adding to

---

*Metaphor representing all the young men of Kalymnos. Text translated by Matroni Dikeakou.

the pressure, the diver who met his high *platika* this season could demand even more the next.

YIATI?

Since high casualty rates continued until the 1970s—long after divers should have known about proper deep-diving technique—I asked all throughout the Dodecanese *Yiati? Why?* Why so many deaths and casualties?

I believe I now know the causes. It is their relative weight that remains so perplexing. The list includes poor equipment, ignorance of proper deep-diving technique, the greed of the merchants and captains, the greed of the divers themselves, the *platika* system, "the poetics of manhood" in Greece—in the inspired phrase of Michael Herzfeld—and the incontrovertible truth that the inhabitants of these beautiful but rock-strewn islands had only the sea to turn to, and what the sea so reluctantly gives up.

> *Oh beloved and renowned mother Symi,*
> *if only you were blessed with vineyards and fresh waters.*
> *Though graced with boulders, you rejoice,*
> *full of good men of generous upbringing.*
> *If only you had fruitful trees and land to cultivate,*
> *olive-groves to tend to in abundance.*
> *You've never been empty or abandoned*
> *by those who emigrate to bitter lands.*
> *A bell-of-stone, a net, the tools*
> *of those aboard your boats.*
> *Such is the trade of young and old*
> *that Symiot men inherit.*
> *We found no fields to cultivate.*
> *In the sea's waves and depths we dive,*
> *in sea we found our olive-groves*
> *our gardens and our vineyards.*
> *In eons to come this is our trade.*

—"Winter Dream"

two

PROTEST

O hear us when we cry to Thee
For those in peril on the sea.

—U.S. Naval Hymn

THE FIGHT AGAINST THE SKAFANDRA

Violent protests against the *skafandra* took place on Symi and Kalymnos. Intellectuals and theologians arrayed themselves against the merchants and captains. My grandfather's poem itself was directed at Ottoman Turkish authorities as a plea that they ban the deep-diving gear.
Bans of fleeting duration were issued, one lasting for two years. Bribes
to Ottoman Turkish officials were the primary but not the sole reason
the bans failed. On the island of Symi the sponge industry was called
The Tyranny. All were locked in its deadly grip.

The explosive protests came in the 1880s and 1890s, twenty or
thirty years after the introduction of the *skafandra*. They came after
the industry had largely, but not fully, been reorganized around the
skafandra and after early attempts to ban the gear had failed. And they
came with memory of the safer, more graceful life of the naked divers
still vivid, before the gear's atrocities had fully "won out."

> *One time the people tried to break the gear*
> *before its strength gained on the land,*
> *before its atrocities prevailed,*

its wings spread like today.
      President of the senate then
was Stamatis Kalafatas,
      old in age,
a wise man faithful to the senate.
      He governed fairly,
suffered for his land and was imprisoned.
      He stood up for the common good,
suffered the prisons of Rhodes and Kos,
      yet returned to public office.
The crowd had gathered of one mind,
      men, women, children in agreement,
swarming the shore like angry bees,
      roads full of men and boys.
A roar was heard in the cafes,
      let's break the gear in storage!
They came to Kalafatas for permission
      to break the gear and rescue
their true livelihood.
      Blessed be his name, he tried to make them pause
and counseled them to change their minds.
      He said, this action is not good,
the senate will pay the cost.
      They were unyielding, very wild,
railing against the gear like rabid wolves.
      The horde didn't listen to the wise
counsel of old Kalafatas,
      but lashed out and took him in their hands,
and carried him to the storehouse in mid-air.
      Set next to helmets and to suits
against his will, he touched the gear.
      And then the throng descended,
and in five minutes
      destroyed breathing tubes and suits.
The people meant no crime.
      They only meant to break the gear
and pay for it, but not buy more.

Indeed, the common bank did pay,
but owners did the opposite.
They took the gold for better gear,
a new invention more refined.
And ever since they flogged the town,
and fanned the flame beneath it,
became destroyers of the land,
took wages from the devil.

—"Winter Dream"

GRAMMA NEKRON: A DEAD LETTER

The "uprising" on Symi came in April 1884 after the first ban, issued in 1881, had become *gramma nekron*—a dead letter, on the books but never enforced. According to Antonios Angelides, those who destroyed the gear torched it as they finished their work: They wanted not only to kill the infectious agent but also to cauterize the wound.

Symi was shaken to the core. The Nomarch of the Islands, the regional governor, arrived from Chios on an Ottoman warship to re-store order. Forty divers were arrested, brought to Chios, and jailed for their part in the violence. As wise old Kalafatas had predicted, the common bank of Symi was forced to pay 60,000 francs to compensate for the destruction. The owners turned around and bought new equip-ment.

On Kalymnos common history tells of a similar attack—people breaking into warehouses, smashing equipment, and hurling it into the sea. One after the other, throughout the sponge fishing islands, as the "accidents" mounted, the fight began to ban the gear: Astypalaia in 1868, Kalymnos in 1875, Symi in 1880. After the outbreak on Symi, regional authorities on Chios recommended to the Sultan that, once again, he ban the gear. And the municipality of Symi asked that this time the ban be enforced directly from Constantinople.

Bans were instituted in 1881, 1884, 1902, and 1911.* Each time the Turkish government issued a ban it was soon revoked. On Symi, merchants conspired with the Turkish police chief, the *kaimak-bey*, to keep a ban hidden until the fleet had set sail for North Africa for its seven-month summer season.

> *Though orders came to us last March,*
> *they've been kept under cover,*
> *   so that the Symiots might sail,*
> *their diving not prevented.*
> *   But five or six spongers heard of it*
> *and argued with the captains,*
> *   and all the women of the town*
> *rushed to the shore with wooden clubs,*
> *   as if possessed by demons.*
> *They rushed the town hall at Kaimak*
> *   and stood on the stairs demanding reasons,*
> *and forced Benyamin and Katrion,*
> *   along with other merchants,*
> *back to their house.*
> *No water would they let them drink*
> *   till they produced the orders*
> *in plain for all to see.*
> *Violent and patient they stood firm,*
> *   exposed the scheming secrets*
> *and Kaimak-bey promised them*
> *   at last, to earn their quiet,*
> *to quit the machines and so they left,*
> *   and wait unto this day*
> *demanding that the diving cease.*

—"Winter Dream"

*I believe these are the official dates of the four bans of the *skafandra* issued by Ottoman Turkish authorities. The 1884 ban and the 1902 ban are sometimes referred to as the 1883 ban and the 1903 ban. I believe the variance comes from the difference in the Orthodox Calendar, between the Old Calendar and the New, and more important, the slowness with which news of the abolitions diffused in the Ottoman world.

Partisan intrigue and bribery played a huge role in life in the twilight of the Ottoman world.

When we arrived on Symi, we checked into the Aliki Hotel in a room that overlooked the Aegean. I am not sure whether the inspiration was the view or that I was finally on my grandfather's island, but my thoughts went to Proust: "When I went to Venice, my dream became my address." The Symiots aspired to be like the Venetians; my aunt who died as a child was named Commissa, others were named Duchissa, names that derived from Venetian royalty. In 1692 the Symiots paid tribute to the Venetians to defend the population and their ships from the attacks of pirates who ravaged the islands of the Aegean. The spirit of Symi was the spirit of Venice and of Genoa.

We had chosen the Aliki because, along with Ben Kingsley, it had starred in the film *Pascali's Island*, set on Symi in 1908 as the Ottoman empire teetered on the edge of self-destruction. Kingsley plays a nervous functionary who survives by picking his way, with Levantine guile, through official indifference and layers of corruption. In this part of the world, here is the proper simile: Corruption like baklava, sweet layer upon layer.

Each morning at the Aliki we threw open the shutters and there, ten feet below, was the sea, lit by the rose-fingered dawn. I could have dived from the window and scattered the black and silver fish. The single Greek patrol boat that circled the island by night would pass under our window in the morning and dock at Symi harbor. With a start, I would be reminded of our closeness to Turkey, just four miles away.

I would be reminded of how the fortunes of Symi, nestled deep in the arms of Anatolia, swelled and declined with the fortunes of the Ottoman Empire. At their zenith the Ottomans were "Lords of the Horizon," writes Jason Goodwin, and their empire comprised thirty-six nations. For more than four hundred years the Ottoman empire held sway. Any qualified, aspiring diplomat needed to know Turkish. But, in the end, there in 1908 on "Pascali's Island," a great empire was reduced to mindless sensuality. Symiot bribes of choice to Turkish officials were silk sponges for the pasha's harem and thick, luscious Dodecanese honey.

According to Karl Flegel, a remarkable champion of the divers' cause for four decades, the Dodecanesians had plenty of reason to be aggrieved with their would-be protectors, both the Ottoman Turks and their own elected island senates, the *demogerontia*:

> The sponge-gathering population of Kalymnos, Symi, Halki, Kastellor-izo, Tilos, Nyssiros, Astypalaia, Leros and Patmos [nine of the twelve Dodecanese islands] had, for a long time, reason to be dissatisfied with the rule of Turkish authorities, having uncovered an unusual degree of negligence and indifference in the face of the prolonged suffering caused by the terrible mishandling of the diving equipment. But the *demoge-rontia* of the above islands were equally culpable in this respect, having proved that they did not know how to handle autonomy for the good of the population and that they [themselves] required benevolent su-pervision, which unfortunately was totally lacking.

ANGEL FROM THE NORTH

Who would expect a professor and journalist from Russia to be in-jected into a story of the Greek sponge divers of the Aegean? Were this Greek theater, which in some respects it is, Flegel would be a god brought in on wires at an improbable moment to rescue the protag-onist from a difficult situation. Most English speakers know the device by its Latin term, *deus ex machina*, but the Romans took it, as they did so much, from the Greeks, who called it *apo mechanis theos*, the god from the machine.

When I arrived on the scene, I did not even know if Flegel, who makes a cameo appearance in my grandfather's poem, was real. After all, the poem is called "Winter Dream," and Flegel is depicted as an angel from Russia. How likely is that? But for six weeks I had a small role to play in the drama as The Naked Diver from America. With the poem as my bellstone, I "dove" many times a day, fetching one or two truths on each dive, and placing them gently—like luxurious sponges—into my net bag, before making my way back to the surface. It was my summer as a sponge fisher.

From my cousin Michael Foreys I fetched the truth that Flegel was, in fact, real and that he had taught for a time at the Castro school on Symi. My heart skipped at finding that truth. But Foreys dismissed Flegel as a foolish idealist: "The naked divers were unproductive. With safe use and the right 'genetics,' *skafandra* divers should have had no problem." He described the practice of gradual ascent used by the *skafandra* divers of Limnos, in the northern Aegean. Divers would put in at twenty-five meters' depth, descend slowly by foot along a sloped bottom to hundred meters' depth, working all along the way, and then return slowly by foot to shallow water before ascending. It was safe technique—making use of gradual ascent—and it could have come straight out of the U.S. Navy Diving Manual. The divers of Limnos had hit on the technique by chance: it worked because of the under-water topography around Limnos. Nonetheless, in Foreys's view, the naked divers were finished once the *skafandra* arrived, and Flegel should have known it.

Only after I arrived on Kalymnos—my next stop after Symi—was I able to gather up the full, unlikely story of Karl Vasilievich Flegel. On Kalymnos, the Island of the Sponge Fishermen, I filled my net bag many times over with fetched truths—and even with what seemed to be *far-fetched* truths—about Flegel.

At the Anagnostirion—the cultural center of Kalymnos—I met Kyriacos Hadzidakis, an intellectual who, for seventeen years, studied the dramatic fight to defeat the *skafandra*. Kyriacos took degrees in Greek and English literature from the University of Athens, the jewel-in-the-crown of Greek education, and he teaches now at the Lyceum on Kalymnos. In beautiful English and in quiet cadences, Kyriacos outlined the difficult problems faced by Flegel and others that fought to ban the deep-diving gear.

In the bright Aegean light outside lay the famed Kalymnian port of Pothia. It was from this port that many hundreds of divers sailed to their death or paralysis. One source, in hyperbole, reports that, between 1866 and 1915, there were 10,000 deaths and 20,000 cases of paralysis among sponge divers of the Aegean, with the majority of victims Kalymnian. What is so interesting about the figures is that there are Kalymnians who believe them. So many were the "hit" divers on Kalymnos, so extreme the agony of the women who awaited return of their men, that it seemed as if 10,000 must have died.

For 125 years paralyzed Kalymnian divers have dragged them-selves on crutches along Pothia's sun-drenched shore, by cheerful blue waters, remembering days when they went unchallenged as the mat-

adors of the deep. In the hushed, darkened interior of the Anagnostirion, in the voice of Kyriacos, I could hear the sadness in my grandfather's voice. It was with perfect pitch the voice in the poem, the voice
I never actually "heard," my grandfather's voice—the voice my father
heard but never "remembered." My grandfather died in 1904, when
his son, my father, was less than three years old.

> Voices ideal and beloved
> Of those who have died, or of those
> Who are lost for us like the dead.
> Sometimes in dreams they speak to us;
> Sometimes within thinking the brain hears them.
> And with the sound of them for a moment return
> Sounds from the first poetry of our life—
> Like music, at night, in the distance, that dies away.
> —C. P. Cavafy, "Voices"

Cavafy, a giant of modern Greek poetry, wrote "Voices" in 1904, the
year my grandfather died.

THE *SKAFANDRA* DIVING EXPERIENCE

"The divers were treated like heroes, and they were heroes," Kyriacos
said to me. Imagine, if you will, working as deep as three hundred feet
beneath the sea, all of that water above you, and your life dependent
on a thin stream of gas, the same gas that can kill you if you ascend
too quickly. Imagine the danger of a tear in your suit or your air hose
from the jagged rocks under the sea or from the propeller of your own
boat, your vessel of safety. Imagine concentrating intently on your
work, with work-time counted out in minutes, amid the constant danger of shark attack. Great whites, in particular, loved the waters between Malta and Tunisia, rich in sponge beds. Herman Melville, imag-
ining such, might recollect these lines from his novel *White Jacket*:
" 'See that white shark!' cried a horrified voice from the taffrail; 'he'll
have that man down his hatchway!' "

Above you, you hope, someone remembers to turn an oversized egg
timer by the half-minute to insure that you are not down too long.

Above you, before the advent of the gas-driven compressor, two strong young men, constantly turn the wheel of the air compressor, from which you draw your life-breath. Above you, the captain or his assistant measures your depth, and, you hope, has not altered the depth meter to trick you to go deeper than you know you should. Imagine the gas-powered compressor that, if defective, can reverse and suck the air *out* of your suit as you alone stand helpless at age twenty, with a mountain of sea above you. Sometimes the compressor, linked to the boat's engine, would feed you carbon monoxide, *in multiples*, and you would swiftly perish from carbon monoxide poisoning. *Palikaria* they were—brave young men.

KARL VASILIEVICH FLEGEL

Karl Vasilievich Flegel was a hero, too—of a different variety—and he was rescued from near historical oblivion by Kyriacos. A large portrait photograph of Flegel hangs in the Nautical Museum of Kalymnos—filled with memorabilia from the island's sponge-fishing past—only because Kyriacos gave the photo to the museum and made the case for hanging it. The story of the sponge fishermen is incomplete without Flegel.

Before laying eyes on the passage praising Flegel in my grandfather's poem, Kyriacos lamented to me, "There isn't even a *street* on Kalymnos named for Flegel." At my request, Kyriacos read the passage aloud in Greek, its fifteen-meter rhymed verse resounding off the walls of the Anagnostirion. He read aloud, too, the last sixteen lines of my grandfather's poem, which begin, "Oh beloved and renowned homeland Symi." When he finished, he raised his deep, sensitive eyes and said: "No such poem exists on Kalymnos. But Kalymnos and Symi were sisters. They have common roots and had a common fight against the *skafandra*."

I feel a degree of contentment that I have done the right thing in returning the poem—with its elegy to Flegel—to the Dodecanese. It belongs there.

Kyriacos has studied the life of Flegel for so long that he calls him *Papous mou*—my grandfather. As he spoke, I thought about how his papou and my papou fought to end the *skafandra*. I thought of how my thoughts, like those of Kyriacos, had been with "the wild pang of the Greek landscape"—sea, rock, and cypress—and valiant young men who put their lives at peril. Playful Greek gods, who have always loved to toy with their charges, arranged for the two of us to meet.

But according to my grandfather, it was God the all-merciful who sent Flegel as his angel.

> *even God the all-merciful*
> *began so to despise it*
> *that, as his angel, sent a man*
> *guileless and full of spirit,*
> *Flegel by name and Russian-born,*
> *in whom I recognized a kind,*
> *masterful benefactor.*
> *Blessed more than once he reached our shores,*
> *studied and learned our torments,*
> *and was so moved by the machine's*
> *criminal miserable results,*
> *he undertook himself the task*
> *to practice good and undo harm.*
> *He gave it all his power,*
> *spent without mercy his own funds,*
> *coming and going first to France*
> *and Italy in tandem,*
> *and then to Crete to meet success*
> *and leave again for Cyprus,*
> *where he found England willingly*
> *coming to our defense.*
> *From there to Egypt without rest*
> *where he delayed Mandroucha.**
> *He wastes no time in laziness,*

*Mandroucha is a port city and province in northwestern Egypt where the country's great Western Desert meets the Mediterranean. Today, Matruh is a resort, known for beautiful beaches. It was in waters off Mandroucha that so many Symiot sponge boats went to fish and that so many Symiots died. On the island of Symi, Mandroucha became synonymous with, and a metaphor for, the sponge-fishing season and a curse word on the lips of Symiot women.

from there he sails to Samos,
  who also swore to ban the gear,
hating its very sight.
  And part of Syria stayed free,
Karman, and Asia Minor.
  May god of Goodness will him grace,
and generous Flegel feel it,
  and reach Constantinopolis
to smite the rabid tiger.
  I too was grateful for his deeds,
brave acts, and wealth of virtues.
  No gift too large to honor him,
a statue I must raise,
  bearing the sign: MAN OF GREAT FAME
FLEGEL WHO FREED *our homeland* SYMI.
  But my daughter, the Elders' Senate, too
suffers from penury,
  worn down by debt, she cannot pay.
her own clerks' wage.

—"Winter Dream"

Beyond my grandfather's words, most of what I know about Flegel I learned from his "grandson" Kyriacos. Kyriacos found in me a soulmate, an American cousin who cared about Flegel's obsession with the divers' cause, and so I left the Anagnostirion laden with information. I squirreled myself away in Katerina's Apartments in Pothia, and I read.

Karl Vasilievich Flegel was born in 1850 in Vilna, Lithuania. Always at sword's point—or in the *cross hairs* of warring nations—Vilna changed hands many times; variously part of Russia, Sweden, Poland, France, Germany, and Lithuania. By nationality Flegel was Lithuanian. A contemporary on Kalymnos described him as having bright blue eyes, a purity and child-like innocence, and very much looking like "the angel from the machine," *apo mechanis angelos.* By training, Flegel was a professor of classical languages and a journalist. He had at his command a dazzling array of languages—Latin, Ancient Greek,

Modern Greek, Russian, French, Italian, German, English, and doubtless others; and he put his languages to work in an international crusade to protect the divers.

Oddly, I felt personally connected to Flegel. After all, he came from
Vilna, from which my wife's four Jewish grandparents came. For 150
years Vilna was the center of Eastern European Jewish intellectual
and cultural life, home of the first Jewish socialists and of the Zionist
movement in Russia. A third of the city were Jews. The Jewish community's intellectual and literary life flourished until the community
itself was destroyed in the Holocaust. Though not Jewish, he was a
member of the intelligentsia of Vilna, a city of leftist politics aglow in
enlightenment, and he was a journalist. Why wouldn't Flegel be interested in the plight of the divers? The pieces were starting to fit:
Flegel's left-wing politics, my grandfather's left-wing politics, and my
father's left-wing politics. They were all part of a certain tradition of
progressive Dodecanese politics, whether homegrown or not.

WHERE ANGELS WALK

The Aegean islands were well known in Russia: The Cyclades islands,
the island group that is closest to the Dodecanese, had been annexed
briefly to Russia in the 1770s. When they were returned to Turkey,
the Sultan issued a highly profitable dispensation, allowing certain
Greek island ships to continue to trade under the Russian flag. The
dispensation became the basis of many Greek shipping fortunes. Flying Russian flags, Greek-owned ships plied Russian ports, and many
Greeks lived in Russia, including a thousand Kalymnians.

"The Aegean is where angels walk," or so the Greeks say. Persis-
tently ill, our angel from the north, Karl Flegel, came to the Aegean
in the 1880s to convalesce. So different from damp and snowy Vilna,
the sunswept Aegean islands beckoned, and Greek acquaintances in
Russia urged him to visit.

Flegel loved the Aegean, and in 1892 he settled on Kalymnos. He
remained a resident until his death in 1928 despite frequent absences
to teach on Symi—and to carry on the divers' cause. Within days of
his arrival, he tells us in his memoirs, he learned "the awful truth about

the *skafandra*." Appalled, he threw himself into the fight. A few years earlier a beloved younger brother had died in Africa of a tropical disease while conducting research; as Flegel himself reports, his actions on behalf of the divers became "the treatment for his grief."

KALYMNIAN SPONGE PRINCE: NICHOLAS VOUVALIS

Today on Kalymnos all summer long you find the Greeks of Pothia out walking along the harbor in the evening: *Mia volta*, a walk with nothing more serious in mind than the breezes that blow in from the Aegean—where the angels walk. If I ever needed to find someone, I could sit at a table outside one of the *kafenia*, leisurely sip an *elliniko kafe*, a Greek coffee, and sooner or later he or she would walk by. It always worked like a charm.

All summer long, tourists too stroll the shorewalk of Pothia, often stopping to buy beautiful sponges at one of the stalls that line the harbor. Amazingly, after millennia, the magic of the sea sponge still seizes the attention of people; it has something to do with what Aristotle said of the sea sponge: "It has feelings!" *It seems to live.* Sponges make wonderful gifts: They are lightweight, squeeze into your luggage, don't break, and cushion all the other gifts headed back to Cleveland or Perth. They are inexpensive and last forever, loyally reminding the recipient of your thoughtfulness. And best of all, they smell of the sea.

Should a strolling tourist duck into the Vouvalis School or into one of several other eleemosynary institutions on Kalymnos, he or she will find a bust of Nicholas Vouvalis, the Prince of Sponges. Under the bust one will read "Nicholas Vouvalis, Great Benefactor." It was Vouvalis's genius that organized the sponge-fishing industry on Kalymnos and helped organize the world sponge market. Brilliantly, Vouvalis established his headquarters in London at the epicenter of the Industrial Revolution. By the late nineteenth century, trade with or through Great Britain consumed all of the good-quality Mediterranean sponge catch. Six large Kalymnian firms had headquarters based in London.

Today, as he would wish to be, Vouvalis is remembered primarily as a great Kalymnian philanthropist. For example, in mid-June, at the end of the school year, Joan and I watched beautiful, healthy Kalym-

nian children perform dances and plays in native costume, before ador-
ing parents, in the schoolyard of the "Vouvalis School of Pothia."
Doubtless many of the children, if not all, have a grandfather or great
uncle who died some awful death at sea: maybe crushed inside his
helmet from the intense relative vacuum created when compressed air
ran out of his suit fifty fathoms under the sea; or maybe in horrible
agony—in multiple spasms from the bends—on the deck of a ship
whose name no one remembers, east of Syria or south of Crete.

Nicholas Vouvalis and his wife, Catherine, twenty-one years his
junior, moved into their new mansion in 1894, the year Flegel left
Kalymnos on his first trip to try to ban the gear. The Vouvalis's op-
ulent home, Pothia House, was furnished in beautiful English Victorian style. Nicholas Vouvalis died in 1918, but his wife Catherine lived
on in splendor until 1959. Their home is preserved as a museum today
and houses an impressive archaeological collection. When I first saw
a bust of Vouvalis, I recalled Lucius Beebe, author of *The Rich and The
Super Rich*: "Behind every fortune there is a crime." Dead divers,
crushed inside their helmets, or dead from the bends, lay in the wake
of Vouvalis's triumph.

I thought, too, of Flegel. No street or statue named for him, either
here on Kalymnos or on Symi. If you want a statue, I mused, you'd
better win; only in the American South did they erect statues to the
defeated. My spirit warmed when I learned from Kyriacos that Flegel's
memory lives on in small ways in folk endearments. One hotel owner
is called Flegeli, a nickname given him as a child by his parents as a
tribute to the man who tried to save the lives of divers. Kyriacos told
me that he had also seen a boat in Pothia harbor the previous summer
named *Flegelis*. "Here on Kalymnos, it is something important, something very good, if people refer to you as *o Flegelis mou*." *My Flegel*.
Better to live on in small ways, among the common people, I thought,
than to have a stone statue.

FLEGEL "THE LIBERATOR"

Once he took up the fight, Flegel realized the need for international
action. Even if a ban were issued for the far-flung seas of the Ottoman
Empire, what did that mean for use of the deep-diving suits in the

waters of Greece, Egypt, Italy, Syria, Crete, Cyprus, or Samos? The merchants and captains could simply shift the venue of diving. And they did, to profitable result. At the very prospect of a ban, the price of sponge skyrocketed on the world market—driven by fear of short-fall as demand continued to rise with the Industrial Revolution.

With any ban in the Ottoman Empire also came an increase in use of the *skafandra* on the Aegean islands of Aegina, Hydra, and Spetses—ethnically Greek, close to the Greek mainland, and belonging to Greece. Greek captains and divers would simply shift their home base from the ethnically Greek *Ottoman* islands to the ethnically Greek *Greek* islands. And with high prices, of course, came a black market for captains and divers. The price of sponges was too high to resist, and who was enforcing this ban anyhow? So they fished illegally; with the bans also came falsifying of records. Kostas Kontos, a historian of Symi, has shown that the number of boats falsely reporting that they were using naked diving or *kangava*, a dragging method of sponge fishing, increased dramatically with news that a ban was now in force. Captains simply fudged the record and sailed out of Symi, Kalymnos, Kastellorizo, or Halki with highly paid, fully complicit black-market crews.

Because of so many deaths, by 1894 the fight against the *skafandra* had reached a state of frenzy on Kalymnos. Flegel hoped the people might now have "the spiritual resources" to beat down the gear. For the first time Kalymnos elected leaders to the *demogerontia* who were opposed to the *skafandra*; the leaders, in turn, dispatched a permanent emissary to Constantinople to lobby for abolition of the gear. In May 1895 the cries of *Anathema! Anathema!* were heard across the island, with the women flooding down the winding streets from Chora, the old capital, into the new port city of Pothia made prosperous by the sponge-fishing industry.

Using his skills as a linguist and journalist, Flegel launched an international crusade, barraging officials with pleas for intervention. He wrote to the Nomarch of the Aegean and all of the great leaders of Constantinople—the Grand Vizier, the Sultan, and the Ecumenical Patriarch, the chief prelate of the Orthodox Christian world. In 1894 he set off on a daunting schedule of personal diplomacy, spanning nearly four decades. As my grandfather reported, he carried his crusade to France, Italy, Cyprus, Crete, England, Egypt, Samos, Syria, and Asia Minor. He also took the fight to Athens, Constantinople, Brussels, Frankfurt, Vienna, St. Petersburg, Washington, and elsewhere. Especially in the early years, much of the travel was done under sail; and often it was done at Flegel's own expense.

Because of Flegel's importuning, the Ecumenical Patriarch of Constantinople visited Kalymnos in 1895 to learn first-hand of the catastrophe. The Patriarch was grieved by the human suffering and by the vandalizing of the sea-bottom made possible by the *skafandra*. The Patriarchate has always taken as holy injunction the second verse of Genesis: "And the spirit of God swept over the face of the water." To the Orthodox Church, humankind has a theological obligation to preserve and protect the waters of the world.

Bob Lange at Brandeis University serves as Coordinator of Science and Environmental Education for the current Ecumenical Patriarch, Bartholomew, whom the press calls "the Green Patriarch." His All Holiness views ecological problems as first and foremost spiritual: it is only humankind's carelessness that has stripped God's creation of its original splendor.

THE HOLY GRAIL: A COMMON AGREEMENT

As if it were the Holy Grail, Karl Flegel pursued a Common Agreement among all countries that had a sponge-fishing industry or that controlled waters where sponges were fished. To him the Grail seemed attainable but always remained beyond reach. He lectured and published in many languages and in many countries, and sponsored endless international conferences and expositions on the plight of the divers and the vandalizing of the sea-bottom.

Although he never attained a Common Agreement, Flegel was right to pursue it. As described in the Prologue to his poem, Metrophanes heard whispers of a ban after sailing his swift *skaphos* into Symi harbor and docking outside the cafe of Xenophon A. Lourtesi. The whispers were about the ban of 1902, which held for nearly two years. It, too, failed but it outlasted the others because it was instituted simultaneously in Turkey, Egypt, Cyprus, Samos, Crete, and Tunisia. A successful Common Agreement would have required the common assent *and* steadfast enforcement of all these parties and of Greece, Italy, and France as well. Diplomatically speaking, gaining and maintaining the common assent and steadfast enforcement of so many parties was, as Kyriacos said, "a very difficult problem."

While working toward a Common Agreement, Flegel promoted other actions to limit the exposure of *skafandra* divers to danger. He advocated banning use of the *skafandra* for a *portion* of the season in March, April, and May. He advocated banning export of small sponges, hoping that doing so would spur regrowth and make large, luxurious sponges plentiful once again in shallower, safer waters. He advocated banning the *skafandra* boats from certain sponge-fishing fields, allowing only naked divers to dive there. He even advocated sponge fish farming, hoping large-scale sponge cultivation could be developed in safe waters.

All of these proposals ended in failure, with the merchant-captains fighting Flegel at every turn because their investment was too great and the stakes too high. The cost of doing business had skyrocketed with the coming of the *skafandra*; two-thirds of the sponge catch coming into the Aegean fishing islands was coming from North Africa or beyond.

As Kostas Kontos pointed out, while captains of naked diving boats borrowed one-third of the money necessary to cover the costs of an upcoming sponge-fishing season, captains of *skafandra* boats routinely borrowed *all* of the money. Although naked diving might be less productive, it was also less expensive, because labor costs were less and risk to the diver was less; equipment costs were less (after all, the divers were *naked*); and crews were smaller.

With the vandalizing of the sea-bottom, *skafandra* captains needed to send divers ever deeper to find sponge. As any recreational diver knows, a diver's bottom time, using compressed air or any nitrogen-oxygen mix, decreases dramatically with depth because of the lurking danger of decompression disease.

Given decreased bottom time—even with divers making three dives a day, seven days a week—*skafandra* captains simply had to set sail with bigger crews because they needed more divers. In 1870, Kontos reports, naked diving boats typically sailed with a crew of ten; but by 1937 some *skafandra* boats were sailing with crews of twenty-five to thirty. With so many divers getting killed or maimed, it was good management to plan for attrition by taking on extra divers. In the early 1950s, one captain was nicknamed Korea—for the war in which Greek soldiers distinguished themselves fighting with U.N. forces— because his casualty rate was so high. Another was nicknamed Nek-rofora, "the hearse," for the same reason.

"UNDIVED SEAS"

Astonishingly, after a sponge is harvested, it can regenerate into a full-sized sponge—assuming that when torn or cut the basal part of the sponge is left attached to the sea-bottom, rock, or other hard surface onto which the sponge had adhered. Regeneration can take five years, but as many as three or four sponges have been taken from the same base. However, the sponge fleet could not wait five years; they sailed every year in search of the golden fleece that made their affluent new lives possible. Captains sailed on past last year's dead sponge beds, leaving devastation behind in the wake of the boat as they sought out "undived seas." They dove in remote places—off the coast of Sicily, off the Balearic islands, off the Azores, and off the Canary islands. Traveling further from home boosted costs, of course, adding to what a captain needed to borrow to finance a trip.

Captain and crew were trapped in a vicious cycle as the supply of sponges ran down. Frantically, they tried diving for pearls, although the Greeks could not compete so easily against skilled Arab pearl divers. And they dove for red coral. In recognition of the huge financial pressures on the captains, and the natural inclination of the widows to blame the captains for the death and maiming, I think it important to invoke the insight of Michael Cantonis of Tarpon Springs, one of the world's leading sponge merchants, who observed: "I never knew a sponge-fishing captain who died rich. I think one hundred percent *platika* corrupted the system. A better idea would have been fifty percent platika, and subsequent periodic payments, while the diver was at sea, to the diver's wife or to the diver's family." Sadly, that did not occur. Nowhere else in the world are fisher folk paid 100 percent of their wages in advance.

In 1905 came news of the ultimate "undived sea"—vast new sponge beds found in the Gulf of Mexico. *En masse* five hundred Aegean sponge fishermen moved to Tarpon Springs, Florida.

As captains carried more divers, paid higher *platika*, and traveled further from home; and as divers dove deeper in search of sponge, the hatred between captain and diver grew, as did tension among the divers themselves. "In the days of the naked divers," Kyriacos says, "all were happy. With the *skafandra* came much hatred. Many divers were killed, left on the bottom too long."

So famed for his dash, the Kalymnian diver would leap from the bow in full gear and spin in the air a full turn and a half before hitting the water. It was as if he were a *zebekiko* dancer. As he slowly sank below the surface, trailing his stream of bubbles, weighing on the captain's mind was the huge debt the captain alone carried for the trip and the *platika* paid to the diver weeks ago back in Pothia. Cultural idiom, *platika*, the economics of a diminishing resource, and the flaws of human nature tragically converged on an occupation where safety should have been the prime consideration.

"Technological progress makes it impossible to go back *sto fisiko*, to the *natural ways* of the naked diver," one Symiot observer wrote when Symi's sponge-fishing industry was at its height. When the bans came, it was difficult for *skafandra* divers to give up the huge money they were making—more money than they had ever dreamed of—and so many signed on to black-market crews, undermining the bans that had been put into place to protect them.

The vandalizing of the sponge beds has its analog in cod fishing in the North Atlantic. Once bountiful, North Atlantic cod grew scarce before World War II because of overfishing, Mark Kurlansky tells us in *Cod*. When war protected the cod from fishing fleets, the cod were replenished. Likewise in the Mediterranean, the two world wars interrupted sponge fishing, allowing sponge fields to repopulate.

COMPENSATION OF INJURED DIVERS

After 1905 Flegel shifted his efforts toward helping and compensating injured divers. In 1911 he created the Society for the Protection of Divers based in Crete. Queen Olga of Greece, Prince Albert of Monaco, and other sympathetic celebrities served on its executive council. But Flegel, as the Society's Secretary-Treasurer, was always the heart and soul of the efforts to aid the divers, inspiring others to act. Queen Olga convinced the Greek government to station a hospital ship in sponge-fishing waters to treat and to shelter victims. The Greek Navy maintained the hospital ship for years. A hospital for injured divers was opened in Tripoli, Libya, and a hostel for paralyzed divers was opened on Crete.

In 1908 Crete began to compensate injured divers, who were, of course, uninsured. Greece and Turkey followed suit shortly after. Flegel secured funds both from private philanthropy and from governments to aid the divers. After the Italians seized the catch of six sponge boats caught fishing illegally off the coast of Tobruk, and after the crews had been convicted, Flegel persuaded the King of Italy to donate the proceeds from the sale of the sponges to help paralyzed divers. In 1922, at Flegel's prompting, a fund was established in the Dodecanese to aid old and infirm *naked* divers.

As Flegel grew older and poorer, and as his health deteriorated, he wearied of the endless trips. His focus narrowed to the Dodecanese, to the fight against the Italians who had occupied the islands in 1912 and had begun to limit their historic privileges. But even at the age of seventy-two, ill and poor, he attempted once again to hold an international exhibition in London on the sponge-fishing industry so that he could present the issues. Flegel never gave up hope: "With my experience, I am the most suitable person to offer a solution to this long-lasting problem, and partly I have succeeded in convincing those who need to be convinced."

Karl Flegel did not end use of the *skafandra*. He died in extreme poverty in 1928. The last *skafandra* boat sailed in 1973.

Ultimately, what brought an end to the deaths from *noso ton diton*— "diving disease"—among the Aegean sponge divers was an end to the sponges. In the late 1960s, one after the other, the North African countries, wishing to exploit their own sponge industries, set high licensing fees for foreign vessels. It made it increasingly costly for the daring, skilled, and highly productive Greek divers to dive. Eventually the North Africans ceased issuing licenses altogether. The Greeks then overfished their own Aegean waters. In 1986, as a final blow, blight struck the Aegean and Mediterranean sponge fields. Sponges turned to dust in the hands of divers.

Many attribute the sponge die-offs to the Chernobyl outflow, making its way south through the Bosporus and out onto the historic sponge fields of the Aegean and the Mediterranean—a vandalizing of the sea-bottom that not even the Russian visionary, Karl Vasilievich Flegel, could have imagined.

three

PENELOPE'S REVENGE

A black day it was
When he took ship to see that cursed city . . .
Destroy, I call it—I hate to see its name.
—Penelope on Troy, *Odyssey* (trans. Robert Fagles)

Mandroucha

—City on the coast of Egypt cursed by the women of Symi

RAGE AGAINST THE MACHINE

One Sunday in May 1895, when news came early that season of many deaths at sea, the women of Kalymnos spontaneously performed the act of *anathema* as they poured out from churches all over the island. Keening women formed circles in the churchyards and squares, touched stones to their foreheads, and cast them to the center, inflicting a collective curse upon the merchant-captains and the *demogerontia*, the island senate. The women then flooded down the narrow winding roads from the high terrain of Kalymnos, from the old capital of Chora, into the beautiful new port of Pothia, built from the boom in the sponge industry that came with the *skafandra*. The women wanted their rage to be seen and known at the new center of money and power. In their fury they reached back to the ritual of *anathema* that pre-dates Christian times; here women symbolically placed at the center of their extraordinary circles those they believed to be outside the human circle; here we have a symbolic stoning of evil-doers.

Where did their rage come from? It came, of course, from their fury at the endless capacity of "Satan's Machine" to spin out death—even as it tossed up the mountains of sponges that filled the warehouses of Pothia; it came from their fury at the greed of the merchant-captains and the silent complicity of the island senate.

TERRIBLE BEAUTY: THE RITUAL LAMENT

> *Oh, I will think of things gone long ago*
> *And weave them to a song.*
>
> —Euripides, *Trojan Women*

Often Greek women transmuted their rage and grief into the terrible beauty of the ritual lament. Ritual lament among Greek women is part of an unbroken oral tradition, dating from the ancients; it was fully evident in my grandfather's "Winter Dream" as a widow sings of her dead beloved, a casualty of the *skafandra*. It is noteworthy to recall with Edith Hamilton that when Greek girls mourned for Adonis every year, "they rejoiced when his flower, the blood-red anemone, the windflower, was seen blooming again." It was said that the crimson flower sprang from where each drop of his blood had stained the earth.* Centuries later, the flower as symbol of a beautiful dead young man appears in "Winter Dream" in the "Widows' Laments."

> *All eyes are dry yet mine still flow,*
> *tears pierce my breast and drench my heart.*
> *Where is my precious hyacinth, my flower of March?*
> *The diving gear devoured it.*

---

*According to the anthropologist Margaret Alexiou, in the ritual laments for Adonis, one finds the refrain *o ton Adonin* that is believed to be of Semitic origin, "meaning simply 'Ah, Lord.'" The Greek Adonis, the youth loved by Aphrodite for his beauty, echoes the Hebrew *Adonai Eloheinu*, the Lord our God. In Judaism, *Adonai* is the word spoken "as a substitute for the ineffable name of God," the *American Heritage Dictionary* tells us. To the Greeks, Adonis was the Lord personified into a beautiful young man who met a violent death.

I turn and look toward the door,
  expect you to appear,
open our wooden chest, put on a shirt.
  In Hades you lie, in Haros' gardens,
  and I still ask if you've been seen
    down near the cafes.

—"Winter Dream"

In Greek mythology, the hyacinth is another flower that came into being "through the death of a beautiful youth," Hamilton tells us. It was not the hyacinth that we know "but lily-shaped and of a deep purple, or some say, a splendid crimson." Hyacinthus was Apollo's dearest companion, killed by accident when playing a game. The god Apollo's "swift cast" of his discus overshot his mark and struck Hyancinthus in the forehead. "Oh, if I could give my life for yours, or die with you," Apollo spoke, overwhelmed with grief. The bloodstained grass turned green again as he spoke, "and there bloomed forth the wondrous flower that was to make the lad's name known forever."

Widows' Laments

Three days a week Calliope Koulia leaves her invalid father in Chora, Kalymnos, and takes a ten-minute bus ride along a winding shore road to the seaside apartments of her friend Irini. Calliope slips off her black kerchief and her black widow's dress, slips on her black swimsuit, and slides into the sea. The sea that has brought her agony now brings her only respite. Within the hour—back in her black dress and black kerchief—she will board the bus and return to care for her father. All of her life Calliope Koulia has cared for and prayed for others; but Calliope Koulia's prayers generally go unanswered.

In 1965 her husband, thirty-two, was diving off the coast of Libya when he was "hit by the machine" and paralyzed from the waist down. Calliope heard the news when a stranger knocked on her door and told her that her husband was in the hospital in Pothia, the port town of Kalymnos. The captain never visited her husband in the hospital, never came to their home, and never said that he was sorry: *"Tipota."* Nothing. *"Kakos,"* Calliope said. A bad captain.

Calliope took her husband to doctors on Kalymnos and in Athens, but none was of help. Unable to work, her husband dragged himself about on crutches until his death twenty years later, at fifty-two. After the accident, Calliope took any job she could find to raise their only child—a three-year-old son. When he was grown, he left for Australia, the Promised Land of Dodecanesians, where he was killed in an accident. Calliope's eyes filled with tears as she spoke of her dead son. She read aloud the Widows' Laments from my grandfather's poem, and said: "It is beautiful, and it is true."

⚱

In March 1962, Dimitris Kopkis's father, thirty, hired on to a sponge boat as a naked diver. On his first dive the captain ordered Dimitris's father to dive to 40 meters—130 feet below the surface on a single breath of air. His chest collapsed from the pressure. He made it back to the surface but died within minutes. He and his young wife had one child, Dimitris, then six months old. The mother of Dimitris Kopkis was only twenty when her husband died on his first dive ever off the coast of Alexandria. She never remarried.

I met Dimitris, now thirty-five, on a small pier at Emborio, a secluded beautiful harbor at the north end of Kalymnos. His two young sons were snorkeling in three meters of water, bringing up giant snails: "Great eating," one said, "raw."

As he baited a fishing line, Dimitris described the details of his father's death with a heaviness that seemed to press down on his own chest. I asked Dimitris what his mother believes caused his father's death. Again, as with Calliope, *"Kakos,"* a bad captain who didn't care. The culture of the naked diver—where *syndrophi* once had nobly cared for one another, comrades and equals all—had been coarsened by the ethos of the *skafandra*. Greed now held sway everywhere.

Dimitris comes from Kalymnos, "the island of the sponge fisherman," where tragic diving stories are commonplace. Kalymnians can spin out entire family trees of tragic diving stories. One woman told me that her grandmother had six brothers, all of whom died at sea.

"On my mother's side the machine hit my grandfather, a *skafandro* diver, in 1955 when he was forty-five years old," Dimitris reported. His grandfather was paralyzed from the knees down, and lived, disabled, until he died at seventy. And the grandfather had three sons—all of whom became sponge divers. Two lived out full lives, but a third was killed in 1968 diving off the coast of Crete. The air hose broke but the hose tender was inattentive; he was talking and not watching as Dimitris's uncle simply ran out of air.

I asked the women of Kalymnos, "What was it like to wait, knowing that one out of three divers might never return or might return paralyzed? What was it like to wait six months out of every year for the return of your husband, son, father, or brother?" *Agonia*. Agony. And so the women of Kalymnos flooded the churches when the men were at sea. In their homes they prayed constantly before the icons of *Agios Nikolaos*—Saint Nicholas, the patron saint of Greek sailors—and *Taxiarchis Michail*—the Archangel Michael, patron saint of Dodecanese sailors. They enveloped their agony in incense, in the mystery of the chanted liturgy, and in the unchanging rituals of the ancient Greek Orthodox church.

The *necrokaikia*, the death boats, never returned with the dead. Few nondivers ever saw a dead diver. The bodies were left behind—buried under the blazing hot sands of North Africa, dumped on rock islands, or tossed into the sea. *Arrivederci*. The widow or mother made her good-bye without even the comfort of burying her beloved. The paralyzed, not the dead, returned to the sponge-fishing islands.

A DIPLOMATIC TRADITION

On the island of Symi the men always hid behind the women.
—Michael Foreys

In my six weeks in the Dodecanese it was the most provocative comment I heard. It came, no surprise, from my cousin, Michael Foreys. In any scanning of Dodecanese social history, however, it is not hard to believe. "It is a diplomatic tradition," Foreys said.

In 1522 Suleiman the Magnificent, the most admired of all Ottoman sultans, lay siege to Rhodes. Sensing imminent defeat of the Knights of St. John, who had controlled Rhodes and the surrounding islands for two hundred years, the people of Symi voluntarily submitted to Turkish suzerainty in exchange for being left to rule their own affairs. The Symiots sent a delegation of women carrying loaves of fresh white bread, beautiful sponges, and the greetings of island notables to Suleiman, encamped nearby in Asia Minor. As William Travis notes, "bread, sponges, women, and courtesy" so impressed the Sultan that he granted Symi virtual autonomy and the sole right to fish for sponges in all the seas of the Ottoman Empire. The granting of that right, more than any other event, shaped the future of Symi for four hundred years. It shaped the whole future of the Dodecanese, in fact, as the Ottomans gradually yielded the right to other islands. At its height, the Ottoman Empire stretched from the Danube to the Nile, from Budapest to the Caspian Sea, and included most of the North African coast, along which lay vast sponge fields—sponge fields that the Greeks of the Dodecanese would one day exploit.

Most Greek men are uncomfortable in speaking about the role of women in shaping political destiny. Foreys was unusual in wanting to talk. Maybe it was because he was eighty-five. Maybe it is because he is a maverick. But here are the facts. Women's protests, sometimes violent, took place on Symi, Kalymnos, and Kastellorizo; they occurred under the Turkish and Italian occupations, and, in the case of Kalymnos, after Dodecanese union with Greece in 1948. In other words there is a continuity that suggests a tradition of women's protests.

SYMI

In 1922 and again in 1930, a *gynekokratia,* "rule by women," was established, with the male leadership ousted, replaced by councils of women. In 1922 Symiot women seized power from the island senate by sit-in, and the Mayor "abdicated," as Foreys says. The Dodecanese delegate in London panicked, and wrote to the British Foreign Office asking for intervention, blaming the "revolt" on Italian infringement of historic Dodecanese privileges. In 1930 Symiot women once again seized power, this time in reaction to the abolition by the Italians of free local elections. Historian Nick Doumanis reports that women marched onto the main square, "armed with rocks and wooden implements." In 1934, he reports, yet again Symiot women rose up when local leaders announced that they could no longer provide free public health and pharmaceuticals because of the declining sponge trade and mass emigration. Church bells were sounded, calling the women into the main square. Violent clashes took place when the women marched toward the town hall. The *carabinieri* held them off, and the Italian *delegato* finally quelled the demonstration by promising to pass their grievances on to higher authorities on Rhodes.

And of course, there is the incident described in my grandfather's poem when Symiot women held the *kaimakam-bey,* the Turkish police chief, and leading merchants captive.

> *Though orders came to us last March,*
> *they've been kept under cover,*
> *   so that Symiots might sail,*
> *their diving not prevented.*
> *   But five or six spongers heard of it*
> *and argued with the captains,*
> *   and all the women of the town*
> *rushed to the shore with wooden clubs*
> *   as if possessed by demons.*
> *They rushed the town hall at Kaimak*
> *   and stood on the stairs demanding reasons,*

and forced Benyamin and Katrion,
  along with other merchants,
back to their house.
No water would they let them drink
  till they produced the orders
in plain for all to see.
Violent and patient they stood firm,
  exposed the scheming secrets
and Kaimak-bey promised them
  at last, to earn their quiet,
to quit the machines and so they left,
  and wait unto to this day
demanding the diving cease.

KASTELLORIZO

In 1934 social protest by women on Kastellorizo also spilled into violence. According to Doumanis and fellow historian Nick Pappas, the women of Kastellorizo rose up, angered at the doubling of import duties on food and fuel. Believing that the Mayor had lined his own pockets and conspired with Italian authorities to permit the increase, the women turned their fury on the Mayor. A group of women in traditional dress pelted the mayor's chambers with stones; as Doumanis and Pappas point out, their dress was a telling sign of a community's moral protest. Panicked Italian soldiers struck rioting women with rifles and, in a related incident, shoved women into the harbor.

As one male eyewitness described the scene, "They would tuck their blouses into their *vrakes* [baggy pants] like men, and go from door to door encouraging people to demonstrate."

KALYMNOS

It is called The Rock War: *o Petropolemos*. It is when the skies of Pothia darkened with a shower of rocks.

For three days in April 1935 the women of Kalymnos fought the armed soldiers of a great nation. That's the way today it is held in memory, in the minds of women who recall it more than sixty years later. The Rock War is the most famous of all the women's protests in the Dodecanese, and it took place on Kalymnos, the Island of the Sponge Fishermen. The anthropologist David Sutton recounts that story in his book *Memories Cast in Stone.*

Kalymnian women, fearing that assimilationist-minded Italians were maneuvering to replace the Greek Orthodox religion with the Roman Catholic, attacked armed Italian troops with a shower of rocks. As Sutton describes, using superior numbers and features of the local landscape—"an abundance of large rocks"—the women hurled rocks down upon the arriving Italian soldiers in the harbor of Pothia. Soldiers were struck in the head, helmets flying into the sea. The "War" lasted three days, and ended when the one Kalymnian man who took an active role was shot dead, a bullet through his head. Kalymnian men had been "allowed" to supply the rocks, but the women cast them.

Anthropologist Juliet Du Boulay captured this view of Greek women in a comment recorded from her fieldwork: Women are "*defteros Theos,*" a second God, reflecting their role in religious life. On Kalymnos women took action when they believed their religion was threatened. Today, The Rock War lives on in Kalymnian memory as the story of proud, free-spirited Kalymnian women defending their religion against the incursion of a foreign power.

In the 1950s, after union with Greece, Kalymnian women protested successfully—and less violently—to insure, as a matter of law, that divers left their wives enough money to live on during their long absence at sea. Another protest followed in the 1960s when, as Russ Bernard reports, one diver divorced his wife and married an entertainer. The women of Kalymnos descended on the Mayor's office, demanding action to prevent recurrence. Wandering musical bands, accompanied by female singers, had been accustomed to arriving on Kalymnos each April to perform at the tavernas before the fleet set sail. Divers often spent their *platika* freely on music and drink; and the female singers sometimes worked as prostitutes in their off-hours. As a result of the protest, a law was passed in 1965 preventing female entertainers from accompanying musicians on Kalymnos.

THE FISHERMAN AND HIS WIFE

Don't the women walk behind the men?
—Commonplace Misconception about Greek Women

Outside of Greece, Greek women are perceived as traditional and deferential to the men. How then does one explain the "revolts" in the Dodecanese? The easiest explanation is to say that "stereotype" is a Greek word and so is "paradox." Anyone who considers the screen personas of such great Greek actresses as Melina Mercouri and Irini Papas would hesitate at the stereotype of *deferential*. Mercouri and Papas are powerful, defiant, and righteous; they radiate the dark energy of Sophocles and the sensuality of Sappho.

In 1999 the Public Broadcasting System in the United States produced a television special on the Greek-Americans, showing highly accomplished, second-generation, Greek-American men and women nervously chuckling over the power of the *nikokyra*, the woman of the house, in the old-country households in which they were raised. Normally it is an interior power—found within the confines of the home— but periodically it surges into the public squares, as happened in the Dodecanese.

In *Inventing Paradise*, Edmund Keeley writes that Greek women tend to be less inhibited than most Anglo-Saxon women in expressing emotions, "sexual and otherwise." While gentle in manner, "what is fiercest about almost all of them is their pride: personal, family, national." They are proud enough, Keeley writes, "not to be shy about *demonstrating* [my italics] their love both for their lovers and for themselves, or for their children, or for their country, and they will defend what they love with a vehemence that is hardly innocent."

In the Dodecanese, the vehemence of the women's protests and their recurrence derived from two cultural currents that, for a time, flowed together in the eastern Aegean, before dissipating and disappearing in the clear blue water. One flowed out of the deep Greek past—a powerful legacy from Greek folk tradition—the other out of the unique history of the Dodecanese.

From the deep past, almost as Jungian archetype, flowed empow-
ering stories of the *andreiomeni*: the female warrior of Greek folk song
and legend. What I know of the subject derives from the work of
Elizabeth Constantinides who wrote of the *andreiomeni* in the *Journal
of Modern Greek Studies*. The *andreiomeni* takes on the male role of
warrior; in doing so, she shares qualities with the Amazon queens of
ancient myth. Constantinides reports that songs about the Greek female warrior fall into three groups:

1. the account of the maiden who arms herself and boldly rides into
   battle against the enemy;
2. the account of the maiden who disguises herself as a man and lives
   among the *kleftes* (warrior-bandits who in 1821 fought for Greek
   independence) until her sex is revealed during an athletic contest
   when her breast is accidentally bared;
3. poems that describe the women of Souli, in the north of Greece,
   who wreak destruction on the Turks and then die a heroic death.
   The women stave off attacks or rescue beleaguered Souliot men.

From the period of the fighting Souliot women, Constantinides recounts the song of Despo Botsis: Barricaded in a stronghold with her
daughters, daughters-in-law, and grandchildren, she could not drive
off the attacking Turco-Albanians. Rather than surrender, she and the
other women blew themselves up.

> "O come, my children, come with me,
> We shall not live as slaves of Turks."
> She touched the powder with the torch
> Engulfing flames consumed them all.

Also preserved in folk tradition is the memory of Leno Botsaris, a
fifteen-year-old who fled her home with male relatives after the Souliot
surrender to Ali Pasha in 1803. During the slaughter of the Souliots,
she joins her uncle in attacks upon the Turks. When surrounded, she
commits suicide to avoid capture.

And etched into the Greek psyche, known by all Greeks, is this
powerful story: Rather than surrender to the Turks when their town

was besieged, Souliot women took their children and jumped off a cliff, singing and dancing the *Choros tou Zalogou*, the dance of Zalago, as they went over the edge.

Songs about the Souliot women include a desire for freedom, personal heroism, and defiance of death. Often in Greek folk song, the female warrior is a valorous young maiden, "willowy and slender," who engages in heroic action in battle prior to the discovery that she is a woman, with an erotic element that ensues with the discovery. Such songs have been found in the Dodecanese, both on Symi and Kos.

In a *kleftic* version, instead of doing battle, the female warrior takes part in athletic contests when her identity is revealed.

> A beautiful girl, but recognized by none
> Until one fine day, a festival day,
> She vied with the men, wielding sword, hurling stone,
> And from her man-like motions and moves,
> Her silver button broke, and revealed her breast.

Constantinides writes that the Greek warrior maiden "arouses admiration, even awe, because of her bravery and daring." She is unlike any other warrior maiden: "As a hero, she transcends the sphere of ordinary human activity, and like her male counterparts, partakes of that superhuman power which separates the hero from his fellow man."

Constantinides asks how we are to interpret the repeated appearance of the female warrior in Greek myth and folklore, from antiquity until the present. If we view it from a historical base, she suggests, "classical scholars have pointed to societies, especially the more primitive ones, on the fringes of the Greco-Roman world, where armed women took to the field." At the center of Greek myth, of course, is flashing-eyed Athena who, motherless, sprang "full-grown and in full armor" from the head of Zeus, as Edith Hamilton tells us. Although likely a pre-Hellenic goddess taken over by the Greeks, the earliest account of Athena is in the *Iliad*, where she is "a fierce and ruthless battle-goddess," who fights alongside the Greek heroes, personifying excellence in close combat. Elsewhere Athena is "warlike only to defend the State and the home from outside enemies."

In *Inventing Paradise,* Edmund Keeley writes of the time that Henry Miller and Lawrence Durrell, friends, spent together in Greece. Miller eulogized Greek women as "not only as heroic as the men but, along with Orthodox priests, responsible for sustaining the Greek fighting spirit through modern Greek history." "For stubbornness, courage, recklessness, daring," Miller says, "there are no greater examples any-where." And Durrell, who was British, wanted to fight *with* the Greeks, which inspired Miller to report: "Who wouldn't prefer to fight beside a Bouboulina (the celebrated War of Independence heroine), for ex-ample, than with a gang of sickly, effeminate recruits from Oxford or Cambridge."

The confluence of a cultural archetype, the female warrior, and the unique history of the Dodecanese gave rise to the women's protests. Not incidentally, the protests of the women coincided with the reign of the *skafandra,* when husbands, sons, and fathers were away for long periods of time, at sea and at risk. And not incidentally, these protests took place on small, occupied islands.

NOWHERE TO HIDE

Although essentially self-governing, and always ethnically Greek, the Dodecanese were occupied almost continuously by foreign invaders from ancient times until union with Greece in 1948. Among others, the Crusaders, the Turks, the Italians, and the Germans all occupied the Dodecanese. Women inferred correctly that if they rather than their men protested, the protest might register with authorities with-out anyone coming to harm. All of the occupying powers, except for the Germans, were sensitive to Great Power opinion, and therefore reluctant to retaliate against local agitation, especially from women.

As Nick Doumanis points out, resistance was never a practical op-tion for the men. Geography alone precluded it: "The islands were small, thinly populated, and very easily traversed by troops searching for the partisans." However, as David Sutton reports, the men were quick to suggest that men were "behind the protests." This was *not* the case. All of the women's protests appeared to be spontaneous, with no one afterward even remembering "leaders," men or women. The women always relied on overwhelming numbers and their wager that no serious harm would come to them or their men.

There is, as well, a history of defiant acts on the part of the men during the occupations. Stamatis Kalafatas, as described in the poem, was imprisoned by the Turks in the Crusader dungeons of Kos and Rhodes, as were other Dodecanese leaders. In the last half of the nineteenth century and in the early twentieth century, before seizure of the islands by the Italians, the Turks made repeated attempts to curtail the historic privileges of the Dodecanese islands in order to bring their governance more into line with the rest of the Empire. When island leaders resisted, they were carted off to prison. Likewise under the Italians, men who resisted similar curtailments found themselves taken off to the old dungeons of the Knights of St. John in the Dodecanese or put into prison on Sicily.

THE BUSINESS WIDOWS

In "The Fisherman and His Wife," Russ Bernard tells us that wives of seafarers worldwide live for long periods without their men and "achieve a certain degree of independence, learning to deal with minor annoyances and major problems." In the spring, when sponge boats made the sign of the cross in the harbor and headed out to sea, the women of Kalymnos became "business widows." These women developed skills in dealing with authority, and were emboldened to act, even in protest. Yet, the role of the business widow was "ambivalent, difficult, and precarious."

> For the sake of her own *philotimo* [honor], and that of her children and of her family, she must preserve her husband's by not appearing to usurp his authority during his absence. Yet, the simple facts of life dictate that she must act in his stead. For six months of every year she must ask herself if she is indeed free to act in her husband's name, or whether she should defer action until his return.

"A Kalymnian woman must understand," Bernard wrote, "that a man's *philotimo* is at stake every time he deals with women. The side of family life which faces on public display must demonstrate the husband's control of the situation. A woman's own *philotimo* depends to a large extent on her not doing anything to harm her husband's *philotimo*."

Bernard, writing in 1966, observed that on Kalymnos, by custom and tradition, "the status of man is defined as superior to that of woman, and everyone must acknowledge this, at least superficially." But women in the Dodecanese had resources, too, in the struggle for personal power in the relationship with their husbands. A Greek woman found empowerment in her traditional right to "a say-so in the disposal of her dower property," as the anthropologist Jill Dubisch points out. On Symi the famed swift ships passed by inheritance to the sons, but the Italianate houses went to the daughters. Oftentimes, women would arrive at marriage literally controlling the house. Uncomfortable at home, the wife's domain—more so if a wife's widowed mother lived with them—men were extruded into their public place, the *kafenia*.

MAD AS THE SEA AND WIND

Women had other resources in maintaining personal power, according to Bernard, including cajolery, argument, withholding of sexual favors, and—important in a seaside culture with men gone at sea for half the year—the threat of infidelity. It was the ultimate revenge that an abandoned Penelope could inflict upon her husband.

As Bernard wrote: "On a boat 33 by 11 feet, where fifteen men live out half a year, the thought of being known as a cuckold is almost intolerable to many individuals." Very rarely, especially on a small island, was the threat ever acted upon. The threat, however, remained a preoccupation of the sponge fishermen at sea.

But the complaint of abandonment is an ancient one to Greek women. Compressed, here is dialogue from Aristophanes' "Lysistrata."

Lysistrata. Don't you feel sad and sorry because the fathers of your children are far away from you with the army? For I'll undertake, there is not one of you whose husband is not abroad at this moment.
Calonice. Mine has been the last five months in Thrace.

Lysistrata. 'Tis seven long months since mine left for Pylos. Instead of enjoying the pleasures of love and making the best of our youth and beauty, we are left to languish far from our husbands.

I have tried to understand the state of mind of the women during the reign of the *skafandra* and especially the fury that revealed itself in protest, not only against the *skafandra* but in other causes as well. Shakespeare's Hamlet, "Mad as the wind and sea when both contend" (4.1.7), flooded my thought one night as I strolled the Kalymnian shorewalk.

And I thought too of Lysistrata, "What matters that I was born a woman if I can cure your misfortunes?"

four

THE POETICS OF MANHOOD

Men are not made for safe havens.

—Aeschylus

Kalymnian divers pay a call to the Cretan port of Agios Nikolaos

It was a Sunday evening and all the Cretans were out promenading—clad in their Sunday-best and walking in that stiff, strange manner of those who are desperately trying not to crease their trousers or skirts, nor ruffle starched blouse nor freshly ironed shirt. Suddenly, without warning, there came down the quay a group of strange beings. Half-bearded, slouch-hatted, thumb-in-belt, lean men—and Greeks, not foreigners. The newcomers settled themselves in the most prominent Kafeneion, slumping down in its chairs and commandeering others on which to rest their spurred boots. Plump waiters flew around like startled quail, cackling excitedly. Trays arrived loaded with beer, which was drunk straight from the bottle, polished glasses ignored, the sun-blackened, hawk-faces thrown far back the better to swallow. The divers, as alien as Martians, seemed superficially equally imperturbable but covertly lapped cat-like at the awe and approbation their bravado presence caused. The young Cretan men appeared shocked and stunned by seeing too many of their precious conventions so easily, so haphazardly, shattered and yet hung around like stage-struck children before a great theatrical performance. For it was theatre—pure Greek drama as played with a flair that only Greeks can carry off. With beautiful timing the group finally rose as a body, toppling chairs and leaving beer undrunk. There was no need to call for their bill, the money was piled ready on every saucer—and they were gone and Agios Nikolaos was left gasping, their Sunday suddenly flat and their staid world in ruins.

—William Travis, *Bus Stop Symi*

Long after knowledge of proper deep-diving technique had diffused, the Greek divers of the Aegean, especially the Kalymnians, continued to employ extraordinarily risky methods of diving. As Russ Bernard reported in 1967 from his own observations, these included "rapid, no-stage ascent; untying of life line and refusal to obey the commands of the tender; and some overstaying of bottom time." Bernard clocked Kalymnian divers, for example, who dove to 120 feet of depth, spent an average of 29 minutes on the bottom, and ascended to the surface in just 3.5 minutes. Given the depth of the dive and bottom time, standard diving tables recommended a gradual, staged ascent of 20 minutes for a *single* dive. The Kalymnians, of course, were doing *repetitive* diving—three dives a day, seven days a week—which upped the risk; modern dive tables in fact discourage repetitive diving over 100 feet. The ascent of the Kalymnian divers was dangerously swift, six times faster than recommended. The Kalymnians were diving with mad daring.

As Bernard asked in 1967: "Given their own cultural framework and knowledge, why do they choose to accept the risks of death and paralysis?" Two cultural factors influenced their choice, he felt: (1) honor of debt, as described on page 73; and (2) the status and role of the diver in Kalymnian society. Over time Russ Bernard shifted his view fully to the first, to a belief that it was solely the *platika* system, the 100-percent prepayment system coupled with honor of debt, that drove the divers to dive with dangerous disregard for safety. It is here, in respectful rebellion, that I break with my brilliant mentor. I think Bernard was right in 1967.

RISK-TAKING BEHAVIORS

Russ Bernard once told me that when he went to sea with the divers he "counted and measured everything" because it had never been done. I smiled when he told me; in my life as a director of admissions I always retained the recruitment visit to Stuyvesant High School in New York, Russ's alma mater and the finest science high school in America. *Why wouldn't he count everything?* As a social scientist Russ also logged everything, including the divers' risk-taking behaviors, which was a blessing for me. Some of the behaviors advanced production while others were pure daredevil stunts. What follows is a sampling.

After the diver was dressed in the 172-pound diving suit, he crossed himself and jumped overboard, sometimes with the embellishment of a one-and-a-half twist. No other diving group in the world, Bernard observed, jumped from a diving vessel into the water in deep-sea gear, and for good reason: it risks fouling lines, breaking hoses, or suffering concussion with the 35-pound brass helmet.

Divers wandered into deep caves in search of sponges despite caves' being the haunts of dangerous deep-sea creatures like octopuses and poisonous sea snakes. In addition, the sharp edges of caves can sever an air hose or put a lethal tear in a diver's suit.

Divers purposely crossed hoses. Often boats worked in close proximity, and so a diver could arrange to land on the bottom with his hose directly over the hose of another diver; this was extremely dangerous, since the diver whose hose was on the bottom could not ascend without first going under the hose above.

Some divers jumped onto the sponge bed of divers from a rival boat. Russ reported that one diver "stealthily" approached another diver whose back was turned and pulled the other's lifeline with the signal "pull me up." The crew hauled the confused diver onto the sponge boat, leaving the other diver alone to harvest the bed of sponges.

One diver yanked on another man's lifeline with the signal for danger; the crew worried for twenty minutes until the man surfaced unharmed.

In a classic prank, two divers met on the bottom and decided to exchange lifelines. Their vessels were within yards of one another. When they surfaced they came up on each other's boats, and their helmets were removed before anyone knew the joke had been played.

In "Fernez" diving, similar to *narghile* diving, the diver wore a wet suit, mask, and air hose fed with compressed air from above. But he did not wear fins; he used his feet to travel along the sea bottom. Despite the danger of skin contact with poison coral, poisonous snakes, or cuts to the feet, divers often refused to wear shoes, which was somehow deemed less manly.

The main cause of death and injury among Kalymnian divers has always been too-quick ascent. As Bernard reported, the single greatest cause of diving accidents among Kalymnians was "controlled blow-up, when a diver, due to come up, allowed his suit to fill with air instead of releasing it through the control valve as he did while working. The more air in the suit, the more buoyant the diver, and the swifter the ascent. Air also expands during ascent so excess air must be vented to control buoyancy. A novice diver could create dangerous blow-up by accident, called *fouska*, when air built up in the suit because the diver failed to release it, and the diver involuntarily *shot* to the surface, bursting up and *out of* the sea. Fernez divers who did not ascend themselves but were hauled up to the surface too quickly also suffered.

Even before the engine-driven air pump was introduced in the 1920s, divers pushed limits. Bernard reports that, with the hand-cranked air pump, adequate air supply could be provided by the pumping crew— two strong young men turning the two cranks on the air pump—to twenty-seven meters, but divers worked beyond that depth, to up to sixty-four meters. The engine-driven pump could deliver adequate air to fifty-five meters, Bernard reports, but with reduction in air quality; the air was often hot, greasy, and tasted of engine vapors. Of course we know that with engine-driven pumps, divers worked at far greater depth than fifty-five meters.

Of eighteen divers Bernard interviewed who had five years of experience or more, *all* had suffered one or more cases of the bends.

Some of the risk-taking behaviors can only be defined as death-defying acts since the men knew the degree of risk they were taking.

As Bernard says, "These men were professionals." Yet, they flirted with death. *Yiati?* Why?

HONOR OF DEBT

Massive credit is the basis of sponge fishing.
—Harvey R. Bernard

I find that sentence the most compelling of all that Bernard so brilliantly wrote about the sponge-fishing industry,

If *skafandra* sponge fishing had become "a Tyranny," as the Symiots called it, the *exchequer* was massive credit. Credit was extended freely to all: the captains, the divers, and even the divers' wives.

During the winter layover captains were happy to oblige the divers by lending them money against the next season's *platika*, Bernard reports. The divers were then bound to the sea by their debt. Bernard reports that captains would actively "cajole" solvent divers into debt or cajole them to go into deeper debt. The system insured a pool of divers for the next season. By winter's end the average diver was in debt and *obliged* to go to sea.

By law on Kalymnos in the mid-1960s no man was entitled to more than 26,000 drachmas ($867) in advance payment, according to Bernard. *Platika* or *prokatavoli* (prepayment) was limited *legally* to roughly one-third of what a diver could ultimately earn. But the divers demanded, and received, the total amount in advance. Because banks would not lend *platika* money to the captains in excess of the legal limit, the captains borrowed the rest elsewhere at usurious rates: 20 to 40 percent. If the trip failed, the captain would be saddled with a debt he could not pay.

The captain, therefore, was driven to adopt a diving strategy that would get him out of debt at the end of the trip and provide an income to live on. Hence the captains sailed for the most lucrative sights, usually off the coast of North Africa. Symiot captains went to North Africa whenever possible; frequently to sponge beds east of Matruh, Egypt, and so *Mandroucha* became the Symiot synonym for the sponge-fishing season. Because the diver had received 100 percent of his wages in advance, one of his strongest motivations was to extricate himself from debt. This was not only because his *filotimo*—his pride and honor and that of his family—depended on it, but also because doing so allowed him to receive equal *platika* or more in the next season. Extrication from debt was the reason "either my hide or the sponge" became the motto of the Kalymnian diver.

Platika took a long time to work off; all the while the diver was in debt to the captain, the captain in debt to the financiers, and the divers' wives in debt to island merchants. Massive credit was the basis of sponge fishing; it is what sealed the divers' cruel pact with the sea.

It is important to note, as Bernard does, that repetitive diving and rapid ascent were not occasional risks taken by individual divers. It was an entire production strategy. Diving seven days a week, three dives a day, was necessary for a diver to earn his *platika* by season's end. The time necessary to get divers dressed, down to the bottom for half an hour, and back up, plus the time necessary to search for new sponge beds, placed enormous pressure on divers to ascend too quickly, given the typical seven divers on board a sponge boat. To follow the ascent tables would have prevented divers from being able to make three dives a day in the available daylight hours.

I once asked John Maillis of Tarpon Springs, affectionately called "the 100-year-old diver" since he was still diving at seventy-six, if the divers followed the ascent tables. He replied, "If you used the tables, you didn't get enough sponge."

And so, as Bernard points out, what evolved was a "production strategy" based on risk-taking; it was a strategy that benefited captains, divers, and the economy of Kalymnos. Before World War II, 70 percent of the economy of Kalymnos rested on a foundation of sponges. Fifteen jobs depended on a single diver's output. As prayed in the litanies of the Greek church, *Kyrie eleison*, Lord have mercy.

STATUS AND ROLE OF THE DIVER

"The divers were treated like heroes and they were heroes," Kyriacos Hadzidakis had told me.

Because of the danger inherent in their occupation, the divers established their place in the Aegean sponge-fishing islands as folk heroes. As Bernard observed in 1968, large sums of money were needed "to validate and revalidate this status." The reputation of a diver was tied to the *platika* he could command. As a diver walked along the shorewalk of Pothia, one could hear his reputation muttered in British currency: "There goes a three hundred pound *platika* man." Not all divers, but many, spent their money wildly, enough for the reputation for exhibitionist spending to stick. The divers were expected to buy drinks in the *taverna*, to be generous to relatives in need, and to dowry sisters, cousins, and nieces.

On Symi I not only learned that some divers light their cigarettes with thousand-lire notes but that others routinely *smoked* thousand-lire notes. Doing so affected the health of the diver even more than the rampant cigarette smoking among divers. So widespread was cigarette smoking that, to test whether a diver had been "hit" during his dive, a crewman routinely placed a lit cigarette in the diver's lips on removal of the diver's helmet: If the diver took a drag and it did not make him dizzy, he was presumed to be fine.

Hadzidakis felt that the divers' lifestyle onshore, heavy with drinking and smoking, might have affected the divers' health and made them more vulnerable to decompression disease when diving. Thus, given the risks taken on- and offshore, there should have been a higher incidence of casualties among the Kalymnian divers. However, Russ Bernard found the contrary. They were, in fact, defying fate.

Tales of exhibitionist spending are legendary. Bernard tells of the diver who reputedly bought a keg of wine, opened the spigot on the floor of the *taverna*, inviting all to fill their glasses, and promised to dance until the keg ran dry. Such no-tomorrow spending underscored poetically, with diver as poet, the danger of their occupation; the divers might not return or might return paralyzed.

The divers were treated like heroes and acted the part. In the *kafenia* of the sponge-fishing islands—on Aegina, Kalymnos, Halki, and Symi—divers told and retold stories of danger at sea; they talked of shark attacks and near shark attacks, of accidents barely averted, of strange sights seen under the sea, and of their sexual exploits in the bordellos of North Africa. Young boys were spellbound.

Bernard reported that adultery on shore in North Africa was taken for granted by all Kalymnians and tolerated, if not accepted, by Kalymnian women. Back on Kalymnos, where a diver's adultery would be known and would humiliate his wife, such behavior was not engaged in. The diver feared retaliation by his wife when he was at sea. In general the divers' wild behavior was tolerated, if looked down upon, since the economy of the sponge-fishing islands so rested on a foundation of sponges.

ACROSS THE GREAT DIVIDE

Why, in fact, do people in a culture hold the ideas they do and act accordingly? I have learned that a Great Divide exists among anthropologists: On one side are those who hold a "materialistic" view in explaining social phenomena; and on the other side are those who hold an "ideational" view. The materialist position explains social phenomena as a consequence of underlying "material conditions." Demography, economics, technology, or other structural factors cause people to hold ideas or even to change their ideas. The material conditions of life explain why one culture is different from another. Those who hold the "ideational" view believe that the ideas harbored by a culture cause people to act the way they do. Why does an admissions officer get mixed up in an ideological debate among anthropologists? Because I want to understand why the divers took the risks they did.

In the case of the Greek sponge divers, anthropologists who hold the materialistic view would ascribe the risk-defying behaviors to the "material conditions"—namely the *platika* or *prokatavoli* (prepayment) system and the production strategy that ensued, which did not allow enough time for safe, staged ascent. The divers never had a chance— *platika* put them at risk every day. Those who hold the ideational view would say that the divers took the risks they did because of some "social capital" that accrued to them: The culture bestowed certain social rewards upon them; it held them to be folk heroes and permitted hedonistic behavior. Like the Colossus of Rhodes, with his legs straddling Mandraki harbor, I straddle the Great Divide: I believe both positions hold truth.

Of course 100 percent *platika*, three-dives-a-day every day, and time-pressure drove divers to take dangerous risks. Bernard shows that in 1965, a year when the skyrocketing price of sponges and a labor shortage combined to send *platika* to runaway heights, the casualty rate among divers soared. Bernard wrote to me, "The *platika* system drove divers to take risks that were statistically guaranteed to result in an escalating death rate." In 1965 the highest *platika* paid was 90,000 drachmas, with 60,000 commonplace, despite the official limit of 26,000. Divers took terrible risks to harvest enough sponge to match the huge *platika* they had received. In my mind, however, another factor in 1965 could well have contributed to driving up the casualty rate; namely, in the panic to recruit divers, men with little or no prior diving experience were sent into the deep. *Forty percent* of divers on Kalymnian boats that year were non-Kalymnian, Bernard reports, as the call for divers went out far and wide.

According to Bernard, structural and infrastructural forces beyond the control of the local people were the cause of the high death rates, not some ideational factor.

But, here's the nagging question: Why did the men buy into the system in the first place? Why did they accept the high full *platika* in advance and press for more if it entailed danger they were fully aware of? What if these sponges were found in the North Sea? Would the Brits or Scandinavians have exploited the resource in the same death-defying manner? Both the British and the Scandinavians fish the North Sea, which is dangerous work; but death rates for sponge divers far exceeded those for any other category of fishermen.

When I posed these questions to the Kalymnians, one British-educated Kalymnian, now retired on Kalymnos, who lived his adult life in the United Kingdom and worked there as a sponge merchant, spoke for all when he said, "The answer is no. The Kalymnians have a *hardness of character* that comes from 'living on a rock,'" which is how Kalymnians refer to their barren island, *agono nisi*. Surely economic resources around the world go unexploited because native dynamism is lacking to exploit the resources. Why was it that it was the Israelis who made the deserts bloom?

In my view, only when yoked together do the materialistic and ideational positions explain the heroic, fate-defying Greek diver of the

Aegean. What upended the solely materialistic explanation for me is what I knew of Kalymnian divers who came to America. When hard times hit the sponge industry in Florida, many divers left diving to become bridge painters. Some died falling from bridges two-hundred-feet-high on perfectly clear days. Remember, this was America, where the "material conditions" of life allowed them to pursue other, safer work—they did not live on a rock—yet they chose a death-defying sequel to sponge diving. Why is that?

What was the "social capital"? What was the "rush"? What were the cultural ideas that impelled the divers? What was, in Michael Herzfeld's brilliant phrase, the "poetics of manhood" in Greece that so shaped their thinking? Surely Homer himself would have recognized in an instant—as if from Odysseus's story—the cunning, daring, and even the recklessness of the divers.

> Sing to me of the man, Muse, the man of twists and turns
> driven time and again off course, once he had plundered
> the hallowed heights of Troy.
> Many cities of men he saw and learned their minds,
> many pains he suffered, heartsick on the open sea,
> fighting to save his life and bring his comrades home.
> But he could not save them from disaster, hard as he strove—
> the recklessness of their own ways destroyed them all,
> the blind fools, they devoured the cattle of the Sun
> and the Sungod blotted out the day of their return.
>
> Launch out on his story, Muse, daughter of Zeus, start from where you
> will—and sing for our time too.
>
> —Homer, *Odyssey* (trans. Robert Fagles)

One icon of anthropology, Ruth Benedict, invoked Nietsche's study of Greek tragedy when she analyzed the cultures of the Native American tribes of North America. In *Patterns of Culture* Benedict discusses Nietsche's "two diametrically opposed ways of arriving at the values of existence." The Dionysian "seeks to attain in his most valued moments escape from the boundaries imposed upon him by his five senses, to break through into another order of experience." With Blake, the Dionysian believes that "the path of excess leads to the palace of wisdom." On the other hand, the Appollonian distrusts all this. He "knows but one law, measure in the Hellenic sense." He keeps the middle of the road, stays within the known map, does not meddle with disruptive psychological states. In North America Benedict saw the Pueblos as Appollonian; the rest of the tribes were "passionately Dionysian. They valued all violent experience, all means by which human beings may break through the usual sensory routine, and to all such experiences they attributed the highest value."

Just so, the Greek divers of the Aegean, especially in the age of the *skafandra*, fell into the Dionysian way of arriving at the value of existence. They sought to escape normal "sensory routine" through their "vision quest." As Benedict writes, the power of the "vision experience" gives "a theoretically unlimited freedom to the individual." The individual who seeks it "might go out and get this supremely coveted power, no matter to what family he belonged."

EASTER BROUGHT TO YOU BY TNT

Yes, in Homer's phrase, *sing for our time too*. David Sutton, in his stunning book on how the past is always present in Greek life, *Memories Cast in Stone*, writes of the Kalymnian fascination with dynamite. The fascination is no more evident than at Easter.

Easter is Greece's most spectacular holiday. In churches all over Greece, at a beautiful moment in the midnight Orthodox Easter service, the lights are turned off. Each member of the congregation holds and lights a candle, one person taking the flame from the next, first from the priest's holy flame: and the priest begins to chant *Christos Anesti*—Christ is Risen. Outside, young men begin to cast firecrackers and set off fireworks—simultaneously all over Greece. On the island of Symi, in the prosperous years, a boat aglow with a fountain of fireworks was sent sailing on a high-wire across the hauntingly beautiful harbor, set against the night sky. Alas, the wire was anchored on one side at *Panagia tou Castrou*, the church my great granduncle Stamatis helped build.

Easter in Greece is both Easter and the American Fourth of July all rolled into one: in Christ's Resurrection the Greeks see the Resurrection of Greece in 1821, its liberation after "four hundred years of slavery." Christ gained new life, and so did the Greeks. Christ's Passion is the Passion of Greece: Birth, Death, and Resurrection. The Kalymnians—never shy about taking to excess—set off, not firecrackers or fireworks, but dynamite. Easter brought to you by TNT. It is an extremely dangerous tradition, as was evident in 1980 when four were killed and four others severely injured when a boy tossed a lit stick of dynamite that had seemed a dud back onto a stack of 250 pounds of TNT.

In classic form the dynamite throwing takes place, in call-and-response manner, as Sutton reports, from the mountains of St. George and St. Stephanos, which face the harbor of Pothia from opposite sides. It is led by rival groups that have "captains"; women are not participants, but they help prepare the dynamite and are spectators. Given the huge crowd at Easter the priest often chants the *Christos Anesti* outside in the courtyard before an overflowing congregation. It is a source of pride to dynamite throwers if the priest is driven inside by the fury of the blasts of TNT going off around him. The Greek army disallows Kalymnians from serving as guards at ammunition dumps for fear of their stealing dynamite for use at Easter and other celebrations. I heard dynamite blasts set off several times in early June of 1997, for no particular reason, while I was sitting out-of-doors at the *kafenia* of Pothia. Sutton reports that in the late 1970s, when then Prime Minister Karamanlis visited Kalymnos, he was given "a traditional Kalymnian greeting." Amid the sound of blasting dynamite Karamanlis turned to his minister, who was of Kalymnian descent, and said: "Kos and Rhodes and other islands have been Europeanized . . . but on Kalymnos the true Greek spirit still resides."

"The road of excess leads to the palace of wisdom," Blake contends. If we follow that road on Kalymnos, home of the Kalymnian penchant for excess, perhaps we can grow wise about the "true Greek spirit." On Kalymnos the road of excess can be a noisy one. Pothia is so densely populated that it is classified as an urban area; young Kalymnian men love to remove the mufflers from their motor scooters and *roar* at deafening pitch through its narrow, winding streets.

GREEK MANHOOD: A POETICS OF THE SELF

In his brilliant study of the tradition of sheep theft in the mountain villages of Crete, *The Poetics of Manhood*, Michael Herzfeld described a social phenomenon he calls "performative excellence"—the ability "to foreground manhood by means of deeds that strikingly speak for themselves." Cretan shepherds steal sheep in order to show those who would steal their sheep that retaliation will definitely occur.

As a fascinating benefit, Cretan sheep thieves develop friendships out of the tradition, from the very "performative excellence" they exhibit. If your theft is done with sufficient cleverness, daring, and flair, you earn respect and possibly a friend and ally in the shepherd whose sheep you have stolen. An example is when one thief served the investigating police officer the cooked meat of the sheep he had stolen, as thief and police officer discussed the perplexing case. What counts is not what men do, but *how* they do it. As Herzfeld writes, the theft

> . . . must be performed in such a manner that it serves immediate notice on the victim of the perpetrator's skill: as he is good at stealing, so, too, he will be good at being your enemy or your ally—so choose! Both the act of theft and the narration that follows it focus on the act itself. They announce the quality of the theft, the skill with which it has been performed and recounted, as primary components of the actor's claim to a manly selfhood that captures the essence of Glendiot, Cretan and Greek identity all at the same time.

To the extent that the Cretan sheep thieves succeed, the act is said to have *simasia*, meaning. The greater the risk the greater *simasia* the actor experiences; and always the *simasia* is associated with heroism, bravery, and insubordination, "which Glendiots associate with being a true Greek." Effective performance comes with "judicious rule breaking, since this foregrounds the performer's skill at manipulating the conventions."

Peter Loizos, in another study of masculinity in Greece, cites the anthropologist David Gilmore's classic definition of the male role in the world: "to procreate, to provision, and to protect." In a country under foreign rule for four hundred years—and in the case of the Dodecanese for far longer—a man's performative excellence can show him to be a true man, revealing his potential to procreate, provision, and protect in the face of indeterminacy. The *eghoismos* of the Greek man, the *self-regard* so often observed, is a poetic statement about being a man. Herzfeld observed that the Cretans say of a man they respect that he is "good *at being a man*" (*kala 'ndras*, well [at being a] man), which suggests something different from "being a good man" (*kalos andras*). It evokes "an unambiguously active condition: the *kala 'ndras* or the *kala eghoistis* ('well man' and 'well assertive man') is not one who rests on his laurels but continues to earn them," Herzfeld reports. It implies the performative: action is transfigured, he suggests, by *how* something is executed, by its embellishment, by the sheer stylistic. The "poetics of manhood" means that action—poetically rendered— can stand for words in the same way that words can stand for action.

When a Greek man gets up to dance—all alone on the floor as Greek men sometimes do—lending to his dance his signature embellishments, it speaks volumes. Any man rising to dance while another Greek man is on the floor dancing his dance does so at peril. I watched my Greek tutor, Christos Stergiou, dance the *zebekiko* in his own living room. He motioned to his mother to place a tall, lit, three-candle candelabra on the floor as he spun and spun again, his leg sweeping the flames. Afterward, I asked if he had seen the maneuver done before. No, it was an improvisation. *Kala 'ndras* is Christos; Christos is good at *being a man*.

In his study of life in Glendi—the mythical name he gave the mountain village he studied—Herzfeld writes: "Life is regarded as a barren stretch of time, a blank page on which the genuine poet of his own manhood must write as engaging an account as he can."

I think of how my grandfather's poem was *all words about actions* and how the divers' daring was *all actions about words*: both were poetically proclaiming, "I am good *at being a man*." Both constituted, in Herzfeld's locution, "a poetics of the self."

THE UNTETHERED LIFE

Among young Kalymnian divers, Bernard reported, lack of prudence is "a definite mark of high status. . . . The ability to face death and to do so purposely is considered a hallmark of manhood in any young Kalymnian diver." Most serious diving accidents happened to divers under twenty-five years of age. Consider what Bernard observed about divers given the signal by the lifeline tender that their time is up and the diver must return to the surface. Bernard noted that in as many as one dive in ten, the diver will not surface but instead will untie his lifeline, which is then hauled up by the tender. The diver continues to gather sponges; and the crew on board is left with no alternative but to wait and see what happens. The untethered diver is in full control. Typically the diver ascends within a couple of minutes, a sign that his judgment was not affected by nitrogen narcosis ("rapture of the deep"), which can cause a diver to be disoriented. Rather the untethering is *ostentation*; it is a deliberate form of insubordination.

Inscribed on the gravestone of Cretan-born writer Nikos Kazantzakis is the epitaph "I hope for nothing. I fear nothing. I am free." The epitaph comes from Kazantzakis's writing. All Greeks know it and embrace the pose the words represent. *I hope for nothing. I fear nothing. I am free.* It is a pose that can keep a race free, as it did the Hellenes— their fate for so long controlled by powers in far-off places—but it is a pose that can kill a twenty-year-old diver off the coast of Benghazi.

One reason anthropologists love Greece is that it is one of the few cultures in the world that has existed continuously in one place since antiquity; it is a place where the burden and glory of the past are always present. In Greece the line between past and present is erased.

On Kalymnos the dynamite throwers have been making a poetic statement successively to the Turks, the Italians, the Germans, and now to the central Greek government: We are the keepers of the true Greek spirit. We are alive. They have been saying, with the Cretan shepherds, "The law doesn't reach here" (*Edho o nomos dhe ftani*).

The Kalymnians take perverse pleasure in other islanders' view of them as "wild." One hallmark of an island is that it is so *insular*—a wonderful place to protect a culture from the sweep of change, as is true of the highlands of Crete. In some real sense Karamanlis was right: the true Greek spirit lives, only more so, on the island of Kalymnos. Daring. Love of freedom. Insubordination. Even recklessness. All are truly Greek.

AFTOKTONIA: SUICIDE FOR SWEET MOTHER GREECE

I was raised on this story, at my father's knee. When the Nazis occupied the Acropolis in Athens, a young Greek officer forced to take down the Greek flag wrapped it around himself and threw himself off the escarpment. *Aftoktonia*, suicide for Sweet Mother Greece. *I hope for nothing. I fear nothing. I am free.*

Other than the Jews of Europe, who were in their own category, no other European ethnic group suffered as many casualties proportionately as the Greeks in World War II. They resisted the Axis onslaught and suffered as the Nazis punished with mass reprisal.

One day, as I searched for *simasia*—meaning—in what I was observing about the Kalymnian divers, who appeared somehow different from other Greeks, David Sutton e-mailed me: "The Kalymnians are not alone in their swagger, and yet they are different from the Koans and the Lerians, and more similar to the Cretan shepherds or the Maniats."

As I reread the e-mail I realized that one reason that I find the scene that opens this chapter so fascinating—a description of the visit of swaggering Kalymnian divers to Agios Nikolaos, Crete—is that the Cretan shepherds from the mountains view Cretan lowlanders with the same disdain as did those Kalymnian divers. The Kalymnians were condescending toward the harbor lowlanders of Crete. The Cretans of the highlands feel *they* are the keepers of the true Greek spirit. They would probably agree with the Kalymnians and with Aeschylus: Men are not made for safe havens. They are made for rugged, fearsome mountains or the fearsome sea.

It was, after all, the ferocious mountain fighters of Crete in craggy fastnesses who fought on against the Nazis long after the Nazis were in full occupation of the lowlands. After the Nazis had taken the Greek mainland, they launched their attack on Crete with a dramatic first-ever invasion by paratroopers. Greeks around the world knew that even the Nazis would have their hands full on Crete. Cretan mountain fighters were wild, and the Cretan landscape terrifying and brutal. My own father in April 1944 wrote a poem, "The Battle of Crete," that included these lines:

> Even if the battle on Mount Olympus is lost,
> even if the Mother of Nations is enslaved,
> Crete, when free,
> will be the graveyard of the enemy.

When on Crete I stared into the eyes of men in their seventies—the generation who fought the Nazis with knife and rifle—as they sat outside the *kafenia*, glasses of fierce Cretan *raki* in front of them. These were men, I knew, that one did not want to tangle with even in their seventies. The Cretan version of dynamite throwing is reckless and wild firing of guns into the air at weddings; the poetics of the action the same as with the Kalymnians: *I hope for nothing. I fear nothing. I am free.*

STEALING A BAD HOUR FROM DEATH

For the Cretan shepherds "a well-lived life is a life of well-stolen moments," according to Herzfeld. The shepherds see Death—personified as *Haros*—as a talented thief, and they respond to the challenge: "We'll steal one of death's bad hours [i.e., one of the hours that Death had instead hoped to steal *from us*]." They mock death out of respect for a worthy opponent.

Here, then, is the essence of the poetics of manhood in Greece: It lies in the *performative excellence*, in the stylistic. In the case of the Aegean deep-sea divers—and especially the Kalymnians—it lies in the daring, in the risk-taking executed as if it has no meaning, and in the improvisation whereby a man is momentarily silhouetted against the crowd. It is through the excellence and eccentricity of a man's actions—through his *eghoismos*, his self-regard—that a man defines who he is. The true *andras*, the true man, takes the fear Death can inspire and turns it into his own weapon, and in so doing, Herzfeld says, gives meaning to his own life. The *skafandra* divers too were "stealing a bad hour from death." Each time their helmets were screwed down onto their breastplates, they were giving meaning to their lives. But it was at a terrible a cost because *skafandra* and *platika* had raised the stakes so very high, and the sea was so unforgiving. Their manhood had become defined through a cruel pact with the sea. The sea that fed them now ate them.

ALAZONIA

Surely, at times the divers' daring spilled over into arrogance, *alazonia*. Early in his poem Metrophanes attacks the merchants for their arrogance, but later levels brutal criticism at the divers for their arrogance.

> *Those who would dive inside the suits*
> *are labeled the Mechanics,*
> > *and carry on with unheard pride*
> *when first donning the helmet,*
> > *as if it were an olive wreath.*
> *They put on airs, look down their nose—*
> > *look close: they piss their trousers.* *
> *They come on two legs, leave on three,*
> > *all strength loosened by water.*
> *Wild olive-limbs they turn to legs—*
> > *it seems their own won't do.*
> *This is their profit and their growth,*
> > *and when they die their alms*
> *are the cost of burial.*

*The reference to the once-arrogant divers who now "piss their trousers" refers to divers who suffered from urological problems after inadequate decompression. Tom Buttolph, the physician who researches decompression disease for the U.S. Navy, told me that their incontinence or impotence was likely the result of spinal cord damage that affected the sympathetic or parasympathetic nerves which control these functions.

They stroll in rich pants, velvet vests,
then leave them to be auctioned.
But now they're fixed, the swine-herd thieves,
the tricksters, the hen-roosters.
Thanks to their pride, their stealing's stopped
their trickery diminished.
No hen would roost inside her coop,
no rooster crow at daybreak.
They too have peace now, and the poor
pigs can rejoice:
their meat is sold at five per weight,
or hawked in the street for four,
where once they demanded and they got
six piasters as a favor—
the thieves had so thinned out the herds.
Now they dress Western like the Franks,
they even wear gold chains.
They want their wives addressed Madame,
no thought that it's all foreign.
Then their poor widows tear their hair,
forget the new, put on the old,
and start to stitch sad dirges
to rip apart the very heart
of anyone who hears.
Morning and night you hear them weep
until your entrails seethe.

—"Winter Dream"

In Scott O'Dell's novel *Alexandra*, set in Tarpon Springs, an old
Greek diver tells his granddaughter that *alazonia*—arrogance—was
the cause of her father's death from the bends:

> . . . a little fear is good, Alexandra. Your father had no fear. And I had
> no fear. . . . But it is best to have a little. The Nereids like to attack those
> who are arrogant and who are without fear. People speak of your fa-
> ther's death as mysterious, caused by this and that. But it was no mys-
> tery. I know the cause. The word *alazonia*, which he spoke as he was

brought home from the Gulf, is proof that by his act of coming to the surface too soon—without fear and arrogantly—he had defied the laws of diving. He had angered the Nereids and they had taken revenge upon him.

As Russ Bernard pointed out in his film *Matadors of the Deep*, adoption of safe diving techniques by the Aegean divers would have involved "an admission of fear that must be avoided at all costs." And so they took risks, their fear at times suppressed by their arrogance.

MATADORS OF THE HELM

In discussing Departure Day on Kalymnos, when the sponge fleet set sail from Pothia soon after Easter Sunday, Russ Bernard beautifully depicted the scene. Before the boats trace out the sign of the cross in the harbor, three times, and head out to open sea for six months, Kalymnian helmsmen put on a display of daring within sight of the quay.

As the divers appear at the dock with their foot lockers and are transported to boats at anchor in the middle of the harbor, a "regular pandemonium breaks loose reminiscent of the American teenager's game of chicken." The boats race up and down the harbor at full speed, coming directly at each other head-on, or sometimes broadside, barely missing one another "by inches." Rarely is there damage beyond scraped hull paint. He records the activity as going on for an hour or more, with the crowd watching the exhibition from the docks and cheering on the "helm matadors."

I grew up along Massachusetts Bay, with its brilliant seafaring tradition. One of my favorite lines in all of literature, a tribute to that tradition, appears in *Moby Dick* when Ishmael utters, "a whale-ship was my Yale College and my Harvard." But I never saw such deft boat-handling as I did in the Dodecanese. In sailing from Symi to Kalymnos, Joan and I traveled on a Kalymnian ferry with an all-Kalymnian crew. As we left Symi, the captain of the *Kalymnos* raced for a tiny strait that separates the north of Symi from the islet of Nimos. Only thirty meters divide the two, and hull clearance, when the strait is at shallow, is *one* meter—as it was that day. The ferry, 185 feet long, carrying a hundred passengers, swept through the strait; sandy bottom and rocks starkly visible in gin-clear water. The crew were all smiles as one called out decreasing depths. Yannis Samarkis, third officer, told me, eyes sparkling, "We are the only ship that will do this." I confess to having loved the scene; after all, the patron saint of Dodecanesian sailors is the Archangel Michael, The Protector, for whom I was named.

RIPSOKINDHINOS

Ripsokindhinos. I adored the sound of the word as I asked my question time and again on Kalymnos. *O Kalymnios eine ripsokindhinos?* The Kalymnian, is he a risk-taker?

After a few days on the island, I had earned an epithet, a sure sign of arrival in the Dodecanese: *Aftos pou rotaei tis erotiseis.* He who asks questions. And when you dwell on a question of risk-taking, you cannot help but ask yourself: "What's the *physically* riskiest thing *I* have ever done?" What flashed to mind was I, Michael at seventeen, a high school long-jumper, four stories up on the flat-roofed house where I was raised, a mile from the harbor, the sea just out of view. A great broad alley of perhaps a dozen feet separated my house from the next: Driven by rush of risk and what I took to be the genius of the act, I backed far from the roof's edge and sped across the tar-and-gravel surface toward the air above the alley and launched perfectly off my *left* foot, arcing high across the chasm and landing with such forward velocity that I fell and rolled, scraping flesh across the roof's rough surface. *Success.* A jump powered by joy, fear, and a push from Hermes the Messenger, whose symbol, the winged foot, I wore on my varsity sweater. *Eine o Michalis ripsokindhinos?* Michael, is he a risk-taker?

ZORBA

So imbedded is he in our culture from the Nikos Katzanzakis novel and the 1964 film, it is impossible not to inject the character of Zorba the Greek into a discussion of the poetics of manhood in Greece.

The story is set on Crete. At the end of the film Zorba says to his half-Greek but British-raised young boss, "You've got everything except one thing, *madness*. A man needs a little madness or else he never dares cut the rope and be free." I picture myself soaring over the alley and a Kalymnian diver untethering his lifeline.

PUSHING INTO DEEP WATER

Not all the deaths of divers, of course, came from risk-taking or from pressure placed on divers by the *platika* system. In the early years of the *skafandra*—in the last decades of the nineteenth century—much was still unknown about safe technique. Torrence Parker, an experienced diver who trained with the Greek sponge divers of Tarpon Springs, has published a history of diving and underwater engineering, *20,000 Jobs Under the Sea*. He points out that "stage decompression," a cardinal rule of deep diving, was not even invented until 1907, long after the Greek sponge divers of the Aegean "were pushing and exploring into deep water." Stage decompression requires periodic stops on ascent to allow nitrogen dissolved in a diver's blood to be expelled safely through respiration. My grandfather never saw a "stage decompression table," nor did the Greek sponge divers who, by the time of his death in 1904, had already pioneered deep-water diving.

In fact, in 1900, when Greek spongers discovered the Ankythera Wreck, which contained full-sized bronzes and marble statuary from the first century B.C., the Greek government had no choice but to hire the captain and divers who found the wreck to recover its contents from 180 feet of water. Parker reports that at that time no navy or salvage company in the world had the capacity to dive so deep as the Greek sponge divers.

While the benefits of stage decompression were unknown before 1907, the advantages of slow ascent were known, and the information made available to Greek divers through a French connection. In 1872 the French physiologist Paul Bert recommended that caisson workers and divers ascend from depth gradually to avoid being stricken with the bends. Torrance Parker adduces evidence that Auguste Denayrouze, a French supplier of diving equipment who corresponded with

Bert, published in the same period a guidebook about safe deep-diving technique that was written in Greek and liberally circulated among Greek divers. He instructed divers not to ascend faster than "one minute for each meter of depth" and not to go deeper than 115 feet.

The Greeks, however, went deeper, came up faster, and dove repetitively—probably more than three times a day in the early years. The only rule they *generally* followed was not to ascend faster than their exhausting air bubbles, which did help limit their risk of the bends.

According to Parker, it was another French physiologist, Leroy de Mericourt, who was the first to compare production of nitrogen bubbles in the diver to that of a bottle of soda water, and with a stark image: "The diver is really, from a physical point of view, like a bottle charged with carbonic acid."

As Parker observes, the Greeks paid a terrible price for their pioneering deep-water work. When I was too ready to ascribe high casualty rates purely to risk-taking, an economic anthropologist at Brandeis, Bob Hunt, wisely warned, "At the early stages of every new technology (railroads, airplanes, automobiles, steam engines) there are terrible things that happen, mostly but not entirely out of ignorance." But as Parker notes, "quick ascent became the rule," and in my view, that is the key that turns the lock: Both before and after knowledge of proper deep-diving technique had diffused, the Greek divers took risks.

KARHARIAS! KARHARIAS! SHARK! SHARK!

I felt as if I were at the Crow's Nest, the bar Sebastian Junger made famous in *The Perfect Storm,* except for a distinctly Greek accent; here you could get an *ouzo.* It was 10 o'clock in the morning in June, and already the blazing Aegean sun was driving the Kalymnians indoors. I sat in a dark *taverna* normally inhabited only by Kalymnian fishermen. It is not a place where a tourist would show up or feel especially welcome. Boats, quays, ship chandlers, and sponge factories lay outside. Just a few steps' walk from the *taverna,* you could hear the familiar *click-click* of scissors, as old men at a sponge factory, sitting on overturned crates, shaped sponges to make them perfect, or at least perfectly acceptable, for shipment to London, Sydney, or New York. *Click-click* of shears is the music of the sponge business. I had listened to it for a moment before entering the *taverna*.

Inside I talked with Nikolaos Kampourakis who had been a sponge diver for more than forty years. Working for so long under the steady beat of the Aegean sun, he was the blackest-skinned Greek I had ever met; his face evokes the "sun-blackened, hawk-faces" of William Travis's description of the Kalymnian divers at the opening of this chapter.

Like all divers who stayed in the business, Nikolaos was cat-quick in alertness and motion, as if his life depended on awareness of his surroundings and deftness of movement, which of course it did. He had spent only three months diving with the *skafandra*, but fifteen years as a *narghile* diver, breathing compressed air and therefore equally at risk of the bends. Later he turned to naked diving. "With naked diving, you can dive all day, five hundred times if you want, with no risk of the bends." Of my list of possible causes for the high casualty rates, Nikolaos said, *"Ola, ola,"* all contributed: poor equipment, greed of the captains, greed of the divers, the *platika* system, and ignorance of proper deep-diving technique. On his ranked list of blame, however, he placed the captains first and ignorance second. The best captains, Nikolaos reports, were divers themselves; if a diver reported that he could not dive today, such captains knew not to force the diver to dive.

Karharias! Karharias! Shark! Shark! is a familiar shout aboard the sponge boats when a shark is spotted. In forty years Nikolaos has seen a lot, such as the time he watched two sharks take off after two divers in the water. Crew mates fired spear guns: the larger shark took a spear in the neck and swam away; the smaller was hit with four spears and still he ate off the fins of the divers as they were yanked on board the boat.

His worst memory is when his uncle—twenty-three and younger than Nikolaos—died in his arms. Alhough his uncle had been signaling to be pulled up, the lifeline tender was inattentive and missed the signal tugs on the rope. Before the trip his uncle had complained of dizziness, a classic symptom of decompression disease, and, Nikolaos believes, never should have been allowed to dive. Nikolaos himself was hit twice in his career with "mapping" or skin bends, extravasations of the skin, and black spots showing on the skin where tissue has died. As a naked diver, on a single breath of air, he has dived to sixty meters' depth, but he brushed off my admiration by saying, "My brother dove to eighty meters."

Like many divers Nikolaos reported having seen *palia karavia*, old ships deep under the sea. For millennia Greek divers have dived deep into ancient seas: the Aegean, the Mediterranean, the Sea of Crete, the Adriatic, the Ionian, and the Tyrrhenian, where the sea-bottom is littered with broken ships and sunken dreams. When the Romans, the Crusaders, the Venetians, and other victors hauled back the booty of their enemies, sometimes their ships were so heavily laden they could not be easily handled, and they sank beneath the wine-dark sea when bad weather struck. It was by coming upon ill-fated ships that the Greek spongers came to be the world's first underwater archaeologists.

THE VICAR'S WIFE

In listening to Nikolaos describe his life under the sea, spanning forty years, and especially in hearing about his *profundito* dives, very deep dives, I was drawn back to *The Sponge Divers*, a novel by Charmian Clift and George Johnston. After talking with Nikolaos, I returned to Katerina's Apartments and reread these lines.

> Of the hidden, secret world of the sponge beds he spoke with an easy familiarity, as if it was an apparent thing, something visible before his eyes in all its shapes and colour and texture—the forty-metre beds of Alexandria where the silky sponges grew; the long, flat shelves of Cyrenaica where at twenty-five metres a diver could stay below for upward of an hour, plucking sponges almost as a vicar's wife might pick flowers from her garden; the dark, deep shafts off Benghazi, where the thick strong sponges clustered at the limit of the air pipe, where no diver, however strong, might for more than three minutes withstand the killing paralysing pressures.

There were many reasons the Matadors of the Deep returned to the sea each Easter; among them the spectral world of the deep, what you might come upon at forty fathoms five, alas "where your father lies." This too from *The Sponge Divers*:

> It was funny the way the good sponges like to live on the things that didn't truly belong below the sea, on wrecked ships and ruins, even of things like wine jars. Once, off the coast of Syria, Christos had found himself confronted by a whole ruined city buried beneath the sea, big square houses, some of them two and three stories high; and it had been a queer feeling, walking through the wide, lost streets picking sponges from the walls.

The Romans, Venetians, Crusaders, Ottoman Turks, Italians, Germans, and British all had their turn at occupying the Greek islands of the Aegean in a sad parade of human aggrandizement. Above the wine-dark sea, dynasties were established; governments rose and fell; armadas and armies came and went; kings, emperors, and sultans died; and frontiers shifted. Deep beneath the sea the Greek sponge divers of the Aegean reigned supreme over a vast empire of the abyss. There, deep in quiet water, their masculinity went unchallenged; they could thumb their noses at the great empires of the Western World.

five

SWALLOWING THE WIND

"Your ancestors harvested sponge when Caesar ruled the world. What they knew is in your blood, Alexandra."

We went beyond Anclote light, but not far. We fished in the shallows in a cove that had not been visited in years, which Grandfather knew about. He showed me how to use the three-pronged fork and the sharp knife strapped at my waist.

He stood up with the tiller between his knees and lifted his shoulder as high as he could . . . and took in a great gulp of air, and another, gulp after gulp, until his chest was twice its usual size. Then he let out the air with a long whoosh.

"It is called swallowing the wind," he said. And because it is important in diving with the sink stone, you must learn it.

—Scott O'Dell, *Alexandra*

Great Mother Ocean brought forth all life. It is my eternal home. But I have been gone into strange worlds so long—countries without currents, countries without tides, countries without depths. I have forgotten how to live in the world that created me. I can no longer breathe the water. I am slow and I am clumsy. I have lost my grace.

But the Deep Indigo of the depths calls me like a loving mother: "Return to the depths. Return to the source. Return to your nature."

—From the film "Blue Water Hunters," PAL Productions, Inc.

Ontogeny recapitulates phylogeny.

It's a principle in biology, and it means that the embryonic development of the individual repeats *all* of the stages the species passed through on its evolutionary journey. That's why you and I as embryos had gills: We used to be fish. Doubtless that's the tug as we roar past the sea on Big Sur in California, at Acadia in Maine, along the Amalfi coast, or why, standing on the prow of a great ship, we feel the compulsion to topple in. The sea draws us still; it is the beckoning mother. We want to return from whence we came. And some of us do.

BLOOD SHIFT

How does it work exactly? How was Symiot Stathis Hatzis in 1913 able to dive to 88 meters' depth on a single breath of air. Or Pipin Ferreras to 162 meters in the year 2000 to set a modern record for the breath-hold dive: 532 feet on a single breath of air. Both did it by calling upon the dolphin within.

The aquatic potential of the human remains remarkable—even though we have lived so long "in countries without currents." During World War II submarines crumpled under pressure if they dove deeper than 85 meters. How then do humans withstand hydrostatic pressure at depth? We humans can because of a throwback to our aquatic past, a remarkable reflex we share with "other" diving mammals—seals, dolphins, and whales. It is called blood shift. In response to pressure, the body constricts the blood vessels in the arms and legs, forcing blood to flood the chest cavity, protecting the core's vital organs. Writing in the *Atlantic Monthly* about "underwater daredevils" like Pipin Ferreras, Colin Beavan tells us that physiologists had calculated that, below 325 feet, a breath-hold diver's chest would collapse "like an empty can of soda." As a diver descends, air in the lungs compresses dramatically. The eight liters of air that Pipin Ferreras "swallows" on the surface before he dives compresses to a mere quarter of a liter at 100 meters' depth. It is called "thoracic squeeze." Rightfully, the diver should die from physics—water pressure crushing in his chest. The Frenchman and free diver Jacques Mayol, who attained international celebrity by way of the film *The Big Blue*, witnessed autopsies of dolphins at the Seaquarium, near Key Biscayne, Florida. He saw no special anatomical structures that protected dolphins from thoracic squeeze. "Mayol was sure that whatever protected them would protect people," Beavan writes. So in 1976 Mayol defied warnings and dove to 328 feet, with scientists finally confirming the existence of blood shift in humans. Says Beavan, "the thoracic cavity becomes not like an empty can of soda but like a full one, blood being incompressible." Amazingly, the body knows that liquid is incompressible.

Because blood shift takes blood from the limbs, burning of oxygen is greatly reduced as a breath-hold diver descends: Only vital organs and the brain are using it, and the heart-rate slows by 50 percent or more at depth. "Diving brachycardia," it is called—the slowing of the heart in response to the temporary cessation of breathing (apnea), water pressure, and contact with cold water. It is what "sometimes allows a near-drowning victim to be revitalized forty minutes after sinking into icy water," as Beavan reports.

In *The Big Blue* the character of Jacques Mayol dives beneath an ice-covered lake in the Andes and positions himself in front of a fluoroscope. Above, a scientist and Rosanna Arquette's character, huddled in a hut, watch the innards of diving mammal Jacques Mayol on a screen. (Physiologists love to study free divers.) All of Mayol's blood not in his chest cavity has migrated to his brain, a phenomenon previously seen only in whales and dolphins. When Mayol finally begins his ascent, he must do so anaerobically since there is no blood in his arms and legs. Blood begins to flow out of a free diver's lungs and back into the arms and legs on ascent at about eighty meters.

Below 110 meters' depth the heart rate of Pipin Ferreras—75 beats a minute on the surface—slows to 7 beats a minute. To potentiate the "natural reflex" of diving brachycardia Pipin adds the fillip of yoga: He commands his heart to slow. Pipin learned to use yoga in diving from Jacques Mayol, the man he calls The Great Intellect of The Big Blue. Pipin's body is conserving energy as he descends deep into the abyss. His heart pumps blood to his brain, knowing he must be alert and thinking to survive; in loving reciprocity, his brain tells his heart to keep beating. Life is reduced to a remarkable co-dependence: brain and heart.

Pipin Ferreras dove to 162 meters on what is called a "no-limits" free dive. The diver plummets straight down on a weighted, rope-guided sled. When the target is reached, the diver yanks off a confirmation tag showing the depth, pulls a pin that releases compressed air from a cylinder into a balloon, which the diver grasps as, in Beavan's words, it "buoys" the diver back to the surface "in a storm of bubbles." No-limits diving involves no swimming and no work. The diver is not trying to fetch sponge, spear fish, or rescue an anchor. The goal is singular: on a single breath of air to dive as deep as possible and survive a perilous ascent back to air.

Below 50 feet, breath-hold divers descend with ease—even without a sled or a sink stone. Increasing water pressure compresses the air-filled cavities of the body, which increases body density. The diver—denser—simply drops into the abyss. But like a bellstone, a weighted sled speeds descent and allows the diver to attain greater depth.

FEET–FIRST

Stathis Hatzis, who well knew the Kalafatas name on the island of Symi and perhaps even knew my grandfather, is a legend among the world's free divers. They talk about him still. His dive in 1913 is said to be the first deep dive in history. In 1989 Pipin Ferreras—curious about Stathis's famous dive—traveled to Rome from his native Cuba to research details in Italian naval archives. The *Regina Margherita,* the ship whose anchor Stathis had rescued in 1913 in Pigadia Bay, Karpathos—in the Dodecanese islands—was the new flagship of the Italian navy. The ship had been sent into Dodecanese waters "to show the flag" because the Italians had seized the Dodecanese islands from Turkey the previous year. It was a last-minute seizing when the Italians bailed out on the idea of invading Turkey itself. Nonetheless, the Italians believed they were en route to empire. The loss of the flagship's anchor on its maiden voyage would be deemed to be a terrible omen, so the Italians went to great lengths to retrieve it. A naked diver from Symi—and a sickly one at that—showed the Italian navy something about an ancient Greek art—breath-hold diving—and in so doing rescued the ship's anchor and the captain's reputation.

In Rome Pipin learned that Stathis was able to dive so deep, to eighty-eight meters, because of technique. While the naked divers of Symi normally dove headfirst, using a flat fifteen-kilo bellstone as a weight and rudder, Stathis tied a fifty-kilo rock (more than one hundred pounds) around his ankles and dove *feet-first.* Diving in the erect position allowed Stathis to descend at an "amazing" speed. Once on the bottom, he cut himself free from the rock and searched for the anchor. On his third attempt he found it and tied a rope through the anchor's eye so the crew could hoist it. Stathis was pulled back to air by the crew, using a second rope he had tied around his chest. His successful third dive lasted three minutes thirty-five seconds.

Before diving Stathis had boasted that he could hold his breath under water for seven minutes. In 1993 a diver who lay motionless on the bottom of a hotel pool for six minutes and forty-one seconds set the modern record for "static apnea."

In *The Conqueror of the Deep Blue*, a tribute to Stathis, University of Athens Biology Professor Yannis Detorakis wrote that, after his successful dive, Stathis reported having felt only "a little pressure on his back." Back on board the *Regina Margherita*, Stathis was asked if he could hold his breath again as a demonstration; he did so only for forty seconds, telling the crew, "I cannot do this outside of the water."

Before his dive, physicians on board the *Regina Margherita* examined Stathis and found his physique unremarkable. Doctors had determined that he suffered from pulmonary emphysema, and they told the captain not to let him dive. The captain let him dive anyway. After the dive, one doctor commented that, on inhalation, his chest looked "like a timpani."

Years later, while watching the free diver Enzo Maiorca descend feet-first, Pipin Ferreras recalled what he had learned about Stathis's technique. So, with the help of Maiorca's aides, Pipin began to experiment with feet-first dives. He quickly learned that he could dive below a hundred meters with relative ease. Feet-first dives are easier, he reasoned, because "the human being is designed and programmed perfectly for eating, digesting, thinking, living, and defending himself in an upright vertical position." Since up to seventy percent of our time is spent in the upright position, important benefits ensue from diving feet-first. Blood shift functions better in the upright position because water pressure first affects the legs, helping blood to "translocate" to the lungs. Equalizing pressure in the ears—critical in diving—is easier since the ears are above the lungs on descent. The heart also loses muscular efficiency and pumping power when the body is inverted. In addition, Pipin believes that in the inverted position a diver's ability to process feelings is diminished. In free diving "feelings are all-important," since, when preparing to dive and when already underwater, "the sensations of alertness, vigilance, and self-assurance come from feelings."

Most of what I know of Pipin, his research, and his diving feats, I learned from "surfing" and diving deep into a *website*—feeling the marine metaphor to the gills. It too was like sponge fishing: the "naked diver" from America again gathering a few sponges and placing them in my net bag. Can you imagine my delight in learning that today's world record-holder for the breath-hold dive was inspired in his technique in part by my Symiot *patriote* Stathis Hatzis?

Of course all that Pipin discovered about the advantages of the feet-first dive, Stathis knew in his bones, etched into them in Greek from antiquity, like an intaglio. The Symiots knew all there was to know, the Alpha and the Omega of the breath-hold dive. In 1610 an English traveler, George Sandys, wrote that the naked divers of Symi were the greatest of all because they learned the craft from childhood. They dove not long after they walked. Drawing upon five thousand years of the art of the naked diver, Stathis willingly tied a hundred-pound rock to his ankles and leapt into the abyss. As for compensation, Stathis asked only for "five pounds sterling and the extraordinary right to fish with dynamite." (The Greeks of the Dodecanese *love* dynamite.) The Italians also presented him with a gold medal and the right to travel for free, for all time, on any Italian ship.

SHALLOW WATER BLACKOUT

Before turning to the Greek sponge divers, the Italians had spent several days in unsuccessful attempts to recover the *Regina Margherita's* anchor. One Italian free diver, who was second in command of another Italian ship, the *Georgio Proli*, was killed in one such attempt. According to Pipin, Italian archives report that the diver died of "blackout." "Shallow water blackout," in fact, is the prime cause of death among breath-hold divers; it is so-called because it often occurs within ten or twenty feet of the surface.

With increasing depth, water pressure compresses the breath-hold diver's chest—giving breath-hold divers, as Beavan notes, "the false sensation that their lungs are full." But, during ascent, pressure drops rapidly and the gas in the lungs expands, creating a kind of vacuum that sucks oxygen out of the bloodstream and into the lungs; it can result in oxygen deficit in the brain and blackout just as the diver nears the surface.

Pre-dive hyperventilation—more than three or four quick deep breaths—can lower a diver's carbon dioxide level to below normal. It is the presence of carbon dioxide, not the absence of oxygen, that tells our bodies that we need to breathe. A diver who has hyperventilated before the dive might be too deep before realizing a need to return to the surface. The swim back to air only uses more oxygen. During ascent the oxygen level in the body can fall below the level necessary to remain conscious, and blackout occurs as the diver approaches the promised land of the breathing world.

Mehgan Heaney-Grier, a model and also one of the world's top women free divers, tells Beavan: "You override your brain's message telling you when to breathe. You're running on your reserve tank and there's no warning before you hit empty."

The second-in-command of the *Georgio Proli* likely "hit empty" on a mission of glory for his country while diving in Homer's wine-dark sea, not far from Symi, in a place he should not have been.

BREATH OF GOD

"Air is the breath of God," writes Catholic scholar John O'Donohue. Why do free divers give it up so willingly for the airless world of the watery deep? Greek sponge divers did so for a reason—they were earning their living from the sea. And most free divers do not do so because they are competitors who are trying to set a world record for a breath-hold dive; rather they are recreational divers.

Why don't they just dive with an air supply? Colin Beavan quotes Tec Clark, assistant director of the YMCA's Scuba Program, on what attracts people to free diving: "The aquatic environment accepts you more as a free diver." You get to see fish that might "shy away from bubbles and the noise of the scuba mechanisms." And while your time submerged is limited to the length of time that you can hold your breath, you can dive as many times a day as you wish without danger of decompression disease. You have more maneuverability than any diver strapped to a tank. Quietly, you can plunge and play, slipping to and fro between the airy world and the world from whence you came.

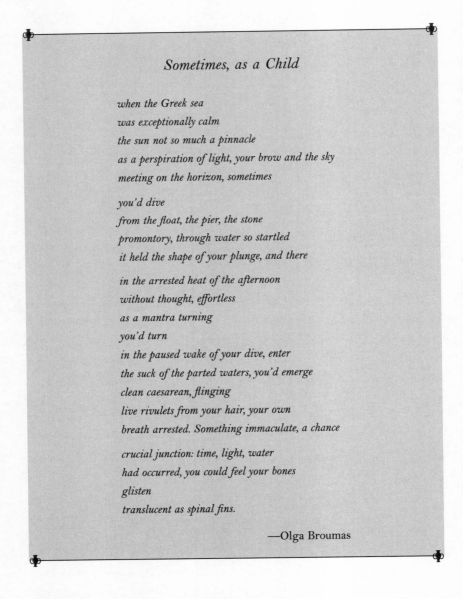

Sometimes, as a Child

when the Greek sea
was exceptionally calm
the sun not so much a pinnacle
as a perspiration of light, your brow and the sky
meeting on the horizon, sometimes

you'd dive
from the float, the pier, the stone
promontory, through water so startled
it held the shape of your plunge, and there

in the arrested heat of the afternoon
without thought, effortless
as a mantra turning
you'd turn
in the paused wake of your dive, enter
the suck of the parted waters, you'd emerge
clean caesarean, flinging
live rivulets from your hair, your own
breath arrested. Something immaculate, a chance

crucial junction: time, light, water
had occurred, you could feel your bones
glisten
translucent as spinal fins.

—Olga Broumas

Terry Maas, an oral surgeon from Ventura, California, is one of the most skillful free divers in the world and one of a small tribe of hunters who fish with spear guns while breath-hold diving. His passion for the dive and the hunt is told in the film *Blue Water Hunters*. A silent stalker, Maas can descend to eighty or one hundred feet and hold his breath for up to three minutes. Normally he fishes in open blue water off the coast of California—nothing below him for hundreds, sometimes thousands, of feet. In quiet cadences—almost religious in tone—Maas speaks of leaving behind the noise, intensity, and smog of Southern California and slipping below the surface into a watery world literally unchanged over thousands of years. He descends noiselessly, patiently waiting for curious "fellow fish" to come to him.

Days can pass without his gun being fired. But in 1982 Maas caught a 398-pound yellow fin tuna. Imagine, if you will, how vulnerable you are, so many miles from shore, suspended under blue water—holding a breath of God in your lungs—as a speared 400-pound tuna turns around, seems to draw a bead on you, and heads straight at you. Just as the huge fish neared Maas, it suddenly veered off, dropping downward, as Maas launched a second spear into the fast-sinking tuna. At sea the line between victor and vanquished is as thin as the film of water between your finger and the trigger of your spear gun.

FIFTY CENTURIES

One of the first books I read when I began to study the Greek divers was the U.S. Navy Diving Manual. It has a wonderful brief history of diving.

As a profession, breath-hold diving dates back more than five thousand years. *Fifty centuries*. Early diving was confined to shallow waters, less than one hundred feet, where divers harvested food, sponges, coral, mother-of-pearl, and other objects of commercial value. Mother-of-pearl inlays dating back to 4500 B.C. have been found in Mesopotamia. From earliest times divers have been involved in military operations, cutting anchor cables to set ships adrift, punching holes in the bottoms of enemy ships, or helping to build harbor defenses. Thucydides wrote of how Athenian divers cut through undersea barriers when Athens launched its attack on Syracuse. And Alexander the Great sent divers into the harbor of the city of Tyre, in what is now Lebanon, to remove obstacles after the city had succumbed to his siege in 332 B.C. Alexander himself went under the sea to view their progress.

In ancient times naked divers developed a salvage industry centered on key ports in the Mediterranean. The U.S. Diving Manual gives the pay scale in one area, fixed by law in the first century B.C., which recognized a fundamental diving principle that risk and effort increase with depth: "In 24 feet of water, the divers could claim one-half share of all goods recovered. In 12 feet of water they were allowed a one-third share; and, in 3 feet, only one-tenth share."

While the advantage of breath-hold diving is mobility, its disadvantage, of course, is limited air supply. So, early along, attempts were made to augment air supply with the use of hollow reeds or breathing tubes extending to the surface. While a diver could stay submerged longer with the hollow reed or breathing tube, he could accomplish little work because of lack of mobility. For the most part, the devices were used to allow soldiers to approach enemy strongholds undetected, hidden by water.

But breath-hold diving as a profession was not restricted to the Greeks. Or even to the Aegean and Mediterranean. As Colin Beavan points out, "Archaeological digs have unearthed widespread evidence of breath-hold diving in seaside cultures."

SEA NYMPHS

In Japan breath-hold diving is women's work.

Luis Marden has written of the whistling "Sea Nymphs of Japan"— fabled women fisherfolk who dive for shellfish and edible seaweed, and have from before the time of Christ.

Holding their breath, the "ama" dive as deep as seventy-five feet many times a day. They are found all around the coast of Japan, except in the far north. Most live along the east and west shores of Honshu. *Kachido*, "walking people," dive in shallow water, tossing their catch into a floating tub; the elite *funado*, "ship people," dive in deep water from an anchored boat. Thirty years ago there were seven thousand women divers in Japan; in recent years their numbers have declined. Their profession is threatened by overfishing, pollution, and the ravages of *El Nino,* according to Bethany Leigh Grenald, a doctoral candidate in anthropology at the University of Michigan who has studied and dived with the ama.

Because the ama dive in water much colder than the Aegean, they tend to be chubby and deep-chested, with muscular legs. They are famed in Japan for their plaintive whistling, in Marden's phrasing, "like the distant crying of curlews on a wind-swept shore." Japanese poets call their whistling *iso nageki,* "the elegy of the sea." According to Beavan, the practice of whistling before a plunge serves a practical purpose; it "increases air pressure in the lungs, forcing blood out and leaving more volume for the next breath."

While some men dive, for the most part the ama are women. Grenald believes that women dive rather than men because, as empirical evidence suggests, women deal with cold stress better. They conserve heat better in the severe cold of the ocean.

The ama search for shellfish, seaweed, octopus, and occasionally pearls "as a bonus in an oyster caught for food." At her University of Michigan website, Grenald reports that, for a period of time in the nineteenth century, the ama of the Shirahama area dove with compressed-air helmets—confirming what Fotis Mastoridis told the naked divers of Symi when attempting to embarrass them into using the new diving suit. In fascinating contrast to the Aegean, the practice of compressed-air diving was outlawed in Shirahama when it was realized "that it would lead to the quick depletion of local oceanic resources." The banning of its use led some ama to move to California where helmet diving was allowed. There the ama developed a thriving business diving for abalone. Sessue Hayakawa, Grenald tells us, nominated for an Oscar for *Bridge on the River Kwai,* came to the United States from Shirahama to become a diver before finding success in Hollywood.

By tradition the ama have dived naked, except for tightly fitted shorts. When I began studying the Greek divers of the Aegean, a colleague at Brandeis, John Hose, asked the logical question of why the naked divers dived naked. I lacked an answer then, but I have one now: Fifty centuries before Speedo's *fastskin*—which simulates sharkskin—was worn by Olympic champions in Sydney, Australia, diving naked was the best method of reducing drag. When the ama began to use fins about forty years ago, Grenald reports, they gained swimming power and could support more drag in the water—so they added clothing that would provide warmth.

Grenald lived in Shirahama, a hundred miles south of Tokyo, while studying and diving with the ama. Proud of their strength and skill—just like the naked divers of the Aegean—the ama of Shirahama actually legislated "that it is the limits of endurance of each individual, unassisted with any but the most rudimentary of equipment, that determine how long each person stays in the water and how successful each diver becomes." Hence, most areas of the town "forbid divers to wear full wetsuits, permitting only very small, thin, torso-covering wetsuits. Thus now, as in the past, ama rely only on their own heart, lungs and willpower."

The ama are sometimes perceived to be different from other Japanese women—louder and more aggressive. According to Grenald, they often yell or speak in a loud voice and in bold, direct ways, and frequently are leaders in the community's women's groups. The ama feel that their speech patterns are no different from all the fishing people of Japan "because you need to yell and speak directly when working near the loud ocean." Like the Greek *gymni*, the naked divers, the ama suffer ear damage from changes in water pressure, which may contribute to their speaking in loud voices. The ama also wear their hair short and have deep facial tans. Hence, as Grenald points out, the ama do not fit Japanese ideals of femininity as "quiet, slender, shy, pale, and self-effacing." Yet, they have become erotic symbols. The most famous ama erotica are woodblock prints—primarily dating back several hundred years, according to Grenald. The shoguns forbade nudity in woodblocks, but since ama dived topless, nudity was justified as realism.

When Kokichi Mikimoto, the genius behind the cultured pearl industry, invented his method for culturing pearls in the 1890s, he opened a pearl-growing farm to attract tourist trade. According to Grenald, Mikimoto hired ama to pretend to dive for pearls although they were not needed for the harvest of cultured pearls. When tourists displayed shock at the ama divers' nakedness, Mikimoto dressed them in white suits that were semitransparent when wet.

In a bizarre twist, real ama divers began to wear the white suits. "Over time," Grenald writes, "the practice of hiring ama to mimic their prior jobs as independent divers while simultaneously serving as clandestine sex objects became more elaborate." In villages where the ama live, for instance, bars and hotels began hiring "ama-geisha." Women who had never dived were hired to pose as ama-geisha in the sexy and invented ama clothing. As Grenald observes, "A profession that once conflicted with the image of Japanese women as geisha or as sex objects has become just that in the lives of many. Reality has been altered to adhere to a fantasy model of Japanese womanhood."

STATHENA ON MY MIND

Unlike the ama in Japan, women in Western societies, as Marden has observed, have traditionally had only an indirect relation to the sea, through their husbands, fathers, brothers, and sons. In the West women have supported men fisherfolk and, since men first went to sea, have been the preoccupation of men at sea. Of course men have also preoccupied the women they left behind, though perhaps in a more concealed way. During the heyday of the Nantucket whaling industry, in the nineteenth century, men were gone from the island for much longer periods of time than were the Aegean sponge divers. "Three years away, three months at home was the rhythm of the whale fishery," according to Nathaniel Philbrick, an authority on the history of Nantucket. Owen Chase, one of the central characters in Philbrick's *In the Heart of the Sea*, was home for a total of five years in one period that spanned twenty-one years and four marriages.

Despite Nantucket's "staid Quaker reputation," Philbrick informs us that an "island tradition claims women dealt with their husbands' long absences by relying on sexual aids known as 'he's-at-homes.'" In 1979, confirmation of this came when "a six-inch plaster penis (along with a batch of letters from the nineteenth century and a laudanum bottle) was discovered hidden in the chimney of a house in the island's historic district."

In an official film made by the Municipality of Kalymnos, one Kalymnian woman recalled how women helped their husbands prepare for their seven months at sea. Dutifully and endearingly each spring wives addressed and stamped ten envelopes since there was no stationery aboard the sponge boats. They packed them in their husbands' small sea chests, so periodically the men could mail letters home during the long absence at sea.

Yannis Detorakis tells a story about Stathis Hatzis that reflects both his alertness as a diver and the preoccupation of the divers with the women left behind. One day Stathis surfaced from a naked dive with no sponges at a site where the captain knew there to be sponges. When a naked diver dived, usually it was only after the captain or another crew member had spotted sponges on the sea bottom by looking through a glass-bottomed bucket, called a *yiali*. When Stathis surfaced without sponges, the captain was angry. *"Oraio merokamato mou kanis!"* (A wonderful day's work you do for me!) "Didn't you see the damn sponges in front of you? What have you been doing all this time?" Stathis replied that he had heard a huge noise. Surely a big fish was nearby, he said, because he had heard the rush of a school of little fish. The captain turned to Mihalakis, the man with the *yiali*, and asked if he had seen anything? "No," Mihalakis said. Stathis snapped back, "I didn't *see* anything. I *heard* the rush of little fish. Let's find a new place to dive."

Another naked diver on board teased Stathis, saying, "You were just thinking of *Stathena*," using the feminine variant of Stathis to refer to Stathis's wife and implying that Stathis had lost focus on the seafloor because he was thinking of his beloved Stathena. Stathis flung his rope at the other diver in anger. The diver tied it around his wrist and dove under the sea. Just after the diver disappeared, the man with the *yiali* leaped to his feet because a huge black shadow at that moment passed under the boat. The diver signaled to be pulled up; when the lifeline tender pulled the rope to the surface, he found only the diver's wrist and hand dangling at the end of the rope.

Despite broken eardrums and doubtless his mind on Stathena, Stathis had heard correctly—the rush of little fish had signaled the presence of a Big Fish.

MARTYRS OF THE LORD

In a long passage in "Winter Dream" my grandfather describes the "Passions of the dive," the methods and the suffering of those who practice the ancient craft of the *gymni*, the naked divers of the Aegean.

A lot of people want to learn
how divers dive into the deep,
    and ask with great desire
to know about sponge harvests.
    First they'll decide to go to sea,
then the best five are chosen,
    these five then choose another two,
making the boat's crew seven.
    They then stock up on rope and food,
and sail where God instructs them.
    And having sailed, seen off by God,
reach an agreed-on spot.
    There, they prepare the sponging gear,
tools they will use in common.
    Our old ancestors, to sink deep
beneath the waves and currents,
    a stone invented, white, oblique,
tied to a thin rope through its core.
    The Bellstone, as today it's known,
by which to plumb the deep.
Hugging it tightly divers sink,
    steering by underwater leaps,
alighting where they want.
    Having prepared exactly so,
and ready now to venture,
    they wake at dawn, their bedding store
along the ship's sharp corners,
    and wash their face and cross themselves,
call God their only helper,
    who instantly heals the open wound,

protects from any danger.
  After this call they sit at stern,
dipping their bread in coffee.
  Then they set out to tack their sails,
coursing toward their work.
  Finding a rock ledge they decide
to drop the iron anchor—
  when iron holds to rock it needs
men of strong will and courage.
  Having decided they disrobe,
call again God most highest,
  God omnipresent, God of all,
save, guard the human race,
  protect your hands' creation,
who bow beneath your feet.
  And naked now he grips the stone,
his sack hung round his chest.
  His sack is strong, webbed of tough string
to wood or iron ring,
  hung from his neck, tied to his waist,
for the uprooted crop:
  Adriatic sponge and light-winged sponge.
This sack we know as Snare.
  He draws his inbreath with command,
and plunges like a sea-bird,
  the bellstone firmly in his hands
until he touches rock.
  His left hand leans the bellstone by
and, crouching, feels for sponges.
  He leaves the bellstone if he finds
good cutting place, uprooting
  as many as will fill his sack.
Two guards stand ready on the prow,
  tied to him by long rope.
His inbreath gone, he tugs the rope,
  and feeling it they raise him—
these guards are known as Oars.

If either Oar suffers a lapse
of his complete attention,
   the diver suffers too.
And if the lapse becomes too long,
   he bids his health farewell.
But the two Oarsmen keep their heads
   and stand with full attention.
The divers tangle in wild plants,
   suffering pain and damage
as piercing rocks puncture deep wounds.
   They feel no pain at seafloor.
They feel it when they plunge back up
   and wipe dry with their sheet—
harrowing pain, unbearable
   throbbing the heart's own branches
Of all the damage there is one
   that causes great misfortune,
they call it Filth. It has its root
   sunk deep under some sponges.
If it's uprooted whole, intact,
   it's harmless but if crushed
and touched or badly handled,
   not even linseed oil and flax
will offer easy cure.
The diver needs razors, a strict fast,
   in pain and tears for his health.
Wanting to give my listeners
   details about the craft
and all the divers' obstacles,
   I'm forced to write its perils
from which they suffer from the start:
   When they set out to first undress,
They must shield from the sun.
   Then in the spot they call the works,
they hazard a few dives
   until they come up with a sponge.
First sponge in hand, they make a cross

upon the ship, this custom
they call Crossing.
   Then raise a flag atop the mast,
reach for some food and drink,
   and bless the work to start.
The days are full of trials.
   Throughout the heat exhausts them,
then the cold
   from which there is no pause.
They burn in sun, shiver in wind,
   have headache every day,
and helpless in the summer sun,
   their whole skin sears and burns.
Blisters fill up and then they break,
   incurable if left exposed,
and they can't bear even a shirt,
   nor touch their backs to mattress,
nor can they lie down on their side,
   but only on the belly
earn precious comfort and some rest.
   Each dive gambles their ears,
which ring with pain and often burst,
   leaving them with insomnia
amidst the pain and torture.
   To guard against this they have found
small ways to ease misfortune:
   They hold their nose for their descent,
two three four times then sink.
   If they don't know about this trick,
they come back up midway,
   spit blood and some are scared
so much they leave the trade
   until their membranes heal.
Before they learn the craft,
   all aspects of their being
suffer such pain.
   These are the Passions of the dive,

the Symiots' craft and symptoms.
They leave the island late
in April, some in May,
and through September suffer,
constant as martyrs of the Lord.

Willard Manus, writing of the Aegean divers, quotes the poet Oppian from the second century: "No ordeal is more terrifying than that of the sponge divers, and no labor more arduous for men." While the naked divers were not breathing compressed air and therefore not in danger of the bends, air embolism, or asphyxia, they were in danger of drowning, especially when encountering strong currents, and, though infrequent, shark attack. When surfacing from deeper dives, as Torrance Parker points out, all too often they were "hemorrhaging from the ears, eyes, nose, or mouth." Many did die. Always there was the beating sun and broken eardrums. But amid arduous labor there was nobility to their work. They were, after all, *syndrophi*—comrades—who were in right relationship to each other and to their God.

In *The Conqueror of the Deep* Yannis Detorakis calls upon the memoir of Giorgos Georgas, a Symiot sponge merchant and writer who took part in the uprising on Symi in 1884—when naked divers and angry compatriots torched deep-diving equipment. Among the forty naked divers sent to prison for the action were some of Symi's most famous naked divers, imprisoned for putting to flame Satan's Machine.

In his recollection, written in 1937, Georgas contrasts the pious life of the naked diver with the morally corrupted life of the helmet diver. Always the naked diver walked humbly with his God, kept to Christian custom and the patriotic way. But the *skafandro* diver lived in "a bad cycle," *favlo kiklo*. His morale low, he worsened the society in which he lived. To describe the "moral degradation" of the *skafandro* diver, "you would need the pen of a sociologist and the strength of Emile Zola." The helmet diver spent without limits and partied wildly. He became such a bad marriage risk that a young woman about to marry a *skafandro* diver "must first think of the death of her future husband and who would be her next husband." As a consequence some divers married Turkish and Arab Muslims, Georgas says, who practiced the Christian faith only superficially "to achieve their goal."

The moral degradation that Georgas describes is captured in a story told me by my cousin Michael Foreys. As the fleet was about to sail, sometimes a *skafandro* diver would refuse to board the sponge boat despite his having accepted the captain's *platika* weeks or months earlier. Steve Katzaras of Tarpon Springs recollects from his youth on Symi that the captain or a burly assistant would round up divers from the tavernas. It was a process that might take several days. Knowing how critical he was to the success of the sponge-fishing season, a diver might stall to eke out some additional benefit in the waning hours before *Mandroucha*. In Foreys's story a *skafandro* diver resists the request of the trip's financier to board the departing sponge boat. "Please board," the financier says. The diver refuses, demanding some additional prize. "Give me that!" the diver says. And the diver is given the demanded object. Still the diver refuses to board. "Give me that!" he now demands, of something else. And he is given it. Still he refuses to board, demanding yet again, "Give me that!" And so on, each demand met, until finally, at the fifth request to board, the diver bellows, "Bring me Isabella!" the wife of the financier.

"That was the mentality," Foreys says, "and the reason 90 percent of the people of Symi were against the *skafandra*, and the reason the theologians and professors were all saying, 'Stop the *skafandra*!' "

THE FIRST TECHNIQUE: A WAY OF LIFE

Many of us have the capacity to "swallow the wind" and dive to the deep on a single breath of air, if only we are willing to take the risks and cultivate our primordial diving reflexes. Mother Sea beckons to us all.

Jacques Mayol, Pipin Ferreras, Meaghan Heaney-Grier, and other free-diving champions have taught us that, to remain down for a long time, you must be at ease and relaxed under the sea. While we cannot be like elephant seals that dive a mile deep, remain submerged for an hour and a half, and, some researchers believe, *sleep* while holding their breath, we can be at peace under the sea. In the end breath-hold diving is a kind of art form, requiring the diver to be in a meditative state, alert and utterly relaxed, when returning to Mother Sea. Jacques

Mayol used yoga and the naked diver his piety to attain that state. Piety put the naked diver in right relationship with his God, with his *syndrophi*, his comrades, and with Mother Sea. "Long live the first technique," wrote my grandfather in 1903. The "first technique" was a means of diving and a method of living. "What does God require of us?" Micah asks, but "to do justly, to love tenderly, and to walk humbly with one's God." Before the arrival of the *skafandra*, the lives of the naked divers, like the lives of the ama, had nobility and serenity. The naked diver's bellstone—his beautiful white sink-stone, handed down from father to son—was a symbol of Inner Weight, a symbol of the Spiritual Rudder that guided the life of the naked diver. To Carl Jung, water is our unconscious—our feminine side, the deep that lies beneath us all, Mother Sea within. As weight and rudder through life's uncertain journey, the naked diver had his beautiful white bellstone—the trigger stone of Kalymnos. It guided his way to the deep, of the sea and of himself.

What resonates about this story for all, Greek and non-Greek, is not only the primordial wish to return to the sea, to our watery birth, but the wish we all have to return to ourselves, to the watery deep of our unconscious, and to know the gifts kept there for us. We wish to return to the first technique.

Like the bellstone that is used as a clapper in the bells of island churches, the naked diver's bellstone connected the naked diver to his God and to his noble forebears. To be hoisted to Paradise, God's safe, airy world above, the naked diver on the seafloor had only to yank on the bellstone's rope, the motion identical with that of the naked diver's *papas*, his island priest, as he rang the church bell, welcoming the faithful to prayer.

MIND OVER WATER

"A quiet mind levels the boat," writes Craig Lambert in *Mind Over Water*, his book about the Zen of sculling. In thinking of the quiet mind requisite to breath-hold diving, my thoughts glide to sculling, my sport as an adult. "There's no such thing as a mindless row," my coach insists. In sculling, a precarious rower perches on a sliver of a boat:

eleven inches wide, twenty-nine feet long. In physics of design the boat "prefers" to be upside down and willingly obliges if the rower—rowing backwards—errs with one of the nine-foot oars. Lambert proclaims a truism of the sport: To have success in sculling one needs to have a quiet body, one that makes *no* unnecessary moves. True too of breath-hold diving. "If you can't do it easily, you can't do it at all," Lambert quotes Steve Fairborn, coach at Jesus College, Cambridge, as saying. Quiet mind, quiet body—in sculling and in the artful breath-hold dive.

A BAD CYCLE

While the naked diver needed inner peace to return to Mother Sea, the helmet diver had no such need. Sealed in a compressed-air-filled suit, the diver "in the box"—as called by those who mocked him—needed alertness and daring, but not piety. He did not need to be at peace with himself, his comrades, or his God. Piety was driven to the wings; daring moved to center stage. Always the Greek divers knew the odds: there were few white heads among the *skafandro* divers, although many could be found among the naked divers. Rightly, the helmet diver perceived that prosperity—his own and that of his island—hinged on his willingness to risk his life. When he dove to fifty, sixty, or seventy meters of depth, breathing the compressed gas that could kill him, fifteen jobs weighed down on him as heavily as the many atmospheres of water above him. Three times a day, seven days a week, the Man in the Box had to answer the question, as few of us do, "How brave am I?" He knew there could be no "Gold Rush" without the mad daring of the Greek helmet diver.

SARANDITES

They dove soon after they could walk. Among the Symiot naked divers, the most respected were those who could dive the deepest and keep under the longest. Good divers were called *sarandites*—from the Greek for forty, *saranda*—because they could dive to forty *oryes*, forty fathoms. A fathom is six feet, a unit of measure used in seaside cultures around the world because a fathom, roughly, is the length of rope a man can hold between his hands with his arms spread apart at full span.

According to Plutarch, ancient naked divers would keep in their mouths a white balm, which they blew out on the seafloor to illumine the sea "like a torch." Today, a similar method is used by "hook spongers" in the western Atlantic, who fetch sponges in thirty to forty feet of water while never leaving their boat. Using an extremely long pole fitted with a sharp hook, the spongers "hook" the sponge and bring it to the surface. By pulling or tearing the sponge from its attachment, it is often so mutilated as to impair its value. Sometimes hookers sprinkle oil-soaked sand onto the water to calm, clarify, and light their view of the sponges below through their "sponge glass" or "water telescope," the *yiali* of the Aegean.

LITTLE MICHAEL OF THE FISHERMAN

Paratsouklia—nicknames—are common on Symi. How else can you tell apart four cousins who share first and last names?

When on Symi, I interviewed an elderly, lively, and diminutive man—under five feet tall. His name is Michael Alexopoulos, but in the *kafenia* he is known only as *Mihalaki tou Psara*: Little Michael of the Fisherman, meaning Little Michael whose father was a fisherman. (*Mihalaki* is the diminutive of Michael, and *tou Psara* means "of the fisherman.")

For most of Mihalaki's long life—he was then well into his nineties—he was a fisherman. But from 1922 until 1931 he was captain of a naked-diving boat that "fished" for sponges off the coast of North Africa. In nine years he never had a diver die, and some of his divers were diving with white hair. One diver with a white beard dove with Mihalaki for seven years; in his last season with Little Michael he was sixty-nine years old. One day the man with the white beard dove to thirty-four fathoms: *204 feet*. With no irony Mihalaki referred to him as *palikari*, a brave young man. Mihalaki had another white-haired *palikari* who, at seventy-five, dove to thirty-eight fathoms and fetched five sponges before surfacing.

Each morning the naked divers would have tea and a little bread. That was all. Their big meal was reserved for the evening. Every day the diving routine was the same. One diver would dive five times, and then rest. The next diver in rotation would do likewise. By day's end each diver would have dived fifteen or sixteen times. Mihalaki took his men to dive at sites all across North Africa, from Alexandria to Benghazi.

Once, when Italy was at war with Abyssinia, Mihalaki's men were diving off the coast of Abyssinia. One diver surfaced very quickly, saying, "I *heard* a big fish!" Mihalaki replied, "You mean you *saw* a big fish." "No," the man insisted, "I *heard* a big fish!" Some minutes later, a short distance from Mihalaki's boat, an Italian submarine burst out of the sea.

THE DEVIL'S WAGES

I hate it, the disgusting thing,
as much as the devil's legions

—Winter Dream

The naked divers called the new diving suit "Satan's Machine" and "Tool of the Devil." The new diving technology had transformed the economic and cultural life of Symi and of all the sponge-fishing islands. The world of the past was gone. Metrophanes and the naked divers grieved at the new world being born.

The anthropologist Charles Stewart drew my attention to the critique of and resistance to capitalist encroachment inherent in my grandfather's poem and in the divers' story. In particular Stewart pointed to the alignment of the profit motive with the devil as evidenced in my grandfather's reference to the "devil's legions" and in the naked divers calling the new technology "Satan's Machine" and the "Tool of the Devil."

Michael Taussig analyzes such alignment in *The Devil and Commodity Fetishism in South America*, in relation to two widely separated rural areas of South America—the tin-mining region of Bolivia and the sugar plantations of Colombia. In Western myth "the devil contract" is an indictment of an economic system that forces men to trade their souls for "the destructive power of commodity." Societies on the threshold of capitalist development naturally interpret that development, Taussig explains, in terms of their "precapitalist cosmogony," in the folk beliefs of the peasants, miners, artisans, or seafarers who are involved in the transition. In the two areas he studied he found a "precapitalist hostility toward the flowering of the market economy." While "the imagery of God or the fertility spirits of nature dominates the ethos of labor in the peasant mode of production, the devil and evil flavor the metaphysics of the capitalist mode of production...."

In the Cauca Valley of Columbia some cane cutters are believed to enter into a secret contract with the devil in order to increase their production and wages. But local folk belief holds that "these wages are inherently barren," that the sugar cane fields will become sterile, sprout no more, and that the man who made the contract with the devil "will die prematurely and in pain." Short-term monetary gain is "more than offset by the supposed long-term effects of sterility and death." Devil beliefs are a kind of "collective representation of a way of life losing its life." One way of life is being supplanted by another—with the devil representing the process of alienation.

Taussig's analysis seemed apt to "my" sponge divers. Had not "the devil's legions" brought the new diving suits to the Aegean in the view of my grandfather and the naked divers? And for what purpose, if not the profit motive? Had not the *skafandro* divers traded their souls for the "destructive power of commodity"? Had not the sponge fields turned barren and sterile, once vandalized by those who employed the Tool of the Devil? And were not *skafandro* divers dying premature and painful deaths?

In the Age of the *Skafandra*, the helmet diver who took prepayment signed his contract with the devil. He took devil wages and paid the price. *Platika* was his contract with the devil. In the Dodecanese islands of the eastern Aegean, Michael the Archangel is patron saint of seafarers—the same Michael who safeguards Christians against the wickedness and snares of the devil. Not even he could protect the divers from the devil—and from themselves.

six

THE SPONGE WARS—
TARPON SPRINGS, FLORIDA

An advertisement for sponge divers was placed in several Greek newspapers. Nowhere was it read with more interest than in the Dodecanese....

    Into staid little Tarpon Springs in the summer of 1905 came some five hundred Greek males, noisy and vigorous and excited. They spoke a strange musical language in rapid-fire staccato, and fairly danced as they spoke. They were powerful, swarthy, keen-eyed fellows of all ages, many with dark curly hair and mustaches.

—Gertrude K. Stoughton, *Tarpon Springs Florida: The Early Years*

They burned the boats of the Greeks to the water.

The Greeks were beaten. They were jailed. Some murdered. The state legislature barred the Greeks from diving in the Florida Keys. This was the reception the "Conchs"—Key West hook fishermen—and hate-filled rednecks arranged for the Greeks when they arrived in Florida. *Welcome to The Sunshine State!*

These were the Sponge Wars.

"In 1918 my uncle's sponge boat was burned to the water in Key West," Denis Cantonis told me. "They tried to kill him and his men, but they escaped." Today, one of my college roommates, John Kreinces, is a physician in Key West; every afternoon at four o'clock he plays the bag pipes in Mallory Square. I imagine John's squeezing out a sad tattoo on his pipes as he watches black smoke twirl upward against a waning Key West sun.

But the Greeks proved as tough as their assailants and swiftly came to dominate the sponge industry of Florida. Their leadership turned the Florida sponge fishery into a bigger industry than citrus. For half a century Tarpon Springs, Florida, was the epicenter of the world sponge industry; success brought by the daring Greek divers of the Aegean.

My family arrived in Florida in 1946–47, the year the music died.

THE FLORIDA KEYS

Until the 1840s the world supply of sponges came entirely from the Mediterranean and its ancillary seas. But in 1841 a French sponge merchant was shipwrecked in the Bahamas where he discovered natives gathering and using sponges. Before leaving he sent a shipment to a customer in Paris. The sponges were a smashing success, and thus began the West Atlantic's role in the world sponge market. By 1849 Bahamian spongers—known as Conchs because of their large daily consumption of shellfish—had moved into the Florida Keys and begun large-scale sponge-fishing operations, using the hooking method. The United States was fast-becoming the leading consumer of sponges in the world. Sweaty, brawny America, awakening to the Industrial Age, found natural sponges a handy tool in manufacturing, the cleaning trades, and elsewhere. Unlike the European market—dating from the Roman aristocracy—the American sponge market was never about the bath and cosmetics. America was about the building of a New Jerusalem—a New Athenian democracy rising out of vast land, plenty, and great industry. What better legatee of the Greeks in the modern world than America, Cradle of Democracy *Redux*: sixteen towns named Athens, ten named Sparta.

As Nantucket seamen long-hauled whale oil back from the Pacific to lubricate the New Nation's machinery and rail system, sponges were needed to clean up at the end of the work day; needed too to make ceramics, finish shoes, wash down horses, and help hospital surgeons sop up the bloody mess: You do not build a New Zion without injury. In *Leaves of Grass* Walt Whitman wrote, "I hear America singing, the varied carols I hear." In 1855 he was hearing the song of America's burly occupations. The workmen of Whitman's America—and later of Carl Sandburg's—reached naturally for the sponge. It was Homer's

Hephaestus all over again—a sponge needed to wash off the smithy's grime. New York could not get enough of sea sponges to bale or crate—dried and pressed—and ship across America by prairie schooner or by rail. But now sponges could be found in the New World, not only in the Mediterranean. From the harbor of Key West, the Conch schooners fanned out, sailing to some of the most beautiful sponge fields in the world. Even the Greeks, so proud of the Aegean, would rhapsodize about nature's bounty as they found it under the sea off the west coast of Florida. "In the sea we found our vineyards and our olive-groves," wrote Metrophanes of Symi; and so the Greek divers of the Aegean found it again, half a world away in the Gulf of Mexico.

GULF

"Here, suddenly, was a fresh livelihood against a fresh background," Jennie Harris wrote of the Greeks of Tarpon Springs. "Sponges had, in a way, reversed procedure; they had sent out invisible hooks themselves and tugged the Greeks here."

Demosthenes Kavasilas was the first Greek deep-sea diver to go over the side and into the Gulf. Reportedly, he stayed down only ten minutes and brought up a full bag of wool sponges. When they lifted off his helmet, his first words were: "There are enough sponges down there to supply the whole world." And the sponges were "the best and sturdiest in the world," according to George Th. Frantzis, who wrote *Strangers at Ithaca*, a history of the Greek spongers of Tarpon Springs. Taking turns, Kavasilas and Stelios Bessis, a second diver, sent up bag after bag of sponges, every ten minutes. At day's end the first Greek sponge boat on the Gulf—the *Elpis*, "Hope"—turned and beat for port, loaded with large wool sponges.

Once again the Greeks had penetrated the sea. This time in a new hemisphere. Within a year of the Greeks' arrival in 1905, there were fifty Greek boats working Florida's waters; within two years a hundred. By 1939, two hundred.

As they peered out of the tiny windows of their helmets, the *palikaria*—"the brave young men"—beheld a world far different from the clarity and simplicity of the underwater scapes of the Aegean.

In the silence of the deep, far from home, here was a New World symphony of form and hue. An overwrought Frantzis describes the scene as the Greeks found it, on the floor of the Mexican Gulf.

> Sponges by the thousands darkened the virgin and untrodden bars. Thousands of corals of all colors and shapes; thick, wild-grape vines hard to get through; multi-colored peacock feathers of the sea; dream-like gardens in which all manner of fish traveled.

Everywhere was "like a garden of flowers or an orchard of fruit," Stoughton wrote. Meadow after meadow, "studded with sponge."

HOOKING

Each Conch schooner carried or towed astern one small skiff for every two crew members. When a promising site was found, the captain dispatched his skiffs—one man sculling while the other peered through his glass-bottomed bucket to scan the seafloor for sponges. If the water was rough, he would pour shark oil onto it to calm and clarify it. The friction of oil on water kept the surface from ruffling, breaking, or being driven by the wind. Using a long pole, twenty or thirty feet in length, he would "hook" a sponge and pull it up on board, hand over hand. The Conchs were after Key wool sponges that were native to the shallow waters between the Keys and the mainland. Like the "right whale" of Nantucket whalers, the Key wool sponge was the "right sponge": it was soft and beautiful—despite a distinctive red hue at the root from iron oxide deposits found off the Keys—and it brought a good price on the market. Best of all, Key wool sponges could be hooked out of twenty feet of water or less. The Conchs never needed to put their lives at risk.

Of the 10,000 varieties of sponges only a dozen are of commercial value. But several of these can be found in the Florida Keys; so the Conchs also fished for yellow, grass, velvet, and glove sponges, but with less fervor since they brought a lesser price. Sometimes the Conchs fished the Gulf coast of Florida—as far north as Appalachicola; occasionally near the Anclote Keys, a few miles down the Anclote River from Tarpon Springs.

Hooking is not easy. The Conchs were good at it—but never quite as good as the Greeks, according to Steve Katzaras, a Symiot by birth and one of Tarpon's top sponge merchants. Like many seaside crafts, the hooking of sponges has been passed down to the Greeks from antiquity, one generation to the next. Boat caulking is another such craft, as in my name, Kalafatas—boat caulker. Since the Greeks were first in pretty much all matters related to the sea, Greek nautical terms have crept into other languages. "Nautical" itself is from the Greek for sailor, *nautis*. As further example, most Turkish nautical terms are Greek, so dependent were the Turks on the Greeks for everything related to the sea. Five thousand people named Kalafat live in Turkey today; the Turkish word for "boat caulker" also derives from the Greek, *kalafatas*. For several hundred years Romania was part of the Ottoman world; so today there is a Romanian city, Kalafat, that sits quietly alongside the Kalafat River.

In the Aegean the hooking of sponges is done to depths of seventy-five feet because of the clarity of the water; in the West Atlantic, never beyond forty feet. Hence, the Greeks honed their skill to a fine point in deep water.

Knowledge of the Greek hooking tradition is far-flung; I bought a model of a Greek hook-fishing boat on Cape Cod in Massachusetts. The boat is called *Spetses* after the Greek sponge-fishing island of the same name. But hooking is hardly genetic; it is a learned skill and very difficult. Steve Katzaras told me that one day, for fun, he tried hook fishing; all of the sponges he hooked arrived on board in shreds. Even a well-hooked sponge is damaged—a clean one-inch hole right through it. A hooked sponge is less sturdy and beautiful than a "virgin" sponge fetched whole by a diver, gently tugging it free from the sea-floor using a hand-held rake, or cutting it clean away from the bottom with a knife or scythe.

Part of the beauty of the natural sponge is the mystery of its being taken. Seawater pulses through a sponge day and night; twenty-five times its own weight surging through it at any instant. As the sea penetrates the sponge, so the Greek penetrates the sea, to steal away the sponge from Mother Sea—Greek and sponge "eloping" to the surface. To the Greeks, for millennia, the sponge has been a gift of the gods, life-sustaining and beautiful, like nectar or ambrosia; the fetching of the sponge itself an ancient ritual.

KAMAKI

Kamaki is Greek for the hook or harpoon used by hook fishermen to fetch lush, ample sponges from the sea. In the Aegean *kamaki* is also a term of opprobrium for Greek men who pursue the non-Greek women who drift into the Aegean on the currents of tourism; typically, the women are from Germany, Scandinavia, and England. Non-Greek women are physically safe in Greece; Greece has the lowest crime rate of the seventeen countries that compose the European Union. Pursuit by the *kamaki* is with charm, irresistible hospitality, and unearned assists from the siren breezes of the Aegean. Derogated by their communities, shunned by Greek women, the *kamaki* spend the winters in the *kafenia* touting their successes to one another. The character of Shirley Valentine—famous in film and on stage—falls prey to a *kamaki*. Some of the women choose to stay in the islands; ever after they are known as "Shirley Valentines." Like *Psarofagomenos* or *Michalaki tou Psara*, they have acquired a *paratsoukli*—a nickname.

THE CADILLAC OF SPONGES

There are two sponge fisheries in Florida: the Key Grounds, lying between the Florida Keys and the mainland, and the Bay Grounds to the north, in the Gulf of Mexico. The Bay Grounds stretch 160 miles, almost without interruption, from Johns Pass, north of Tampa Bay, to St. Marks on the Florida panhandle.

In 1873 vast beds of wool sponges were discovered in the Gulf by accident. While working waters off the Anclote Keys, turtle fishermen from Key West found their nets fouled time and again by growth on the bottom. When brought to the surface, the growth was identified as sponge. As it turned out, there were nine thousand square miles of sponges in the Gulf of Mexico. These virgin sponge fields, as exploited by Greek daring, would make the Gulf of Mexico the center of the world sponge trade for the first half of the twentieth century. Ninety percent of the U.S. sponge catch would be brought into Tarpon Springs, almost all of it on Greek boats. The Bay Grounds were "thickly studded" with Rock Island wool sponges. The Rock Island wool is the Cadillac of sponges, the most famous in the world. It is soft and strong, highly absorbent, 90 percent round, and it brings the top price—higher even than the Key wool sponge. Brushed against your face, a wet Rock Island wool feels like lamb's fleece. That sponge would make some Greeks rich, build a Mediterranean town on the coast of Florida, and send out an "invisible hook" that would tug my father, born in Lahania, Rhodes—where *"Winter Dream"* was written— to Tarpon Springs. He would come with his family, including three-year-old Michael, the grandson of the poet. We stayed only a year but I feel the hook in me still.

FISHING THE DIVER

Captain Love Dean, who conducts nature and history cruises in the Florida Keys, has written in *Oceans* magazine of the dramatic rise of the West Atlantic sponge fishery. That fishery includes the waters of Jamaica, the Bahamas, Cuba, Honduras, Nicaragua, Mexico, and Florida. A favorite painting of mine is a watercolor by Winslow Homer owned by the Museum of Fine Arts in Boston, "the Athens of America." (Not to be confused with Nashville, "the Athens of the South.") Painted in 1889, *The Sponge Diver* shows a muscular, black Bahamian sponger, fresh from a breath-hold dive, clutching a dark raw sponge as he clings in recovery to a dinghy. Naked diving continues in the Bahamas, although never a possibility in the Gulf because of the strong currents.

The Florida fishery was by far the most valuable in the West Atlantic, and the Conchs controlled it until the arrival of the Greeks in 1905. The Conchs felt "very territorial about their sponging beds," Dean writes, and they were not about to let the Greeks move in. They attacked the Greek boats like swarming bees. When the Greeks arrived in Florida, the Greeks were the world leaders in the use of deep-sea diving gear. Cavaliers of the deep, in full armor, they had been pushing the limits of the new diving technology. So, when the Greeks undertook "machine diving" off the coast of Florida, they outdid the Conchs four to one. Native-born Americans have never been good at being outdone by new immigrants; a sorry flaw in the American character. A modern example is violence inflicted upon Vietnamese shrimp fishermen when they began to work the waters of the Gulf in the 1980s; the bad behavior of native-born Americans is portrayed in the film "Alamo Bay."

The Greeks outproduced the Conchs by working smarter and harder; by using a system similar to the one developed in the Mediterranean; and of course by taking risks. They had transported their poetics of manhood from the Aegean to Cedar Key, along with the rubberized-canvas diving suit and the hand-cranked air pump. The technology allowed them to work productively; their daring allowed them to dive deep—far beyond the reach of any hooking pole—to where the best sponges lay. And the Greeks outpaced the Conchs by using boats powered both by sail and engine while the Conchs clung too long to sail-driven schooners and hand-rowed skiffs. The Greeks were also willing to work under tough conditions; in the Gulf, they braved some of the most unpredictable, squall-driven weather in the world. The Greeks dove on days that kept the Conchs snug in safe harbor—in wind and rain that muddied shoal waters and kept the Conchs from even seeing the sea bottom through the "water telescope."

"Men are not made for safe havens," Aeschylus wrote, and so the Greeks dove in all but violent weather—although Gulf weather often *is* violent. Tampa, twenty-eight miles southeast of Tarpon, has ninety days of lightning a year; in effect, every day all summer since summer is when lightning strikes. Florida is the lightning capital of America, and Florida's west coast a prime target of ripping lightning. Gulf weather was of critical importance to the sponge fleet; of this the thirty-five sponge boats that sank in a hurricane in St. Joseph's Sound in 1918, close upon the Anclote Keys, are a stark reminder. Hurricanes brush or hit Tarpon Springs with regularity. Gertrude Stoughton writes of boats "flung into the tree tops a few miles up the coast by one of the hurricanes that could be expected in the summer months of every year." One of the early stories from my childhood is that of my father helping a man pull his boat to safety in a Gulf hurricane. I learned to love "weather" from my father.

OUR ETERNAL ODYSSEUS

Beneath the Gulf waters our Eternal Odysseus—helmeted and in full battle gear—leaned into the swift Gulf current, carrying a net bag and a heavy three-pronged hook into his wars with the Phrygian cities of the sea. He trotted along the sea bottom at a forty-five-degree angle—air hose tucked between his legs to reduce drag—scoffing up puffball after puffball of sponge from the virgin bars. Sometimes he trotted along for several miles, the boat above obliged to follow the diver's lead. "Fishing the diver," the Greeks call it. The Greeks were doing "live diving," which is the most dangerous kind of diving, with the boat moving, and the whirring propeller a constant threat to the diver's air hose and to the diver himself. *Time* magazine called the work of the sponge diver the most dangerous job in America; the poetics of manhood given new life in the home of the brave. Until a wire cage was invented to encase the propeller, most accidents to Greek divers in Florida's waters came, not from the bends, but from the unforgiving propeller.

Greek spongers were experienced, brash, and completely threatening to the Conch hook fishermen, even though there were nine thousand square miles of sponge fields and plenty of sponges for all, at least in the early years. The Greeks faced constant harassment by the Conchs, as if the work and the weather were not dangerous enough.

In 1953 Hollywood made a film about the sponge wars—*Beneath the Twelve Mile Reef.* It was the second Cinemascope picture ever made, and it was nominated for an Academy Award for its spectacular underwater photography. You simply can't go wrong with a diver wrestling with an octopus on a Cinemascope screen in Technicolor.

My whole family traipsed off to see the film. I love it still. The Greeks win all the fights—at least most of them—and get the girl. The film starred Gilbert Roland as the *paterfamilias* who dies of the bends; Robert Wagner, with jet-black hair, as the cocky but adorable young Greek; and Terri Moore as the beautiful daughter of an influential Conch fisherman. It is *Romeo and Juliet* on the west coast of Florida. In the end Robert Wagner wins the hearts of the Conchs and gets the American Girl, Terri Moore. *Yay!*

Also deserving of an Academy Award Nomination for Best Boat in a Feature Film, the Tarpon Springs sponge boat, *Eleni* appeared in the film strung stem-to-stern with beautiful wreaths of Rock Island wool sponges.

TARPON: "THE SPA PERIOD"

What was John King Cheyney thinking?

Surely that question must have been asked by the wealthy Northern elite—people with backgrounds similar to Cheyney's—when he invited five hundred Greek men to come live in the spa resort of Tarpon Springs in 1905. The town had only a few hundred year-round residents, so when the Greeks arrived they instantly became the majority. *What was Cheyney thinking?*

For a quarter century Tarpon Springs had been a winter haven for wealthy Northerners. In the late fall they arrived by train, some in private railroad cars, others by yacht. In the 1890s "railroading was in the air," Stoughton reminds us: four transcontinental railroads had been laid down, sprouting smaller lines in all directions. One of these, the "Orange Belt," reached Tarpon Springs in 1887, making it possible for passengers to travel from New York City to Tarpon Springs in just thirty-six hours. Tarpon Springs was the southernmost Florida reach of the U.S. rail system; even a decade later Teddy Roosevelt and his Rough Riders were forced to abandon the troop train at the new rail terminus in Tampa and board a ship to Cuba.

Tarpon Springs had "all the elements of a successful, healthful resort," Stoughton reports, including "a mineral spring of remarkably unpleasant flavor" at the head of Spring Bayou that was "enshrined under a pagoda." Dozens of millionaires built the Golden Crescent, a semicircle of elegant Victorian homes round the head of Spring Bayou, each with its own boathouse. The wealthy brought governesses and domestic staff, and hired black Tarponites as additional servants. Tarpon Springs was "a polite and decorous town" with values shaped in part by evangelicals who frowned upon drinking and rowdyism.

The Northern elite strolled around Spring Bayou, the women in their grand sun hats. Steam launches took wealthy vacationers down

the winding Anclote River and out into the Gulf to view the spectacular sunsets. There was sailing, golf, and bicycling; garden parties,
dinner parties, and dances. Thousands of invalids came too, Stoughton
reports, sent by Northern physicians to enjoy the sunshine, seabreezes,
and smell of the pines. Far from snowswept Philadelphia and New
York, they rocked away in comfort on "spacious porches."

John King Cheyney was the son of a wealthy Philadelphia Quaker.
In 1886 he came to Florida to watch over his father's business interests
and to identify wholly new ventures. While cruising the Florida Keys
on his yacht in 1889—the year Winslow Homer painted his Bahamian
sponger—Cheyney hit upon a new business: supplying sponges to the
U.S. market. The United States was still importing most of its sponges
from the eastern Mediterranean, Cuba, and the Bahamas. Cheyney
began buying up sponges and learning all facets of the sponge business: sponge fishing, processing, and marketing. In 1891 he launched
the Anclote and Rock Island Sponge Company, with offices in Tarpon
Springs and Philadelphia. He hired buyers and technical experts.
Among them was a clever young Greek, John Cocoris, from Leonidion
in Arcadia, Greece. Leonidion lies on a lush plain famous for its egg-
plants; but it has a bright pebbly beach that shines by the sea, across
from the sponge-fishing island of Spetses. Blocked on its inland side
by the abrupt rise of Mt. Parnon, with its sheer red cliffs, Leonidion's
livelihood has always relied upon sea communication and the success
of its merchants abroad. Cocoris had been working for the Lembesis
Company in New York as a sponge buyer in Key West. Cocoris also
knew everything about bleaching sponges with chemicals to turn them
into the golden color that so appeals to the buying public.

Cheyney hired Cocoris in 1897. Together they would revolutionize
the sponge industry, shifting its center from the Old World to the
New, from the eastern Mediterranean to Tarpon Springs, Florida. As
Stoughton writes:

> They were to play different roles—Cheyney the investor, employer, and
> man of affairs, and Cocoris the leader of the hard-driving, competitive
> colony of Greek spongers who were to come to Tarpon Springs.

The Greeks have never hesitated to uproot for economic opportunity; *diaspora*, after all, is a Greek word. That is how tiny Symi ended

up with a population of more than 22,000 in the late nineteenth century, Greeks uprooting and coming to Symi from the Turkish mainland and from the islands to take part in the booming sponge business. Sensing a new world being born, John sent for his three brothers, George, Louis, and Gus. The four brothers worked in Cheyney's packing house, but in their spare time they began to survey the Gulf and found it rich with sponge at all depths. They themselves began to harvest sponges and accumulate a stash. Convinced that more and better-grade sponges could be taken from the Gulf using deep-sea divers, they sold off their sponges to bring in a crew and diving equipment from the island of Aegina. George bought a boat for $180, refitted it with a hand-cranked air pump, hose, and lifeline, and hung a ladder over the side; he rechristened the boat *Elpis*, Hope. On June 18, 1905, "Hope" made its way down the Anclote River and out onto the Gulf, inaugurating a new phase in the life of Tarpon Springs. It was "the beginning of the end of the city as a winter spa for wealthy Northerners," wrote the anthropologist Edward Buxbaum. Within a generation the transformation was complete. By 1920, Buxbaum tells us, "most of the easterners who had come to Tarpon had died, were very old, or had returned to the north." A Greek sun was arcing through the Florida sky.

THE GOLD RUSH

News of the rich sponge fields spread swiftly through the sponge-fishing islands of Kalymnos, Halki, Symi, Aegina, Hydra, Spetses, and the others—spurred on by newspaper articles and advertisements telling spongers that travel expenses would be paid by "an American gentleman." Fortunes were to be made on the west coast of Florida, if only they would seize the golden moment. Cheyney stood behind the offer, convinced by Cocoris that a bonanza lay ahead if the Anclote and Rock Island Sponge Company boosted production using the *ska-fandro* method. My grandfather, by this time dead for a year, would have wept at the prospect.

In the summer of 1905 the 500 spongers arrived. All were men—

either single or having left their wives and children behind to follow the Gold Rush, the Rush to the Golden Fleece.

Within a year 1,500 Greeks arrived. The first Greek woman to come was John Cocoris's bride, Anna, who gave birth in 1906 to a daughter, Stamatina, the first child born to the Greeks of Tarpon Springs. The Greek population skyrocketed; by 1940 three-quarters of the residents were of Greek descent, Buxbaum reports. Here was a community without equal in the United States; while other cities might have more Greeks, no city was so Greek. From 1905 onward the Greeks either were in the numerical majority or, in alliance with black Tarponites, could dominate the politics of Tarpon Springs. The political influence of Greeks in this part of Florida remains strong. In the 2000 election Congressman Michael Bilirakis—of Dodecanese descent, Kalymnian and Karpathian—won reelection with a whopping 82 percent of the vote.

In the beautiful, quiet park by Spring Bayou, there is a lovely war memorial where one can read the names of young Greek men who fell in battle in the world wars, giving the last full measure of devotion to their new country. "Blessed is the match consumed in kindling flame," wrote the soldier-poet Hannah Senesh. And so the blessing, too, for these young Greek men, sons of Pericles, for keeping lit the flame of democracy first kindled in the country of their ancestors.

ANATOLIA MY LOVE

After 1905 Greek spongers flooded into Tarpon—especially from the Dodecanese and especially after 1912 when the Italians seized the islands. Having taken Libya from Turkey in 1911, the emboldened Italians intended to invade Turkey's vast Anatolia peninsula; but they got cold feet at the last instant and "settled" for the Dodecanese, the archipelago off Anatolia's shore.

By the seizure Italy slashed the Dodecanesian lifeline to the Anatolian mainland: the Dodecanese were part of Turkey no more. The Italians also initiated a program of "de-Hellenization" to make the islands into Italian colonies, as Russ Bernard points out. In reaction the Symiots and Kalymnians began to organize "subversive groups whose purpose was to undermine Italian authority and bring the Dodecanese situation to world opinion." In retribution the Italians barred the Dodecanesians—for a time at least—from sponge fishing off the coast of Libya. Hence, the seizure dealt a twofold blow to the Dodecanese: no lifeline to Anatolia and no lucrative Libyan sponge fields to work. Wealthy families from the Dodecanese, especially from Symi, lost extensive landholdings and grazing rights on Anatolia; the boatyards of Symi and Kalymnos lost their supply of lumber. A century earlier the Symiots had stripped their forests bare to build boats for the Greek war of national liberation against the Turks, although the Symiots themselves remained under subjugation, except for a fleeting period of freedom. Ever after, the Symiots depended on the forests of Anatolia for materials to build their swift boats.

Imagine, if you will, an early Nantucket or Martha's Vineyard suddenly sliced away from the United States, told not to fish or hunt whales, and made to learn Italian. Offshore islands cannot survive without connection to a mainland, and for the Dodecanese, Italy was too far away. Recall, too, that the tie to Anatolia was economic *and* cultural, a tie that even preceded the four hundred years of Ottoman Turkish rule. The perimeter of Anatolia, including its northern perimeter along the Black Sea, was dotted with large Greek communities dating from the great period of Hellenic colonization.

Once aboard a Greek vessel, I noticed that we were passing what I thought to be the Turkish port of Bodrum, where they fish for sponges. It sits on the southern coast of Anatolia, just across from the Dodecanese island of Kos, the birthplace of Hippocrates. I asked the Greek captain if what I saw was indeed Bodrum. "No," he snapped, "It is Halicarnassus," the ancient Greek name for the same port.

When a Symiot sailed his swift *skaphos* the four miles to Anatolia, when a Rhodian sailed the short distance to the mainland, he would say to family or friends, "I am going to '*Symaiki Perea*'" or "to '*Rodiaki Perea*,'" in old Dodecanese dialect—to "Symi a little further on," to "Rhodes a little further on." These were places that were a regular and necessary part of the life of the Dodecanese, for agricultural products and for other staples of life and livelihood. The Dodecanese are beautiful rocky outcroppings from the sea, "jewels" as residents are quick to say. But geologically, they are an extension of the mountains of Anatolia, jutting out of the Aegean between Asia Minor and the island of Crete. Even the weather of the Dodecanese, by and large, is the weather of Anatolia.

So Anatolia was the lifeline. Once cut, hunger, even starvation, prevailed in the Dodecanese. Mothers committed suicide. Fleeing and bewildered Dodecanesian refugees roamed the Greek port of Piraeus. Photos of desolate refugees abound. My widowed grandmother, Anastasia, saved my father's life by lying about his age—making him a year older—and enrolling him at an orphan school in Piraeus. The date on my father's papers leaps out at me every time I look at it: "Enrolled at the Eleni Zannis orphan school in Piraeus in April 1912," the very month the Italians seized the Dodecanese. There, fed and protected, my father remained until 1917, when he graduated and went on to shine at the naval engineering college of Greece. The day he graduated, the Queen of Greece presented him with a medal. In 1997 I visited the orphanage and said a prayer for my father and for my grandmother Anastasia.*

HEMORRHAGE

The population of Symi plummeted from 22,000 in 1912 to 7,000 in 1917, Kalymnos from 23,000 to 15,000, and Kastellorizo from 4,000 to 2,000. As microhistory, it is a hemorrhaging (also a Greek word) that evokes Ireland in the Great Famine. The disaster was made worse

---

*My father survived, but he would never forget his ties to the Dodecanese or his love and hope for the common people. In the late 1920s, he served as president of the Greek Educational League in Chicago, an organization that appeared on the Attorney General's list of Communist-front organizations. Chicago had 150,000 Greeks at the time, the largest Greek community in the United States. My father spoke on the same platform with William Z. Foster and Earl Browder, presidents of the American Communist party; and in 1927 he led the Greek contingent, when ethnic groups and leftists put a hundred thousand people on the streets to march on behalf of Sacco and Vanzetti.

A love for social justice was handed down from the poet Metrophanes to his son Nikitas; a dream deferred.

by the food shortages and disruptions in maritime trade and sponge fishing that came with World War I. In both world wars, innocents aboard sponge-fishing boats were strafed.

Whole sponging crews, with long experience and tradition—large portions of the Aegean sponging fleet—left from Symi, Halki, and Kalymnos for the west coast of Florida. Gifted spongers, "aces" in Tarpon talk, also came from Aegina, Spetses, Hydra, Limnos; from Rhodes, Kos, Leros, Kastellorizo, Nissyros, Karpathos, Tilos, Lipsi, Astypalaia and Kassos, and from the other Aegean islands. Roughly, very roughly, one-third of the spongers in Tarpons Springs were from Kalymnos, one-third from Halki, and one-third from Symi and the other islands.

Swiftly following the spongers came representatives of great sponge houses—like that of Nicholas Vouvalis of Kalymnos and London—who established warehouses in Tarpon Springs. Buyers arrived from France, Italy, and beyond, and investors from around the United States to finance sponge-fishing trips and boat building. The boats built were adapted from designs the Greeks brought with them in their heads. The early boats were traditional Greek double-enders, with a high bow and stern; later models sliced off the stern—to allow a Diesel engine to be mounted and to prevent the boat from "squatting." The *kaiki* had been built to nine meters at the water line to match the wavelength of the Mediterranean Sea. How exactly do you adapt a Greek *kaiki* to the squall-driven Gulf?

"Supplying the industry was a network of trades and crafts," Gertrude Stoughton writes; this included a sail loft, ship chandlers, machine shops, and packing houses where one could hear the "clipping away at sponges all day" during the good years. Among the craftsmen of Tarpon was Gabriel Peterson, whom Lee and Eileen Rozee describe in *Sponge Docks* as "a Turk by birth and a Tarponite by choice." Peterson is credited with devising the method by which the air compressor worked off the sponge boat's engine, making it more powerful and more reliable than the old hand-cranked air pump. In the 1920s Peterson—the Turk by birth—invented the removable propeller cage that saved the lives of many Greek divers.

A power elite emerged in Tarpon Springs to represent the sponge industry's interests at the state and federal level, and in the many court cases that grew out of the sponge wars that broke out sporadically. Homegrown sponge merchants like Nicholas Arfaras and George Emmanuel joined blue-blood John Cheyney in representing the industry and helping it to grow into a booming force in Florida's economy.

"DEADPAN FLATNESS"

Before the Greeks arrived, quiet Tarpon Springs comprised only a few streets and stores. When the five hundred Greek men arrived, native Tarponites were "frankly nervous," Stoughton writes. Indeed, a mutual wariness held sway. Accustomed to the "noisy, colorful ports of the eastern Mediterranean," the Greeks were "amazed at the cool deadpan flatness of American ways, with no passion or laughter that they could see."

John Cocoris was the patron of the newly arrived Greek spongers; he made sure that they were housed, fed, paid, and able to send home letters and drafts of money. The Greeks worked hard, kept to themselves, and "piled up the sponge catches." And they struck up a friendship with the African-Americans. "Coming from the Mediterranean area where many people are dark-skinned, and they themselves often being very swarthy, the Greeks had none of the southern white's ethnocentric attitudes," Buxbaum noted. As the sponge business grew and a need for labor developed, the Greeks naturally hired on African-Americans. They became cooks, lifeline tenders, and even divers; they learned to speak Greek, often with a Dodecanese accent. The Greeks and the African-Americans slept in close quarters on the *kaikia*. The friendship of the Greeks with the African-Americans did little to endear the Greeks to the wealthy Northerners or to the Southern whites. The worst case of redneck justice toward the Greeks themselves came in 1931, when as Stoughton reports, three young Greek sponge divers, who had been arrested, were found "apparently burned to death in a jail cell at Cedar Key." Two officers of the law were later convicted "of stabbing and bludgeoning the men to death, and then setting fire to the cell to conceal the crime."

"KNOCK IT A LITTLE, KALAFATES"

Surprisingly, there was no cleared-off port in this part of the Gulf, Frantzis tells us; only on the banks of the Anclote River at Tarpon Springs, three miles up from the Gulf of Mexico. But the Anclote River lacked a deep channel, so each trip up and down the river proved dangerous.

President Calvin Coolidge and his wife once visited Tarpon Springs. A reception committee took the esteemed visitors on an outing to the Anclote Keys. A flotilla of sponge boats, festooned with flags and patriotic bunting, took the three-mile trip down the Anclote river to the Gulf. The sponge boat *Calvin Coolidge* carried the President and his wife. At sunset the party started back, led by the *Calvin Coolidge*.

Condensed from George Th. Frantzis's account in *Strangers at Ithaca*, the following is a report of what happened on the return trip.

When they entered the intricate, narrow, and shallow canal of the Anclote, John Douglas (John Kananes of Halki), leader of the reception committee for the President, went to the stern and approached the captain, John Kalafates. "Knock the boat a bit and drag it on the sandy-shallow bank of the river." The captain looked at him with terror and surprise. Upon collecting himself he continued to pay attention to his course in the labyrinth-like river that makes its three-mile distance into the Tarpon Springs port.

"Knock it a little, Kalafates," Kananes whispered again.

"What are you saying? Can't you see the President and his wife? Are you crazy, or do you want us all to hang?"

"Knock it a little on the side," urged Kananes. "I didn't tell you to get stuck in the sand completely. Listen to me, I am telling you this for your own good."

As the President and Mrs. Coolidge were busy admiring the green banks of the river, the calm, and the gilt edge to the setting-sun waters, suddenly the diving boat shook. But only for a moment. The captain, with a steadied jerk of the tiller, sent the prow to the left and the boat back on its course. The President and his wife surprised—and jarred a bit—looked around to see whether the boat had collided with anything. The bodyguards too were shaken and apprehensive.

"Do not worry, do not worry," they were assured by the steady-voiced John Kananes.

"But what happened?" asked the tall guest.

"Mr. President," answered Kananes, "just a slight wrong twist on behalf of the captain. The canal is very shallow and narrow, and, especially at night, it becomes dangerous to navigate."

Mr. Coolidge shook his head understandingly, and, turning to his secretary, instructed him to remember this incident and to remind him of it when they returned to Washington. Smilingly, John Kananes looked at the captain and winked.

The headshake of the President brought to Tarpon Springs a few days later big government drag lines that began dredging. And so Tarpon Springs acquired a deep and wide canal that continues up to the mouth of the river where it meets the Gulf of Mexico. The cunning of Greek Odysseus will live forever and everywhere.

In the year before the Greeks began diving, the Florida Keys landed about 266,000 pounds of sponges and the Tarpon Springs area about 67,000 pounds, reports Love Dean. In 1918 the Conchs landed 108,000 pounds of sponges while the Greek divers of Tarpon Springs landed more than 344,000 pounds. The percentage of total catch of the two regions had nearly reversed, as Dean points out. The effect of the Greek spongers on the economy of Tarpon Springs was "immediate and immense," wrote Andrew Carras in the November–December 1996 issue of *Odyssey* magazine. "By 1908, the Greeks had converted a $100,000-per-year sponging industry into a $1,000,000-per-year gold mine—the largest industry in Florida." While Tarpon Springs was not founded by the sponge-diving Greeks, Carras observes, "they put it on the map." Clearly, sponge fishing had become Tarpon's signature industry.

MEDITERRANEAN PORT-OF-CALL

May there be many summer mornings when,
with what pleasure, what joy,
you enter harbors you're seeing for the first time;
may you stop at Phoenician trading stations
to buy fine things,
mother of pearl and coral, amber and ebony,
sensual perfume of every kind—

—C. P. Cavafy, "Ithaka"

There is no more exotic Mediterranean port-of-call than Alexandria where the great Greek poet Cavafy was born, when a hundred thousand Greeks lived and flourished there. In that queen of Greek cities lived the great cotton traders of Egypt, all Greek. But had Cavafy put in at the harbor of Tarpon Springs in the first half of the twentieth century, he would have thought himself at a Phoenician trading station or a colorful Greek port.

Two hundred gaily colored sponge boats bobbed and glinted in the sun when sponge fishing was at its zenith and the fleet safe at home; *kaikia* with high bows and open decks, recalling the ancient boat designs of the Mediterranean. Some *kaikia* dock there still; enough to make a *kalafatas*, a boat caulker from the Dodecanese, feel pride-of-craft. God bless the boat caulker who keeps boats from leaking when slammed by gale-force winds; his tools pine tar, cotton, and the endless tattoo of his hammer.

In 1947 Jennie Harris captured the profusion of colors, as she scanned the painted boats of the Greek sponge fleet: "Bright orange and black; all blue; or red, white, blue, and black; or white, gray, orange, and green." No deadpan flatness here.

"AMERICAN GIRL"

Crevecoeur, DeTocqueville, and others have written of the creation of a wholly new American. The evolving loyalties and loves of the new Greek-American sing out in the boat-names of Tarpon Springs: *Poseidon, Nike, Kalliope, Demetra,* and *Socrates* from the ancients; *St. Nicholas, St. John, St. George, St. Paul,* and *Santa Maria* from the Church; *Democratia, Boubalina,* and *Venizelos* from the Greek polity; *Sparta, Crete, Kalymnos, Halki, Hydra, Nereus,* and *Symi* from sweet Mother Hellas; *Anna, Angeliki, Eleni, Chrisula, Katina,* and *Bessie* from their beloveds. From the adopted homeland were *Uncle Sam, George Washington, Lincoln,* and *Roosevelt; Mayflower, Liberty, Century of Progress,* and my favorite, *American Girl.* And from American places, *St. Augustine, Appalachicola,* and *Dixie.* In flush times the boats were tied up four deep at the sponge docks. And these Greeks love their boats; the Dodecanese islands alone sent forty-seven ships to the war against Troy.

"UNDENIABLE GREEKNESS"

Had Cavafy ambled along what is now Dodecanese Boulevard, by the sponge docks, he would have felt comfortable—as if in the Greek pur-lieus of the Alexandria of his youth, Smyrna of yore, or in any of scores of Greek ports in the Aegean or the Ioanian seas: "Hot sugar and butter fragrances from the Greek bakery mingle with the coffee house smells," wrote Jennie Harris. Greek was spoken everywhere; all around the poetic eyes and faces of grace. All the shops were Greek, some selling souvenirs from the sea—sea fans, coral, and sponges of every variety and phantasmagoric shape; some of the sponges of shock-ing size. In the *kafenia* men played cards and smoked the Turkish water pipe—the *narghile* that gave its name to a kind of diving. Outside the *kafenia* men sipped thick sweet Greek coffee or nursed an ouzo while twirling *komboloi*, a string of amber worry beads. Greek music wafted out of tavernas; sounds of "the lyre, the clarinet, zither, violin, or man-dolin" were heard everywhere, Stoughton writes. Had Cavafy leaned into a taverna to listen more closely to the *bouzouki* music, he would have seen men on their feet, twirling and leaping as they did the dances of their homeland. In prosperous times there was "a holiday air," Frantzis tells us, pretty-girl dancers, sounds of castanets, and laughter. "One felt the virility and vigor of the spongers, and saw their open-handedness, which was characteristic of their trade," he writes.

But whether spirited or mournful, Greek music dwells largely in the minor mode, like the music of the Jews: two peoples who know in the end that the world can break your heart. The Greeks speak of Constantinople, lost in 1453, and Smyrna, burnt and destroyed with its Greek inhabitants in 1922, the way the Jews for many centuries spoke of Jerusalem: The City of Peace. Sad to say, alas, *holocaust*, too, is a Greek word.

The first event that brought Greeks and Americans together was the christening of Stamatina, the daughter of John and Anna Cocoris. After the Greek Orthodox priest performed the baptism, the guests retreated to a feast with "all the delicacies of local fare plus imported wines and choice confections ordered from New York," Stoughton re-ports. Then came the Greek dancing, with the Cocorises "such irresistible hosts that the Americans found themselves joining the swaying lines and dancing too. This was an important first step on the long road to mutual understanding and esteem."

THE CHURCH OF SAINT NICHOLAS

Brave and proud as bullfighters, the "matadors of the deep" were humble before their Church and gave willingly to support it. The Greek Orthodox Church had bound Greeks together through four hundred years of slavery and had been the tie that binds in diaspora. The incense and icons, the chanted liturgy, the priests in lofty hats and ornate robes, the gold and silver everywhere; all evoke the splendor of Byzantium and the timelessness of Greece. In church the Greeks are borne back ceaselessly into their past as they gaze at row upon row of candles wavering in soft flame. The Church is why Greeks believe deep in their hearts that Constantinople has not been lost forever; it is why Constantinople, the City of Constantine and of Helen, remains the country's spiritual capital; and why Smyrna will never be forgotten.

In 1907, on the west coast of Florida, the divers built the Church of Saint Nicholas, named for the patron saint of Greek seafarers, the legatee of Poseidon in the Orthodox Christian world. *Syncretism*—the fusion of different sets of beliefs—is also a Greek word.

Clearly, the Greeks were in Tarpon Springs to stay; few spongers returned home, although many had come thinking they would remain long enough to accumulate a stake and return to the Aegean. Their families soon followed them to the "gilt-edged" shore of the Anclote river.

DELIVERED BY SCHOONER

Steve Katzaras loves to tell the story of his older brother's arrival in Tarpon Springs. Most Greeks came into the United States by way of Ellis Island. "Not my brother John; he came on a schooner from Cuba," Steve says with a grin. John Katzaras came into the United States soon after immigration laws tightened in 1921, just after my own father's arrival. (My father left from the island of Rhodes in 1920 and arrived, of all places, in Rhode Island.) The tightening came on the same wave that brought the Palmer Raids and the Red Scare; after both world wars, nativism flared in the United States—the tightening an attempt to keep radicals from southern Europe out of the United States. John Katzaras traveled to Cuba as a merchant seaman, hoping he could hitch a ride to Tarpon on one of the Cuban fishing schooners that worked the Gulf. He was right. But as the schooner neared the Anclote Keys, the captain—fearing shallows—told John to jump overboard and swim. The swim no problem to a Symiot, Steve's brother leaped into the sea and swam to the Greek sponge fleet anchored near the Keys; the Greeks brought John to a safe-home in Tarpon Springs. John Katzaras became one of Tarpon's ace captains; he knew where to find sponge and how to assemble top crews. And he became a U.S. citizen.

THE SPONGE EXCHANGE

In 1908 the first Sponge Exchange was founded to store and auction sponges; a percentage of all sponges traded was turned over to the Church of Saint Nicholas. Ever practical, the Greeks built the Sponge Exchange close upon the sponge docks; all the business of sponging could now take place within a tight, tiny locus of activity.

Stoughton reminds us that the environs of Tarpon Springs made the Greeks feel rather at home: "the blue-green sea, the beaches and the palms and pines, the oranges and lemons and the sun." No surprise. Sponges flourish only in semitropical climates: the Mediterranean, the Caribbean and the Gulf, and the waters of the South Pacific—Micronesia, the Philippines, and Japan.

While other factors were at work, the arrival of the Greeks spurred the departure of the Northern bluebloods; the tone and tempo of the city had forever changed. As Edward Buxbaum observes:

> Greek gregariousness was foreign . . . and the Mediterranean habits of facial expression and gesture combined with loud and rapid talk made the evenings noisy. The quiet refinement of northern cultured society

was entirely lacking. The Greek custom of visiting with friends and family occupied many of them till late hours in their homes. Holidays and name days were celebrated with typical Greek enthusiasm and uproariousness.

And rapidly, Greek industriousness led to acquisition of real estate; the Greeks edging out of Greek Town and toward the "fine old homes" around Spring Bayou.

"The undeniable Greekness of Tarpon Springs is the town's most alluring, and by far its most vibrant, feature," Andrew Carras observed. In the 1940s, undeniable Greekness combined with undeniable Americanness to charming result: the local high school football team, "The Spongers," openly called their plays in Greek, giving them advantage over their confused opponents.

DIVING IN THE GULF

Gulf waters were "heavier" than the Mediterranean, the ace divers of Tarpon reported—less saline, less buoyant, warmer, and harder to work. In actuality the water was less dense and lighter; it was the divers who felt "heavier" in the less dense water. Divers now had currents and tides to deal with as opposed to the tideless Mediterranean. While divers needed to descend to less depth to find sponges, they felt equally at risk in the shallower water of the Gulf. Despite rapturous beauty all around, diving in the Gulf was a sweaty, rough, and dangerous business.

George Billiris is of Kalymnian lineage, an international sponge merchant, and a diver. His family has been involved in the sponge business for four generations, on both sides. George is unofficial ambassador of the sponge docks and a frequent spokesperson for Tarpon Springs. Sea water runs in his veins, and the people of the press sense it instantly. George loves to talk about "hard-hat" diving: "Some people say that the hard-hat helmet is almost as hard as George Billiris' head," he says in sweet self-mockery. He once narrated a National Geographic film about the spongers of Tarpon Springs and hit his mark with the easy grace of a professional. George is a strong and bluff man; you feel protected in his presence.

George has fought hard to keep sponge diving alive in Tarpon

Ready for the Passion of the Dive. Soon he will don the thirty-eight pound helmet and descend into 120 feet of water in his well-worn diving suit. He is the poet of his own manhood. *Photo by Hamilton Wright.*

A dashing Kalymnian captain and his crew work on a successful haul of sponges somewhere off the coast of North Africa. *Photo courtesy Kyriacos Hadzidakis.*

Paralyzed by the bends. For 125 years such scenes were commonplace in the harbors of some of the most beautiful islands in the world. The terrible beauty of sponge fishing. *Photo property of Kalymnos Nautical Museum.*

The plight of the sponge divers highlighted in a newspaper. Caption on photo reads: "A 19-year-old who was hit by the bends last year in Benghazi. He has recently started taking a few steps. His doctors are optimistic." *Photo from Kirannis Photo Shop.*

We few, we happy few, we happy band of brothers. Cameraderie was a regular harvest from the sea for all the brave young men. *Palikaria* all. *Photo from Kirannis Photo Shop.*

Karl Vasilievich Flegel, the Angel from the North. A professor of classical languages and journalist from Vilna moved to the Aegean and for decades made saving the lives of the divers his cause. *Photo courtesy Kyriacos Hadzidakis.*

My father the *morfomenos*. Those who were educated were believed to have metamorphosed: they looked and sounded different. His elegant attire and striking pose were suitable to the salons of Western Europe. The *morfomeni* were national patriots all. *Photo in author's collection.*

Women of the Dodecanese in traditional local costume. *Photo courtesy Denis Cantonis.*

The General Sponge Fishing Company was once the largest sponge house in the world. George Kandounias, father of Michael and Denis Cantonis, was manager of operations at the Symi branch. George is the well-dressed man with a necktie directly under the "Y" of SYMI. *Photo courtesy Denis Cantonis.*

"Splash of a Gold Cross Thrown into Spring Bayou Sends Greek Youths Diving for the Church's Blessing," wrote Jennie Harris in *National Geographic.* This was Epiphany Day, Tarpon Springs, Florida, 1947. Aged three, I was present in the crowd of 15,000. *Photo courtesy AP/WIDE WORLD PHOTOS.*

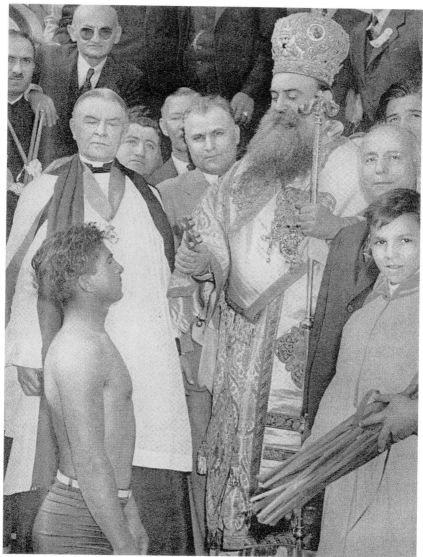

"To the Victor Belong Good Luck, Happiness, and the Blessings of the Church," reported Jennie Harris in *National Geographic.* Archbishop Athenagoras bestows his blessing upon the winner. *Photo by Bill Abbott.*

In the sponge industry the *click-click* of shears was the sound of money as workers trimmed sponges for the market. In flush times the sound could be heard outside all of the sponge warehouses in the Aegean and here too in Tarpon Springs. *Photo courtesy Tarpon Springs Area Historical Society Collection.*

Gorgeous sponges in sweet profusion. Natural sponges have always been in short supply. For a time Tarpon Springs held a monopoly when red tide shut down the West Atlantic and World War II shut down the Mediterranean. *Photo by Herb Davies.*

These children are from Kalymnos, "The Island of the Sponge Fishermen." Everyone who sees this photo says, "Three Michaels." They all look like photos of me in the late 1940s. *Photo from Kirannis Photo Shop.*

Beneath the Gulf waters our Eternal Odysseus—helmeted and in full battle gear—leaned into the swift Gulf current, carrying a net bag and a heavy three-pronged hook into his wars with the Phrygian cities of the sea. *Photo: Courtesy, Tampa–Hillsborough County Public Library System.*

The author reliving history. "The magic of retelling this story has been passed to me. It is the story of a man I never knew, my grand-father, and a place that I never lived in, the Dodecanese, but some-how his story and this story have become my story. *Photo in author's collection.*

This statue of the beautiful boy, a Cross Day victor, stands outside St. Nicholas Cathedral in Tarpon Springs. It captures the courage, grace, and piety of the Na-ked Divers of the Aegean. *Photo in au-thor's collection.*

Springs. He understands that the city's multimillion-dollar tourist trade is tied to its daring divers—to the stories they fetch from the seafloor, along with the sponges. In the tourist industry, as in the film industry, you can't go wrong with a story of a diver wrestling with an octopus.

Tourists coming into Tarpon Springs are transfixed by the stories of Greek divers and their historic courage handed down father-to-son. Some scholars believe that Shakespeare visited the Greek island of Corfu before writing the *Tempest*; Greek mariners from Corfu and elsewhere—divers included—have felt connection to these lines:

> Full-fathom five where thy father lies;
> Of his bones are coral made
> Those are pearls that were his eyes.
> —Shakespeare, *Tempest* (1.2. 397–399)

SPONGE DIVING 101

Demand for sponge always exceeds supply, eight to one at times, Billiris avers. So he wants more people to dive for sponge. George Billiris has even taught a course in sponge diving at St. Petersburg Junior College to retrain displaced Florida net fishermen and turn them into sponge fishermen. "Sponge Diving 101" people called it, eyes a-twinkle. But it was more than a classroom course: the men learned to walk the bottom.

While the diver in the Mediterranean typically works in deeper water, the diver in the Gulf constantly works against the strong currents. The currents are set off by inflow from three sources: the warm river-like current of the Gulf Stream that enters from the Caribbean, drainage from the Mississippi, and drainage from the Rio Grande. All spin about in the basin of the Mexican Gulf while the diver, breathing compressed air, tries to harvest sponge with his three-pronged hook. Imagine, if you will, knowing that your legs are pumping against the power of the mighty Mississippi or the Gulf Stream while, alone, you work under a mountain of water. "You have to have stamina; you have to have legs; you have to have a good eye to spot sponge," says George.

When the sponge industry in the Gulf was at its zenith, divers dove deep, to 120 feet. Today's divers work in 30 to 60 feet of water. The old-timers were more organized, more prepared to dive deep, and more willing to take unfathomable risks. The poetics of manhood can cross an ocean, but in a land of plenty it has trouble crossing the generations. The deep-water diver no longer exists in Tarpon Springs.

While diving in the Gulf is dangerous, only twenty divers have been killed working off the west coast of Florida. "We're really lucky we didn't lose more men over the years," George Billiris says. Many more, of course, suffered paralysis or disabling injury from encounters with the propeller or with the other hazards of the sea. Why else would sponge divers carry rules in their heads, like this one noted by Jennie Harris: "In case of sharks, stand still! Fold your arms, hide your bare hands under your arms, and don't move till the sharks depart."

On July 10, 2001, the *Boston Globe* reported, "According to the International Shark Attack File in Gainesville, 34 of the nation's 51 reported shark attacks were in Florida. One of the attacks was fatal: A 69-year-old-man was killed near his St. Petersburg home last August." St. Petersburg is on the Gulf of Mexico, some twenty miles south of Tarpon Springs.

WHY FEWER DIED IN THE UNITED STATES

There were relatively fewer deaths among Greek sponge divers in the United States for several reasons. Diving to great depth, followed by rapid ascent, is the surest way to die of the bends. In the United States Greek divers dove in shallower water. Doing so cut their risk. Repetitive diving also increases risk of decompression disease. Gulf divers did not dive at the ceaseless pace of the Mediterranean divers: three times a day, seven days a week, for six months. In the Old World the Greeks dove in the *Meltemi*, the strong northeast winds of July and August that can topple tourist tables; but in the New World not even the weather-defying Greeks dove in violent squalls. The ceaseless pace was interrupted. "Perhaps because they were less fatigued, they were less likely to be hit," Michael Cantonis of Tarpon Springs mused early along as we discussed the difference in diving between the Mediterranean and the Gulf.

"Massive credit is the basis of sponge fishing," Russ Bernard wrote of the sponge industry on the island of Kalymnos. Massive credit drove some captains to abuse divers and put huge pressure on the 100 percent *platika* diver to take risks. In the Mediterranean high capitalization of diving ventures was a necessity because of unique circumstances. Divers were gone for a half-year in clusters of a mother boat and several diving boats that had sailed to distant sponge fields; diving deep required large crews, expensive equipment, and 100 percent *platika*. From high capitalization followed a simple, stark rule: *You better find sponge!* But in the United States, the sponge fields were not so distant. The system of a mother boat and several sponge boats was not necessary; you did not need to bring so much with you or to store so much sponge since you could get to port more easily. Coming into port more often also interrupted the ceaseless pace; repetitive diving was reduced. Sponge catches were sold off with greater frequency; hence, there was less debt. Risk was spread around since captains owned and operated their own sponge boats and sponge ventures, no more clusters: a phenomenon spurred on by material conditions and by American individualism.

Divers did not receive 100 percent *platika*. Payment was spread across a system that involved some *platika*, some payment to the diver's family while he was at sea, some pay as he went along, and some pay at season's end—*"ta resta,"* the rest. The whole American system cut away at the more lethal heavy-upfront expenditure of the Mediterranean system. Debt burden on the captain's head and on the financier's was not so great; pressure on the diver below not so immense.

By 1905, thanks to the daring Greeks, more was known about safe diving procedure than in 1863 when Fotis Mastoridis pulled his stunt and lowered gravid Eleftheria into Symi harbor.

Divers could get out of harm's way. Recall that they were fishing for sponges off the coast of Florida. They were not diving off the coast of Libya, Corsica, or the Azores. If the American sponge boat put in at another Florida harbor, the under-skilled or abused diver could simply quit. He telephoned his wife, and said, "Come pick me up." Suddenly, a diver destined for paralysis or death was preempted from the casualty list.

Last, workers in twentieth-century America were not treated so harshly as were workers in the nineteenth-century Aegean. Political pressure from Eugene Debs, other American Socialist and leftist leaders, and fervent labor unionists, like my dad, helped to ameliorate the lives of working men and women in America. What was it that Debs said? "The cross is bending, midnight is passing, and joy cometh with the morn."

SYMIOT DARING

Michael Cantonis, eighty-six, is a Symiot by birth who built the Acme Sponge Company from scratch into the greatest sponge house in the contemporary world. Always daring, at age twenty-three, after only three years in the sponge business in Tarpon Springs, Michael struck off on his own. By 1943 Michael Cantonis, age twenty-eight, and his new company, Acme Sponge, was the largest buyer of sponges in Tarpon Springs when the U.S. sponge industry was at *its* acme. Always Michael's life and work were characterized by discipline and imagination. For example, Michael was the first person of Greek descent to show up in Key West to buy sponges from the Conchs *after* the outbreak of the Sponge Wars: He was Daniel in the lion's den. In 1936 he went alone into Key West and won the respect of leading Conch captains by telling them: "Look, I will not fish for sponges. I will be a third buyer, added to your two local buyers. A third buyer will create competition, raise sponge prices, and help you. And me." As always, Michael was right; everyone prospered.

MOTHER SEA AS SEDUCTRESS

Risk aside—or because of it—the Greeks found diving in the Gulf rapturous, even irresistible. A siren voice once again called Odysseus to a dangerous destiny. Always Mother Sea has been the Great Seductress of Greek mariners: they become all-forgetting in her presence. Mother Sea whispers into the "unwaxed ears" of the Aegean divers, *"Forget the risk.... Your Mother calls you to the Deep.... Come to me, Come to me."*

Diving holds a "tremendous fascination" for the Greeks, Jennie Harris observed. "The Greeks have a saying," she noted, " 'A diver for two years is a diver for life.' " But she also depicted the diver's hard life:

> The deep sea diver spends two months out of nine *under* water, in everlasting twilight, walking the floor of the sea.... His 35-pound shoes give back no sound of footfall, arouse no echoes as he treads these gloomy miles of solemn water, peering through the glass windows of his helmet.

Today in Tarpon Springs there are only a half-dozen boats that fish for sponge on an organized basis; fifteen or twenty men—and a few husband and wife teams—who dive for sponge. Billiris reports that there are still plenty of sponges in the Gulf; all he needs are more trained divers. Diving for sponge was a father-to-son business, sponger born of sponger, but periodic kill-offs of sponges from outbreaks of red tide "broke the chain," as Billiris says. The younger generation opted out for more reliable and safer occupations, and they headed off to college. Among ethnic groups in the United States, Greeks stand first in educational attainment and second in income.

Always confident, George Billiris believes sponging in Florida has a future. He reminds us, "World demand for sponge is eight times bigger than supply." "Quality pay will bring quality men who will find quality sponges," he says; it's lines like that that keep the media rushing up to George Billiris.

SUPERSTITIONS

In writing about the Greek spongers in *National Geographic,* Jennie Harris reported on some of their superstitions. "Suitcases bring bad luck. Try bringing one on board and the captain will throw it overboard," she writes. The boats are crowded, she concedes, leaving no room for a suitcase; each man brings just two big seabags.

Russ Bernard reported on similar superstitions among Kalymnian sponge boat captains, such as those that controlled when a captain set sail for the season. "Saturday was the first of May, a day when no boat can leave Kalymnos if luck is to be courted. The first of the month is always a dangerous time, and it is best to avoid doing important things on those days if possible." Nor could a boat set sail on Sunday since "men should not leave their families on Sunday." Tuesdays are the unluckiest days of all "since Constantinople fell to the Turks on a Tuesday." He reports that one boat was taking off "when the church bells tolled the death of a citizen, a shoemaker. The boat turned on its stern and headed for port because the captain heard the death knell."

EPIPHANY DAY

Now when Jesus was baptized, as soon as he had gone up from the water the heavens were opened, and he saw the Spirit of God descending like a dove and coming upon him, and lo, [there was] a voice from heaven saying, "This is my beloved Son, with whom I have been well-pleased."

—(Mark. 3:16-17)

If I had had a daughter, I would have wanted her named *Epiphany*. The beauty of the word rings in my ear. As a holy day, "Epiphany" is all about the Sanctification of the Waters for the Greeks. It is hard to imagine a people for whom such a rite would hold greater significance. Always, the Greeks have been attracted to the seaways and slipways.

Before Christianity, Greek mariners prayed to Poseidon, after to Saint Nicholas. The blessings of the Nile were celebrated in ancient Egypt; and elsewhere in the world people had similar rites. But in the bowl of the Mediterranean, "The custom of revering water, germinating in pagan days, intertwined with the later flower of Christian religion to become the full-blown splendor of the Greek Church's day of the cross," as Jennie Harris observed. That day is January 6, Epiphany Day, the holy day marking Jesus' baptism in the River Jordan by John the Baptist. *Agiasmos.* In Orthodox Christianity it marks when Christ's divine nature was finally revealed in "an epiphany": The Spirit of God descended in the form of a dove, and a voice from the heavens proclaimed, "This is my beloved Son, with whom I have been well-pleased." To Roman Catholics and Protestants Epiphany marks the appearance of the Magi.

While Epiphany is celebrated in Greece, the observance in Tarpon dwarfs all others; partly because of the spongers, partly because of the proximity of St. Nicholas Cathedral to beautiful Spring Bayou, and partly because of *nostalgia*—"the pain for home."

In Tarpon Springs the daylong festivities begin with a morning service at the Cathedral of St. Nicholas, completed in 1943. The Cathedral was built during flush times in the sponge trade to replace the old wooden-frame church of St. Nicholas, twice burned by fire. The beautiful yellow-brick Cathedral was designed to evoke Agia Sophia in Constantinople, the greatest church in Orthodox Christianity with its great dome, lavish colored marble, and gilded mosaics.

I visited Agia Sophia to see the spot, The Omphalion, the little navel, where—I swear—the eleventh-century Byzantine Emperor Michael Kalafatas was coronated. The Muslim Turks, after they seized Constantinople, were forced to build the luminous Blue Mosque nearby simply to reply to the grandeur of Agia Sophia.

The Cathedral of St. Nicholas was built when sponging was at flood tide, money pouring into Tarpon Springs during World War II. Oddly, the two world wars and the Great Depression brought boom times to the Greek spongers of Tarpon Springs. The wars shut down the sponge industry in the Mediterranean, and the no-new-construction, just-paint-up, fix-up, of the Depression years required much squeezing of sponges.

The yellow-brick Cathedral of St. Nicholas inspires prayer. Up early one morning, in the gentleness of first light in Florida, I strolled to the Cathedral and read the marquee:

Prayer is so simple. It is like quietly opening a door and being in the very presence of God.

My thoughts went to the piety of the naked divers. I was reminded that, in life, piety can carry you deep into an abyss and bring you back. Outside the Cathedral stands the statue of a beautiful boy, wet but full of triumph, holding high the cross that he, the young Greek hero, had retrieved on Epiphany Day. The beauty of the world can make you weep.

Dr. Thomas Lacey, an Episcopal clergyman from Brooklyn, took a liking to Tarpon Springs and for years never failed to come to Epiphany Day. Jennie Harris captured his description of the liturgy of the

Greek Orthodox Church, its gravity and glory: "In the solemn chanting of the Liturgy, we catch the cadences of the Athenian tragedians reciting the sonorous lines of Aeschylus on the classic stage. We catch echoes of the Byzantine music such as filled the dome of Saint Sophia in the days of Constantinople's splendor."

After the liturgy on Epiphany Day comes the Sanctification of the Waters. (In Lacey's time, the archbishop and clergy adjourned to a marble kiosk in the courtyard, as we learn from Stoughton. An inscription carved in Greek on the fountain, where now stands the statue of the boy, read the same backwards and forward: "wash your sins, not only your countenance." (*Palindrome*, too, is a Greek word.)

"Making the sign of the cross over a symbolic bowl of water, the priest prays for calm seas and the safety of all sailors, and for blessings on all the faithful," Stoughton tells us. The clergy and choir then form a procession with the congregation that passes through the main streets of the city to Spring Bayou where the cross-diving ceremony takes place. Among the procession is a young woman dressed in white, bearing a white dove that symbolizes the Holy Spirit. At times up to 25,000 people have poured into Tarpon Springs for Epiphany Day. As I sat at dinner in Tarpon Springs one evening with Anita Protos, the former mayor of Tarpon Springs, and her husband, George, I listened to the dizzying detail necessary to carry off a festive and safe Epiphany Day.

A police motorcade leads the procession, followed by clergy and altar boys in glorious vestments, carrying gilded and jeweled religious standards. Then come school bands, representatives of the societies of Kalymnians, Halkites, Symiots, Aeginites, and representatives of AHEPA and other Greek organizations, veterans groups, the Archbishop of America, the Governor of the state of Florida, city officials, and girls and boys of the Greek school, dressed in colorful Greek national costume—among them, at times, African-American children who opted for Greek parochial school over public school. Spectators line the shore of Spring Bayou to watch the "cross-diving" ceremony.

Jennie Harris describes the scene in 1947 when, as fate would have it, three-year-old Michael Kalafatas was in the crowd, held high by his dad, Nikitas of Rhodes—son of Metrophanes, the poet of the Catastrophe of the *Skafandra*.

Archbishop, clergy, and choir descend long steps and board a barge that takes them to the middle of the bayou. . . . Thirty or more divers in shorts, their bodies lithe as though sculptured by Lysippus, wait poised in rowboats. Their gaze never wavers from the archbishop's face. Someone reads . . . "and lo, the heavens were opened unto him, and he saw the Spirit of God descending like a dove, and lighting upon him."

At these words the white dove is liberated. Up over the crowd it flies, with a whir of white wings, a flutter of blue ribbons tied to its feet.

Then the archbishop throws the cross. It flashes—an arc of light— and is lost in water. At once the divers plunge.

Teen-age boys churn, dive, and vie for the cross in chilly 65-degree water. Greek Orthodox Christians believe that the boy who retrieves the cross is the chosen of God; blessed with a year of good fortune. Some believe that good luck will follow the young hero for the rest of his life. "Dripping and shining," the victor kneels before the archbishop and receives the blessings of the Church.

After the ceremony, past cross retrievers fall in behind today's hero. All parade through the streets carrying silver trays, but on the hero's tray lies the gleaming white cross. The parade of winners stops all along the way, collecting gifts for the needy, paper money piling high upon the trays. People touch the hero for good luck.

As the Rozees write:

> The tossing of the cross in the restless water represents the gospel message coming into the midst of the troublous world and the nations reaching after the word of hope and cheer.

After the ceremony there is a *Glendi*—an afternoon of Greek food, music, and dancing at nearby Craig Park—and an Epiphany Ball in the evening.

THE DANCE OF THE BENDS

Charles Rawlings was a writer who settled in Tarpon Springs, and used it as a base to write stories, including sea stories, that appeared in the leading magazines of his time. His wife was Marjorie Kinnan Rawlings who wrote *The Yearling*. In 1932 Charles Rawlings wrote a

List of Cross Divers since 1920

Since 1920, young Greek men have dived into the waters of Spring Bayou in hopes of capturing the Epiphany cross. The names of those who succeeded are:

1920–1949	*1950–1976*	*1977–2002*
1920 Steve John	1950 Nick Faklis	1977 Alex Allisandratos
1921 Zacharias D. Zacharias	1951 Mike Ergas	1978 Jimmie Nicholas
1922 Steve John	1952 Nick Cutsuries	1979 Basil Assimack
1923 Steve John	1953 Tokey Samarkos	1980 Steve Stavrakis, Jr.
1924 Ierotheos Athanasiou	1954 Deno Moutsatsos	1981 Andrew Tsongranis
1925 Ierotheos Athanasiou	1955 Mike Skaroulis	1982 John Korfiatis
1926 Ierotheos Athanasiou	1956 Bill Kotis	1983 Tony Grigoris
1927 George Kakkalis	1957 John Georgiadis	1984 Dean Theophilopoulos
1928 Vasilios Pokratis	1958 Mike Stergos	1985 Jerry Theophilopoulos
1929 Demosthenis Kananis	1959 Sammy Mack	1986 Chuck Kyriakiou
1930 Eleftherios Athanason	1960 George Georgiadis	1987 Manuel Koutsourais
1931 Vasilios Pokratis	1961 Jim Demet	1988 Alex Joanou
1932 John Eliou	1962 Manuel Kamarados	1989 Manny Cladakis
1933 John Cardullias	1963 Costas Pappas	1990 Trevor Meyer
1934 Mike Eliou	1964 Jim Mouzourakis	1991 Anestis Karistinos
1935 John Athanason	1965 John Tsavaris	1992 Andrew Nikiforakis
1936 Athanasios T. Athan-	1966 Emmanuel Tsavaris	1993 Michael Saroukos
ason	1967 Emmanuel Pondakos	1994 John Kapaniris
1937 Demetrios Psarakos	1968 Jim Marcus	1995 Thomas Dellis
1938 Tony Houllis	1969 Pete Kondodiakis	1996 Christian Koulias
1939 Stanley Polychronis	1970 Stacy Zembellas	1997 Theo Koulianos
1940 Theo Lelekis	1971 Nikitas Manias	1998 Theo Mamouzelos
1941 Theophilos Katras	1972 George Vouvalis	1999 Jason Kolbe
1942 John Cortessis	1973 Nick Kondodiakis	2000 Hrisovalantis Pilatos
1943 Manuel Houllis	1974 Nikitas Lulias and	2001 Luke Pappas
1944 Mike Sturgis	Manuel Karvounis	2002 Achilles Houllis
1945 Mike Koulias	1975 Phillip A. Stavrakis	
1946 Theophilios Karas	1976 Manuel Kontodiakis	
1947 Nick Kosely, John	and John Saclarides	
Georgiadis and		
Mike Koullanos		
1948 Mike Houllis		
1949 Hercules Ypsilantis		

Source: Cultural and Civic Services, City of Tarpon Springs.

remarkable piece for *The Saturday Evening Post* called "The Dance of the Bends." It was about the daring Greek divers of Tarpon Springs and especially about the legendary diver Steve John. As you read below, see if you can separate the dancer from the dance.

I first learned about the dance of the bends from my cousin Nikitas M. Kalafatas of Rhodes. Tragic, dark, and powerful, the dance is a story within a story—stories within stories, nestled like so many Russian dolls. The innermost doll, the tiny core doll, is the poetics of manhood in Greece. When Nikitas first saw the dance, he thought the dancer drunk, before realizing that the dance is all about a diver as he is hit by the bends.

If you scan the list of the young cross-diving heroes of Epiphany Day, it is impossible to miss Steve John: Stephanos Ioannou. He retrieved the cross at the first cross-diving ceremony in 1920 and was victor three times. When Steve John became a deep-sea diver, he was much sought-after by the ace captains of Tarpon Springs.

Following, condensed, is Charles Rawlings's account of Steve John's "Dance of the Bends" at Louis's place.

A crippled diver appeared in the doorway and leaned on his cane. The men made a path for him and one gave him his chair near the musicians. He moved forward with the stiff-jointed hitching step characteristic of . . . "the bends". . . . Steve John poured him a drink. "Next week I go into deep water myself," he said. "Tonight I will dance for you." . . . The loud voices quieted.

Only a diver would dare the dance of the bends. If a life-line man or a seaman should attempt it, he would be knocked down for insolence. It is a diver's destiny and only a diver can laugh at it. . . .

The music began. . . . The tune . . . a folk song from Tilos. It begins slowly. There is at first a haunting beat, like a ground swell swinging through a reef. The dance opens with the first permanent symptoms of the affliction. There is a slight indication of the stiffening feet. The step is a shuffle. Then the paralysis climbs slowly up the legs. The dancer changes from a shuffle to a jerk. The tempo increases. Anguish begins to show in the face.

Steve John, his face twitching in mock pain, moved close to the crippled diver. He had arisen and stood simpering in sympathetic suffering. Steve John snatched away his cane. A bellow of laughter drowned out the music. The simper died suddenly. The crippled man tottered forward and back, then far forward, squealing like a hurt dog.

He made a tremendous effort and slowly recovered his balance. He fell gasping into his chair.

The dance finished in a bedlam. The flute howled and the strings twanged as loudly as the picks could beat them. The dancer tugged in frenzy. His feet seemed nailed down. The stolen cane beat a frantic tattoo on the floor. His face mirrored pain just short of madness. Then came madness, with drooling mouth and unfocused eyes. When there could be no further tension the music gave one shouting note. The dancer plunged to the floor in simulated death.

George Lessus did not cheer. . . . "That man—he pointed a bony finger at Steve John—he mocks everything! Now he mocks the devil!"

The following week Steve John sailed into the Gulf aboard the *Poseidon* to dive in deep water on the eastern slope of the Middle Ground Bank. After finishing a dive at 120 feet, with a Gulf squall fast approaching, Steve was hit. The crew recompressed him, like Drossos Saroukos, bringing him from unconsciousness to consciousness, from the world of the dead to the world of the living. Steve John survived, to return some weeks after to Louis's place.

Louis poured the coffee and walked to the door. "Steve John comes down the street," he called back. "He walks with a stick like an old man. Poor Steve."

"The doctor in Tampa bored holes in his spine," Tommy stated. "He says he may get better."

Louis shook his head. "He may be all right for shallow water, but for deep water, *fineesh*! It is hard. He is a proud boy. A good diver too. . . ."

Steve John pushed the screen open and hitched into the room. He tugged at a chair and lowered himself wearily. His eyes swung about and rested on George. He looked at the old man and slowly nodded his head. . . .

Steve John's eyes refused to waver. A slow smile swept over his still slightly twisted face. He brought his cane up from his side in salute.

George studied him for a moment. "You have your own stick now. There is no need for you to snatch one."

Steve regarded the cane. "I have borrowed it. In two, maybe three weeks, I shall give it back and go into deep water. Maybe I will give it to you. You want it?"

The old man's red face took on a deeper shade. "You will wear out that cane. Have you learned nothing? Did the pressure fail to push some wisdom in your head."

"You have no fear? You are not afraid?"

"Fear? Why should I have fear? Did Markos Bozzaris kill ten thousand Turks while he was afraid? Fear is for old men."

Steve John's head cocked to one side. He pulled a coin from his pocket and tossed it at the zither player. The coin slid across the floor.

"Play . . . the Tilos dance. . . . Play something, you Turk. I have paid." . . . The slow, tinkling music began.

Steve John hauled himself erect. He came up slowly, like a bow deck buried in a head sea, shouldering off the heavy water. Pain twisted his mouth, but his eyebrows arched over his eyes that gleamed. His spirit transcended all pain. Twenty fathoms can paralyze the body of a man so that he goes with spastic gait and a numbness in his bones. But if by chance his heart is brave and gay, the deep waters wash impotently over it. A nose may still be thumbed at the devil as long as the insolent will desires. The boldness of man goes deeper than the fathoms.

With horrible, macabre steps, lifting slow legs of stone, Steve John danced.

When Steve Katzaras arrived in Tarpon Springs from Symi in 1937, Steve John befriended him. Katzaras recalls that Steve John walked with no limp, no trace of decompression disease. Perhaps John was lucky, and he was able to dive again in deep water, despite thumbing his nose at the devil. Many who were so bold were not so lucky.

Enslaved for four hundred years, yet the Greeks survived. Who is to say, exactly, that tragedy and glory are not one, that what is engraved upon the marker of Nikos Kazantzakis is not in the end what saved a people: *I hope for nothing. I fear nothing. I am free.* Who has the daring to contradict?

THE YEAR THE MUSIC DIED

What could be more of a Greek tragedy than to be struck down when at the height of your powers? Lincoln, Kennedy, an athlete dying young would be an American restatement. So it was with the Greek spongers of Tarpon Springs. Red tide, first spotted in the mid-1930s in the Bahamas, swept westward, killing off sponge fishery after sponge fishery. In fact, it destroyed all marine life in its path; beach resorts hired special crews to cart off sea carcasses piled up to the wrack line each morning. By 1939 red tide was in Florida's waters. But the Tarpon spongers continued to dive for sponges at a furious

Declining Catches and Soaring Prices

Year	Quantity in pounds	Value in dollars
1936	628,226	1,035,429
1946	156,916	2,945,831

Source: George Th. Frantzis, *Strangers at Ithaca.*

pace "in spite of the reduced beds, because of the high prices," as Ed Buxbaum tells us. By the war years Tarpon had a monopoly on the world sponge trade.

The Mediterranean fishery had been shut down by the war and red tide had killed off competitors in the West Atlantic—all burnt in their sponge beds. Blight was present in the Gulf all during the 1940s, but some divers felt it was disappearing. Life must be lived forward but it can only be understood backward.

Greeks in the United States continued to be drawn to this Mediterranean port-of-call on the west coast of Florida. These were boom times in Tarpon Springs. In 1946, the war over, my father brought his family to Tarpon Springs, finally to be with the people of the Dodecanese. Finally, for his family, here was a fresh start against a fresh background. But it was not to be: 1946–47 was the year the music died.

The anthropologist Ed Buxbaum interviewed one diver who reported that, while red tide was bad in 1939, during the war years the sponges seemed to be returning—until catastrophe struck.

> In 1946, the "red tide" came back and cleaned out everything. People left Tarpon Springs. If you were forty to forty-five years old, you couldn't get a job. I could see little worms under the water that were very thick. Something was wrong with the water and as a little bit of water always seeps through the suit, I could taste something that burnt my lips. . . . People ran away as from the cholera.

In 1948 the Tarpon Springs sponge catch plummeted to 74,000 pounds—a token of the 500,000 pounds a year of a decade earlier.

Panic struck Tarpon Springs. Church services were held at the proud yellow-brick Cathedral of St. Nicholas; prayers said to end the fire that seemed to be burning the sponges in their beds. When the diver touched a sponge with his three-pronged hook, it disintegrated. The rhapsody of color under the Gulf turned to a gray monotone. Gone were the "dream-like gardens." Even the rocks on the bottom of the Gulf turned black.

Families became desperate. Stores suffered. Coffee houses emptied. Young men left in droves, headed north to good jobs in the steel mills of Youngstown, Ohio, and Gary, Indiana, Buxbaum tells us. Some divers turned to bridge painting; their daring exercised in the ether high above. Diving crews scattered, the chain in a father-to-son business broken, forever. The tradition of sponger born of sponger had ended. The characters of Robert Wagner and Terri Moore doubtless raised their beautiful children in a neat little house in Youngstown or Gary.

To make matters worse, after the war, "lower-priced Mediterranean sponges were imported into the United States, and Dupont's newly developed synthetics were being retailed for a third of the price of natural sponges," Torrance Parker reports in *20,000 Jobs Under the Sea*. "By 1948 two-thirds of the fleet had been forced out of the business due to blight, imports, and synthetics," he writes.

It took "more than ten years for the beds to recover in the 10 fathoms range, and nearly twice that long for the deeper bars, where the seed beds had been hit hardest by the blight," Parker tell us.

Even when the sponge beds recovered, Tarpon Springs could not regain its glory. No longer was it the Rhodian Colossus standing astride the world sponge trade. As Buxbaum writes,

> Life on a sponge boat is hard and wearing and the younger generation did not look at sponge fishing through the eyes of their fathers. Thus, when the sponges came back in the years 1954 to 1957, the industry was unable to supply the crews for the boats.

When healthy sponges returned, the captains and crews who knew how to dive deep for sponges were gone. As Parker tells us, in valediction, "The golden years of sponge fishing were over."

DREAM DEFERRED

Edmund Keeley writes that Lawrence Durrell and his wife "found it difficult from the start to imagine any strict dividing line in Corfu between 'the waking world and the world of dreams.' " And so it has been for me since Olga Broumas first spoke to me of the beauty and passion of my grandfather's "Winter Dream." My first journal entry after our meeting was from George Seferis's "Mythistorema #3"; it haunts me still.

> I woke with this marble head in my hands;
> it exhausts my elbows and I don't know where to put it
> down.
> It was falling into the dream
> as I was coming out of the
> dream
> so our life became one and it will be very difficult for it
> to separate again.
> —*George Seferis,* "Mythistorema #3"

I am the legatee of dreams. Of my grandfather's "winter dream" that Mother Symi would regain her glory as a place of beauty and of social justice, where "the naked dive will bloom, our forefather's art will flower . . . where the divers will again be strong"; that sweet Mother Symi would stop her weeping. "The time has come the end is near." And I am, as all sons are, the legatee of my father's dreams. My father left behind the dash of a naval officer's uniform and likely a career of distinction as a marine engineer—first in his class—to join his brothers in America; a career of distinction had he survived Greece's many wars and tribulations in the twentieth century. In coming to Tarpon Springs with his family, he was trying to return to the Dodecanese, to find his way back to the people of the seaways and slipways. Like salmon—perhaps like us all—the Greeks try furiously to swim their way back to origin. Perhaps Greeks and Americans are more spirit-twins than we think. The last lines of *The Great Gatsby* speak of time and of the watery journey of our collective unconscious: "So we beat on, boats against the current, borne back ceaselessly into the past." My father was answering the Greek mariner's call, the siren call of the sea, the call to origin. But it was not to be. There were no jobs for the skilled machinist he had become in his American restatement; the jobs burned away with the sponges. He returned to Cambridge, Massachusetts, joined General Electric, and built jet engines; and, like his father, he fought for social justice, the FBI tap, tap, tapping at our door because of his advocacy of the UE as the union-of-choice at General Electric.

> What happens to a dream deferred?
>
>> Does it dry up
>> Like a raisin in the sun?
>> Or fester like a sore—
>> And then run?
>> Does it stink like rotten meat
>> Or crust and sugar over
>> Like a syrupy sweet?
>>
>> Maybe it sags
>> Like a heavy load.
>
> Or does it explode?
>> —*Langston Hughes*, "Harlem (2)"

Or might dreams unfulfilled in one generation be transmuted through the alchemy of time and family and be left to the next generation; left for a son and grandson wandering around with a marble head in his hands, trying to find a place to put it down? Left for a grandson to tell a story of children dying in the sea and the need for us all to be outraged at injustice. Left for us to realize, as Thucydides did, that "Justice will not come to Athens until those who are not injured are as indignant as those who are injured."

seven

SEA FEVER

It is the Meltemi *which give the Aegean its unique quality. Every day they begin to blow at dawn, reaching their maximum round about noon, and usually dropping off at sunset. It is their cool invigorating rush which dissipates that bugbear of so many Mediterranean lands—the noonday lassitude and the high humidity which curb thought and action alike. At midday, in an Aegean island, one can stand on a rocky peak or sit in a quayside taverna and feel, in a shade-heat of 90 degrees, the stimulating wind that helped to make Aegean civilization. . . . in the open sea one can see the small boats taking the wind on their beam, and carrying the wine and oil of one island to exchange it for the sponges and citrus fruit of another.*

—Ernle Bradford, *The Companion Guide to the Greek Islands*

They had sea fever. They loved the sea and the wind that blows. These were the Greeks of the Aegean—these were the Greeks of the Dodecanese, ready to pick up the *Meltemi* as it blew down off the coast of Anatolia. The winds swept south from March until November; cool, dense air from Russia, scented by the pine forests of Asia Minor, rushed in to replace the air over the Aegean as it heated and rose in summer. A certain piquancy in the air doubtless reminded Karl Flegel of his youth, far to the north. Because of the *Meltemi*, Bradford writes of the Aegean, "The blue of the sky is sharp, and broomed by the wind."

BEL TEMPO

The *Meltemi* taught the Greeks to sail—first island to island, then outward with greater daring. Navigation began in the Aegean, and the Greeks gave it to the world. "The Greeks and Romans traversed the Mediterranean and the Black Sea and crept out into the Atlantic before the birth of Christ," the *Boston Globe* once wrote. But the Aegean mariners sailed only in the season of good weather, *Bel Tempo* in the Venetian, *Kalokeri* in Greek. As Ernle Bradford writes, "During the winter the islands reverted to their native loneliness. They look inwards towards their own small lives, and not outwards—as in summer—towards the extrovert activities of trading and sailing." It follows that the Greeks came to pay heed to the balanced life, to "the active social life of man and to his inner spiritual needs." With such northerly winds they could easily sail south to Egypt in summer, and return in the spring with a homebound cargo before the *Meltemi* began its strong blow.

Below is a ship's manifest showing a cargo that arrived in Alexandria around 250 B.C., after the ship had first loaded up in a Syrian port. It appears in Lionel Casson's *The Ancient Mariners: Seafarers and Sea Fighters of the Mediterranean in Ancient Times.* The gourmet tastes reflected in the manifest suggest, as Casson observes, that the cargo was bound for the wealthy Greeks of Egypt or for Apollonius, a high-ranking official of Ptolemy whose secretary, Zenon, retained the ship's

Ship's Manifest of Cargo Arriving in Alexandria, ca. 250 B.C.

table wine	138 jars, 6½ jars
dessert wine	5 jars, 15½ jars
olive oil	2 containers
dried figs	9 jars
honey (6 varieties)	14½ jars, 1 crock
wild boar meat	4 containers
Black Sea nuts	1 jar
pomegranate seeds	4 baskets
venison	2 jars
goat's meat	2 crocks
Chian cheese	1 crock
rough sponges	1 basket
soft sponges	1 (?) basket
pure wool	22½ lbs. in a box

manifest in his records. The manifest also underscores the active trade in sponges that dated from classical times.

My father was born on the Island of Roses: Rhodes, in the Dodecanese. Of the Twelve Islands of the Dodecanese, Rhodes is the largest. It lies at the crossroads of civilizations, East and West, Orient and Occident. So much of its fate is explained by geography. When I was a boy, my father raved about the island, its beauty and its flowers. I never paid any attention; I was worried about whether the Boston Red Sox would ever get any decent pitching. Teary-eyed, in June of 1997—my father dead for eighteen years—I watched at Rhodes Town the Anthistiria, the flower festival, as a parade of children from Rhodes and the other Dodecanese islands, dressed in colorful native costume and laden with bountiful bouquets of gorgeous flowers, marched by. In Greece the children are at the center of everything; this is doubtless why the country has the lowest crime rate in the E.U. Among the marchers were children from Embona, one of the quaintest villages on Rhodes, where many still dress in traditional Rhodian costume. My grand-mother Anastasia—"the Resurrection"—was from Embona. Today, few cruise ships in the Aegean miss a stop at Rhodes. It is *de rigueur*, like the stop at Myknonos and Santorini. People come not only for the beaches, history, and the Valley of the Butterflies, but also for the flowers: Rhodian hillsides lavish with rock roses. The writer Michael Volonakis was the first to invoke for me the name: The Island of Roses and her Eleven Sisters. *The Dodecanese.*

The Dodecanese are an 'archipelago'—meaning 'the Chief Sea'; per-haps, as the *American Heritage Dictionary* says, it is "a misrendering of the Greek *Aigaion pelagos*, the Aegean Sea." The list of islands that compose the Dodecanese has changed from time to time, but always it has included more than twelve islands—far more if one counts the many islets.

The people of the Dodecanese owe everything to the sea. Otherwise the islands would truly have been what the historian Fernand Braudel called the islands of the Mediterranean—"lands of hunger"—because of their limited natural resources. Certainly this was true of Symi and Kalymnos, dry rocky islands that produced some of the world's best sailors and, along with Halki, the world's boldest divers.

Ed Buxbaum recalls a well-known Greek myth: "When God was sifting the soil of all nations, he separated the rocks from the whole world's soil. These rocks he threw over his shoulder and they became Greece and her islands." While Rhodes and Kos had extensive farm-lands—85 percent of all arable land in the Dodecanese—they too were dependent upon sea communication.

Braudel had the larger Mediterranean islands in mind—Sicily, Sardinia, Crete, and Cyprus—when he wrote of their limited natural resources, as Nick Doumanis points out. They faced the constant threat of famine, the Dodecanese even more so because they are far drier than the other Mediterranean islands and can support less of a population. In the summer of 1997, when I was in the Dodecanese for six weeks, it rained for two minutes: the tally of two separate "rainstorms." The Dodecanese are essentially rainless from May until October, although Rhodes and Kos "enjoy a comparatively plentiful water supply" and suffer less from the effects of rainless summers, Doumanis reports. Consequently, the Dodecanese have always been thinly populated; but, as Doumanis notes, "By the nineteenth century, some of the more barren islands had been transformed into thriving trading centres, and this was particularly true of Kalymnos, Simi, Kastellorizo, and Halki, where the main impetus for economic growth was sponge fishing and merchandising." Because of the flourishing sponge trade and merchant marine activity, the islands were supporting a far higher population density than would otherwise have been possible. The boldness and skill of its sailors and divers—the poetics of manhood in action—were making a prosperous life possible on "lands of hunger."

EIGHT GOOD HARBORS

I write now of Symi out of homage to my grandfather's *patrida,* his "homeland." But much of what I say about Symi holds true of The

Twelve Islands and the other Greek islands of the Aegean—"where angels walk." As for mood, Symi evoked in Ernle Bradford this remembrance from Tennyson:

> For now, the noonday quiet holds the hill.
> The grasshopper is silent in the grass:
> the lizard, with his shadow on the stone,
> Rests like a shadow, and the cicala sleeps.
> —Alfred Lord Tennyson, "Oenone"

"The cicala or the cicada, spell it how you will, is for me the symbol of the Mediterranean just as much as the olive," Bradford writes. The shrill noise emitted by the male, Bradford learned from the *Encyclopedia Brittanica*, is a sexual call, a sexual "song" that can be heard in concert a quarter-mile away. The "high-pitched buzz" of the cicadas is the music of the Aegean, a sound as familiar as the zither or the bouzouki. On a blazing hot afternoon in the Aegean islands, during siesta, "if one has lunched well (but not too well) and drunk well (but just enough)—then is the time to summon Aphrodite into the golden-net of Hephaestos."

Past and Present are a unity in Greece: a golden circle without beginning or end, a timelessness that evokes that chant of the Orthodox Liturgy, "Now and ever, and to the Ages of Ages." Pliny wrote of Symi's "eight good harbors," which the island has to this day. As ferries make the abrupt turn into Symi's main harbor, passengers let out a collective gasp—having been lulled into lassitude, after league upon league of aquamarine sea and dry barren islands. "Inevitably, there's a fusillade of clicking camera shutters and purring of camcorders when the ferries swing into Symi's main harbor, Gialos, one of the most breathtaking sights in Greece," writes Dana Facaros in *Cadogan's Greek Islands*. "Few other islands have Symi's crisp brightness and its amphitheatre of imposing neoclassical mansions, in soft ochre or traditional deep shades, stacked one on top of the other up the barren hillsides." The harbor's crowning glory, of course, is *Panagia tou Castro*, the beautiful church that my great granduncle Stamatis helped build. From its lofty aspect one could have watched Fotis Mastoridis lower his pregnant wife into Symi harbor in 1863 and change the course of history in a Greek archipelago.

When I first entered Symi harbor in 1990—the year after my "maiden trip" abroad to England—what rushed to mind, oddly, were Matthew Arnold's lines about Oxford: "That sweet city of dreaming spires, whispering the last remembrances of the Middle Ages." Symi harbor whispers the last remembrances of Symi of the nineteenth century, itself an echo of Venice's wealth and glory of earlier epoch.

Symi's major characteristic is her numerous safe, natural harbors, "great tongues of water which penetrate the land through narrow mouths and then suddenly widen," write Kostas Farmakidis and Agapi Karakatsani in *Symi: a Guide*. Some harbors retain names from deepest antiquity: Pedhi-Pedhion, Nymborio-Emborion, Panormos. In the twentieth year of the Peloponnesian War, Thucydides tells us that the Spartans triumphed over the Athenian fleet off the coast of Symi; the Spartans then sailed into safe anchorage at Symi and erected a monument to their victory. Today, the original of Thucydides' *History of the Peloponnesian War* resides in a "safe harbor" in the Dodecanese; it can be found in the underground library of the monastery at Patmos.

Metrophanes writes of Symi's safe harbors, by way of Mother Symi's proud reverie:

> *Gifted with priceless goods I was,*
> *and wealthy in all I needed.*
> *I am surrounded by safe ports*
> *and greatly praised by sailors.*
> *To the northeast of my island*
> *Pedi and Aigialos rule over all.*
> *All boats are harbored there,*
> *others are moored ashore.*
> *From Kampos and Aigialos ships sail*
> *perfected by shipbuilders.*
> *Another winter port to the southwest*
> *has always been famous for its length.*
> *The Panormitis monastery*
> *holds its feast to high praise here.*

To my north, St. Aimilianos, another safe port,
surrounded by piers and a domed church
for fishermen and carpenters, a serene place.

We learn from legend that the sea-god Glaucus married the nymph of Symi and they made their home on the island. Why wouldn't a sea-god choose to settle with a beautiful nymph on an island with "eight good harbors"?

From these harbors the Symiots ventured forth to distant seas: They found fortune, gold, sophistication, and wisdom; when all opportunity vanished, from these harbors they sent their scions off to Rhodes, Alexandria, Athens, Marseilles, Paris, London, New York, Tarpon Springs, Darwin, Perth, Sydney, and Melbourne. As Michael Cantonis said of the Symiots: "They were always wide-thinking." I think of Fotis Mastoridis diving with British equipment in the East Indies in the early 1860s, and returning with his new diving suit and new knowledge to Symi.

In returning "home" to Symi it is no surprise I would feel pride of origin when I read the following written by British Naval Intelligence—about Symi, Kalymnos, and the Golden Age of sponge fishing.

> A century of this exceptional prosperity developed exceptionally vigorous, intelligent stocks, curiously different in build and temperament, in the two main communities; while they have adopted different varieties of sailing-craft, and are prepared, like good seamen, to defend their choice.

I once met a Greek living in the United States who said: "I can tell by the square-cut of your shoulders that you are from Symi." All my relatives on Symi and Rhodes, as do my own sons, have the same cut of shoulders. In swimming through the frothing surf of the Aegean, in diving to its depths with a fifteen-kilogram diving stone, it is helpful to have strong square shoulders. On Symi the diving stone was called a *kambanellopetra*, a bellstone; on Kalymnos, a *scandalopetra*, a trigger stone, it triggered the dive. On Symi the stone was bell-shaped; on Kalymnos, more rectangular, a slight trapezoid—like one of your front teeth, a white incisor that sent divers in a fierce plummet to the seafloor.

Doumanis recalls that in 1687 an English traveler to Symi wrote,

"They will dive 15 fathoms under water, being brought up to this profession from their childhood; they reckon those the best of men who can longest keep under water." Doumanis goes on to say that "Simian divers traveled throughout the eastern Mediterranean, and their merchandise found its way to all corners of Europe."

As I read the report of British Naval Intelligence, I could only think, in a delirium of self-flattery, of King Nereus of Symi whom Homer called, "second in handsomeness only to the great Achilles." Nereus was an ally of Agamemnon who led Symi's three ships to the war against Troy. Alas, Nereus, like Achilles, fell in battle beneath the walls of Troy.

THE PRIVILEGED ISLANDS

After vigorous resistance to the Turks, in 1522 the Symiots voluntarily submitted to Suleiman the Magnificent in the last struggle of the Crusader Knights of St. John, who had controlled Rhodes and surrounding islands for two hundred years. Seventy years earlier Constantinople had fallen to the martial Turks; ethnically Greek islands in the northeast Aegean had succumbed; Crete and Cyprus too. The Crusaders were in retreat. Suleiman the Magnificent was not to be denied. The Knights had preyed on Muslim shipping far too long, interfering with the flow of Egyptian grain to Istanbul and harassing Muslim pilgrims bound for Mecca. It was the Sultan's sacred duty to protect the pilgrims. Suleiman II was determined to be rid of the nuisance: he lay siege to Rhodes and ordered that his war tent be built of stone as a symbol of his resolve. Having shut themselves up in their citadel on Rhodes—which they believed impregnable—the Knights abandoned Symi and the surrounding islands to the mercy of the foe. Suleiman's encampment was directly across from Rhodes near Marmaris, along the Asiatic shore, not far from the peninsular arms of Anatolia that enfold Symi.

The future was written. The wily Symiots sent a delegation of women to Suleiman II to offer the island's voluntary submission to Turkish suzerainty; the women came laden with loaves of white bread and luxurious sponges. The message was clear: although the Symiots came from a rocky island of little arable soil and even less water, they lived from the sea and prospered. The women of Symi also voluntarily supplied the Turkish besiegers of Rhodes with bread. The Sultan was impressed and replied with gratitude. Since the Knights had granted special privileges to Symi to encourage maritime and mercantile activity, the Sultan offered similar privileges to Symi and then to the other Dodecanese islands that also submitted voluntarily to Turkish rule. In the end all did, except for Rhodes and Kos, which eventually fell to Suleiman's will. The Kalymnians also sent sponges and white bread to Suleiman, for "the sponge diver does not raise corn, but buys flour and buys of the best." The final settlement appears in the British Naval Intelligence's history of the Dodecanese.

Included in the *vilayet* of the islands, of which the seat of government was in Chios, and under the supervision of a Turkish *mutessarif* in Rhodes, and the protection of a Turkish garrison there and in Kos, they were to govern themselves with a collective tribute (*maktu*) that was not heavy.

The people of the "Privileged Islands" could govern themselves. While the light *maktu* was primarily used to support Muslim institutions, the Greeks could observe their own religion undisturbed, like other Orthodox communities under the Ecumenical Patriarch. Endowed schools were to be maintained on Patmos, Symi, and Kalymnos; as it turned out, they would be superb schools, attended by students from afar until founding of the National University of Athens in 1837. Students "from abroad" were no strangers to the Dodecanese: Cicero, Cato, and Julius Caesar all had studied at the famed school of rhetoric on the island of Rhodes.

Suleiman II granted to the Symiots the exclusive right to fish for sponges in *all* of the seas of the Ottoman Empire, a right that would be extended to the other Privileged Islands. As the boot of Turkish conquest marched on, Ottoman seas would reach beyond the distant horizon. The vast and rich sponge fields off the coast of North Africa would belong to Dodecanesian spongers.

"The Ottoman empire lived for war," Jason Goodwin has written in *Lords of the Horizon*. He quotes the Venetian Morosini on the martial spirit of Ottoman troops: "They never show the least concern for their lives in battle." The Ottomans died willingly. It is the reason polygamy was so attractive to the Muslim Turks: they could repopulate their armies. Under the Ottomans, Goodwin writes, "even madmen had a regiment, the *deli* or loons, Riskers of their Souls, who were used, since they did not object, as human battering rams, or human bridges...."

Almost half of Suleiman the Magnificent's 200,000 troops were killed during the siege of Rhodes to rid the island of just 5,600 Crusader Knights. Ottoman hordes lie buried in cemeteries outside the Old City; but in the end, Rhodes and the eastern Mediterranean belonged to Suleiman the Magnificent.

At their zenith, the genius of the Ottomans was their ability to be a minority within their own empire. They ruled over "thirty-five million people of whom twenty-three millions belonged to alien creeds," as Joan Haslip wrote in *The Sultan*, her biography of Abdul Hamid II, the sultan to whom my grandfather directed his poem. The Ottomans were at their finest when they let subject peoples rule their own affairs in exchange for fealty. "Wherever they met talent they gave it scope," Jason Goodwin observed.

From 1522 onward, in *firman* after *firman*—written decree after written decree—Sultans through the ages confirmed the special status of the Privileged Islands. Only when the Ottomans began to lose their imperial confidence, in the latter part of the nineteenth century, did they move to curtail the historic rights of self-governance of the Privileged Islands. The attempts at curtailment coincided with the period of exceptional prosperity on the islands. When Turkish policy changed, "Symi was one of the first islands to protest and give trouble," British Naval Intelligence reports. Symi was occupied by Turkish troops or blockaded by Turkish warships in 1855, 1869, 1885, 1887, 1896, and 1909. Other Privileged Islands resisted as well, especially Kalymnos. Turkish troops, for example, were dispatched to Kalymnos twice in connection with the Cretan uprising of 1867 and were garrisoned there again in 1896. Whenever Dodecanese island leaders gathered to consider their position or to develop a political strategy, they did so on the island of Patmos, where Saint John heard the Word of God and recorded it in the Book of Revelations, the Book of the Apocalypse. The leaders of the Dodecanese, sophisticated and well traveled—some educated in Western Europe—knew of the seriousness of their undertaking. The writer Frances Fitzgerald would choose a phrase from the Book of the Apocalypse to describe the Viet Nam war, a war of national liberation, as "the fire in the lake." Dodecanese leaders were no fools; they knew they were defying a world power, even if one slipping in strength.

Denis Cantonis of Tarpon Springs told me the story of Symi's daring rescue of one hundred boys from the island of Crete in the 1870s. Ottoman forces, in yet another attempt to suppress the refractory Cretans, were about to slaughter one hundred boys. A large Symiot ship arrived, flying the Turkish flag. With stealth and swiftness, the Symiots rescued the hundred boys, sailing them to safety and a new life on the island of Symi. In gratitude the Cretans named twin towns for Symi: one in the mountains, Ano Symi, High Symi, and the other in the lowlands, Kato Symi, Low Symi, located in the northeastern Prefecture of Iraklion, near the town of Vianos.

Among island leaders who repeatedly protested the clipping away of historic privileges was my great granduncle Stamatis.

> *President of the senate then*
> *was Stamatis Kalafatas,*
> *old in age,*
> *a wise man faithful to the senate.*
> *He governed fairly,*
> *suffered for his land and was imprisoned.*
> *He stood up for the common good,*
> *suffered the prisons of Rhodes and Kos,*
> *yet returned to public office.*

When Suleiman II died in 1566, Constantinople was Europe's largest city, Goodwin reports. Starting in the seventeenth century, however, the Ottoman empire began a long slow slide into the second division of world powers, its currency depreciated, its bureaucracy bloated, its soldiers poorly led, its economy and technology outclassed, and its sultans diminished by mental illness and dissolution.

Sultan Abdul Hamid II, to whom my grandfather directed his poem, was so ill-informed and paranoid that he banned the electric light in the empire because, as Goodwin tells us, "he had mistaken the word 'dynamo' for 'dynamite.'" He feared explosions.

Goodwin gives us a view of the diminishing Ottoman star:

Rich in talents still, the empire no longer provided a glittering stage for their expression. Its most brilliant sailors were all Greek. Its canniest merchants were Armenian. Its soldiers were ineptly led, while everywhere admired for their courage. Imperial statesmen operated at home in an atmosphere of intolerable suspicion. Yet the empire lingered into the twentieth century with no white cliffs to shield it, like England; no single language to unite it, like France. . . . The Ottomans seemed to stand, in their final years, for negotiation over decision, for tradition over innovation, and for a dry understanding of the world's ways over all that was thrusting and progressive about the western world.

The Ottoman empire survived so long in decline because no world power wanted its chopping up to benefit any rival power. Abdul Hamid II spent his years as Sultan nervously playing one power off against another. Still, during his reign, which lasted from 1876 until 1909, Ottoman Turkey lost half of its European possessions. In the end Abdul Hamid II would be overthrown from within, despite his daily ritual of reading dossiers sent to him by personal spies throughout the empire.

The vitality of the warrior Turkmen had been sapped; it was a sorry fall from Suleiman the Magnificent.

ABDUL HAMID II

Abdul Hamid II was a direct descendant of Ibrahim the Mad. Need I say more? The praises Metrophanes sings to the Sultan were part prayer that the 1903 ban might be ever-lasting, part gratitude, and much Levantine guile. The efforts of Flegel and others, like my grandfather, to secure the international abolition of the diving gear were dependent on the good will and support of "the Sultan of Sultans, the Lord of Two Continents and the Two Seas."

When I think of the Dodecanese, I think of the looming dark mountains of Anatolia, so close upon the islands, an emblem of Ottoman might. I think of the powerful reach of Ibrahim the Mad or of Sultan Abdul Hamid II, who was also known as Abdul the Damned and Bloody Abdul.

We praise his Highness our Ruler with pure hearts,
with hymns and adorations,

> *his good will abolished the machines*
> *and sent them from our land.*
> > *Untouched they stayed, idle from work,*
> *in Turkey's seas and shores.*
> > *Long life we wish our Ruler's Heart,*
> *Sultan Abdul Hamid,*
> > *inspired by God to ban the gear*
> *and punish all its murders.*
> > *In 1903 he did decree*
> *against such gear in Turkey,*
> > *and sent them as far as Spain.*

Metrophanes sang his disingenuous praises to the Sultan for nought. The 1903 ban, though the longest lasting, was rescinded shortly after my grandfather's death.

THE GOLDEN CAGE

"What can you expect of us, children of slaves brought up by eunuchs?" Adbul Hamid II once confessed to a British businessman who had become his friend, Joan Haslip tells us.

The Ottoman empire had come to be ruled with the fear and madness cultivated in the Sultan's harem; it was the chrysalis out of which flew deformed butterfly after deformed butterfly—sultans expected to govern wisely the lives of thirty-five million people.

Princes-in-waiting were kept isolated, idle, and ignorant in the so-called Golden Cage, a set of rooms that adjoined the harem. The father of Abdul Hamid II never saw a map of the Ottoman empire until his own father lay dying, according to Goodwin. Writing in *Harem: The World Behind the Veil,* Alev Lytle Croutier—herself Turkish—tells us that life in the Golden Cage was "wracked by fear and suffused in ignorance of events outside. . . . If a prince lived long enough to ascend the throne, he was, more often than not, unprepared to rule an empire."

Haslip reports that, "Not only politics, but also history were taboo in the curriculum of the 'princes' school.'" Their education "was confined to readings from the Koran, a superficial knowledge of music

and of French, and fabled stories of the glories of the Ottoman Sultan."
Outside the Golden Cage, awaiting Prince Abdul Hamid II, was the
rising modern industrial world.

The princes in the Golden Cage found diversion in concubines and
drink, often the powerful *raki*. My mother's father, Stelianos, the only
grandparent I ever knew, was raised eighty miles from Constantinople;
powerfully built, he was capable in his seventies of wrestling my
seventeen-year-old brother and his friend to the ground simultaneously. After he emigrated to the United States, Stelianos used to brew
raki in his cellar. Periodically, he would bring the *raki* to our home in
washed-out bleach jars. On Sunday afternoons, my father would serve
it to visitors from an elegant crystal dispenser on our mantelpiece. I
imagine princes of the Seraglio in gold-embroidered uniforms, sport-
ing the red fez, sitting in our parlor in Irish South Boston, tossing
back glass after glass of *raki*.

BROUGHT UP BY EUNUCHS

Black eunuchs oversaw the harem. If the women of the harem were
watched over by eunuchs, Sultanic logic suggested, they could not
become impregnated; and if somehow they did, the black father would
instantly be revealed in the child's dark complexion. This was not a
healthy environment in which to raise a world leader; the health of
the environment was in no way improved by the mothers of the
princes' being captured slave girls.

DEAD AT TWENTY-SIX

Abdul Hamid II's mother was a Circassian dancer and slave girl who
died of consumption at age twenty-six, when the prince was seven.
The loss and loneliness cast a long shadow of suspicion across his
reign. Always he would be sad, fearful, and full of horror at disease;
often he himself would be sick in mind and body. This was the man
upon whom my grandfather pinned his hopes for the rescue of the
divers.

Above all, Joan Haslip tells us, Abdul Hamid II would "crave security." It would elude him. After thirty-three years as Sultan, Abdul Hamid II was ousted by the "Young Turks" and was exiled to Salonica.

By any standard Abdul Hamid II was unprepossessing, his manner furtive, his eyes heavy-lidded, his nose so wildly hooked that he was the darling of political cartoonists in the Western capitals. Wary and melancholy, he sought comfort in mysticism. "Ministers were kept waiting for an audience while dervishes and astrologers were admitted at all hours into his presence . . . ," Haslip reports. And Croutier writes that Abdul Hamid II "was obsessed with parrots, believing the birds could warn him of evil spirits threatening his household."

DEAD HAREM GIRLS

If you were a harem girl, getting pregnant could either make you famous as the mother of a Sultan or get you killed. Sometimes you were drowned in the Sea of Marmara, sometimes in the Bosporus.

In Ottoman Turkey, the Sultanate passed, not from father to son, but to the oldest living male member of the family. Today, we would call that "bad law": often it led to a deadly melee among a passel of brothers and cousins. The law resulted in "such atrocities as the murder of Mehmed III's nineteen brothers in 1595, some of them infants, at the instigation of his mother, or the stuffing into sacks of seven of Mehmed's father's pregnant concubines and throwing them into the Sea of Marmara," Croutier tells us. A mother in the Seraglio often acted with deadly ferocity to remove any threat to her son's becoming Sultan; or, were her son slated to become Sultan, to remove by death anyone who might aspire to succeed him. Killing off challengers, even *in utero*, enhanced a potential successor's legitimacy. It is no surprise, then, that the concubines of princes-in-waiting were often sterilized by removal of their ovaries or uterus. "If, through some oversight, any woman did become pregnant by an outcast prince, she was immediately drowned," Croutier informs us. Many harem women were drowned, willy-nilly, out of the diverse intrigues of the harem. Those "to be murdered were seized by the chief black eunuch," Croutier writes, who "stuffed them in sacks, tied the neck tightly, and loaded them in a rowboat. After rowing out from the shore a little way, the eunuch assisted in throwing the sacks overboard."

FOUR THOUSAND SPONGES

For nearly four hundred years—from 1522 until 1909—the island of Symi sent four thousand choice sponges annually to the Sultan's harem as tribute, following the island's voluntary acceptance of Turkish rule. It was a small price to pay—along with a low tax—in exchange for being able to run your own affairs and for having exclusive access to all the sponges in the Ottoman seas. Each year, the Symiots shipped off four thousand beautiful *melatia* sponges, "Turkish cup sponges," so called because they were shaped like a cup without a handle. I could never shake from my head the question: Exactly what were the four thousand sponges used for?

THE BATH

The Fine Arts Museums of San Francisco owns an oil painting by Jean-Leon Gerom, called *The Bath*, ca. 1880–1885. The painting is set in a Turkish bath, a *hamam*, the walls adorned with lyrically beautiful Arabic calligraphy, as a half-clad voluptuous black woman slave washes down a beautiful nude white woman. In the black woman's hand, overflowing with luxurious suds, is a Turkish cup sponge—one of the four thousand *melatia* sent by the Symiots to the Sultan's harem. Alev Lytle Croutier includes a stunning color plate of this painting in *Harem: The World Behind the Veil.*

ODALISQUES

The word odalisque, the *American Heritage Dictionary* explains, comes from the Turkish *odah*, meaning room. These were "women of the room," restricted to the Seraglio. Deprived of personal freedom, their daily trips to the baths were a source of joy, renewal, even euphoria. The women would spend endless hours at the baths. I understand why. When in Istanbul, I went to the famed Cemberlitas's Bath, one of the most treasured examples of sixteenth-century Turkish architecture, built in 1584 when the Ottoman star was at its zenith. I was sudsed, scrubbed, pummeled, and doused with buckets of hot water by my attendant *Mustafa*, strong enough to have been on the Turkish national wrestling team. The only English word he knew I had taught him: *Boston*. He would say *Boston* repeatedly, whacking me each time with his heavy meaty hand. I was in the men's section of Cemberlitas's Bath; there is also a women's section, doubtlessly attended to by equally strong female staff.

ROMAN BATHS

The tradition of the *hamam* dates back to Byzantium and, before that, to the baths of Rome. When in Israel, I toured the remains of Roman baths high atop Masada, the natural hill fortress where Jewish Zealots took their own lives rather than surrender. Herod the Great, king of Judaea under Roman suzerainty, built a well-appointed bathhouse on Masada. Roman generals would distract garrisoned troops from boredom and blazing heat by allowing them to spend endless hours making their way through a complex set of bathing rooms. The Turkish *hamam* was a direct descendant of such baths.

FRENCH SPONGE BATH

On the island of Symi a woman gave me instructions on how to take a *French* sponge bath. You wash down as far as possible. You wash up as far as possible. And then you wash . . . *Possible!* This sophisticated little instruction somehow provides a segue to the exotic, erotic goings-on at the baths of the Seraglio.

SEX

Imagine being a concubine, exquisitely trained in the erotic arts, who rarely attained the Sultan's bed. It's like being dressed up with no place to go—except they did have a place to go: to the *hamam*, to the Turkish baths.

While Sultan Abdul Hamid II had comparatively few women in his harem, his father Abdul Mecid had five hundred; here were many women dressed up with no place to go. Croutier quotes Edmondo de Amicis who wrote of the Seraglio in 1896, during the reign of Abdul Hamid II: "Women have the most ardent relationships with one another. They wear the same colors, same perfumes, put on patches of the same size and shape, and make enthusiastic demonstrations."

Croutier observes that for women of the harem the baths were "a chance to feast their eyes on beautiful bodies and satisfy each other." She writes, "Women of the harem were renowned for their luminous complexions and satin skin. To wash and purify was a religious obligation." Harem women rushed to the *hamam* at the first sign of body hair since it was a sin to have any. Searing depilatory pastes were applied, and hair scraped away with seashells; the skin flushed clean with fresh flowing water squeezed from sea sponges. "While washing and massaging one another, while scrutinizing closely for the first signs of emerging body hair, the women became lovers as well as friends," she writes. It is hard to imagine that women, engaged in pleasuring one another, did not use as an aid the world's most luxurious sensual sponges, so readily available at the *hamam*.

Following the bath, Croutier tells us, the women repaired to "a resting room" to relax on mattresses, nap, sip coffee, groom one another, and gossip. There they applied perfumes and spices to enhance their seductiveness. For women of the harem, so lacking in personal freedom, the *hamam* "became an all-consuming passion and a most luxurious pastime." In the resting room, Croutier reports, harem women smoked their "bejeweled chibuks," very long pipes, "nibbled on slices of melons or savored delicately perfumed sherbets."

The Seraglio was a world of opposites, of deadly intrigue and high hedonism: it was a world of pools and baths, of suds and sensuality, of perfumes and spices, of incredible debauchery behind the veil. It was in this world that Ibrahim the Mad spent much of his time in bizarre diversions. According to Croutier, the Sultan would toss pearls and rubies into the water of the pool and watch the women of the harem dive for them. Goodwin reports that Ibrahim "rode his girls like horses through rooms lined in fur from ceiling to the floor" and that once he had "all the women in his harem sewn alive into sacks and thrown into the Bosporus."

BARRIER BIRTH CONTROL

It was into the world of the Seraglio that the Symiots sent their four thousand beautiful Turkish cup sponges year in and year out for four hundred years. The women of the harem used the four thousand sponges for cosmetics, the bath, and doubtless to pleasure one another; but they also used the sponges for quite another purpose: as barrier birth control devices.

In his *Medical History of Contraception*, Norman Hines reports that the birth control method of choice among women of Constantinople was the insertion of a sea sponge "moistened with diluted lemon juice." It was "one of the most effective contraceptives to be found in the whole range of literature on folk medicine.... so clever, one may legitimately doubt whether it belongs in the folk-belief class at all." After coitus, women "replace the sponge, thus impregnated with citric acid, with a paste made from aloes, rue, and rubber; or else they rub the os with tobacco juice."

As late as the 1930s, when Hines was writing, no modern clinical contraceptive had surpassed using a sponge soaked in diluted lemon juice as a vaginal tampon. As Hines reported, "Citric acid ranks high as a spermicide."

Recall that in the Seraglio an inopportune pregnancy might mean another dead beauty in the Bosporus. For the women of the harem effective birth control methods were limited: sterilization, abortion, or use of a sponge soaked in diluted lemon juice. Abstinence was not an option.

GOLD FEVER

The Greeks of Symi loved gold. I met an elderly woman on Symi who had worked as a seamstress for the Kalafatas family many decades earlier. Without prompting, she recalled seeing "barrels of gold coins" in the home. My cousin Nikitas of Rhodes told me that gold coins were the classic Kalafatas family wedding gift.

Michael Cantonis once told me that, during the Turkish Rule, "There were no banks on Symi or Rhodes, and no safes. They used no paper money. They dealt only in gold and silver coins that they kept in solid metal containers." I thought of how Marco Polo had sewn gems into the ragged robes he wore as a disguise when he crossed the Asian steppes, rife with bandits. I thought of how Jews' fleeing the Holocaust were best off carrying diamonds, lightweight and valued everywhere: Trade a gem for the safety of your family. If you distrusted the currency of an empire run by dissolutes, if your fate might be in the hands of boors or murderers, precious gems or precious metals could protect against catastrophe—even be a passport to freedom: Toss a barrel of gold coins onto a swift Symiot sail boat, let the lateen-rigged canvas billow out with the *Meltemi*, and follow the sea-blue sky of the Aegean toward the horizon.

TRADING SILVER AND GOLD

"Few people understand bi-metallism," my cousin Michael Foreys told me, "but it was the way the old Symiot families built their wealth. It was not from sponge fishing, shipbuilding, or commerce. They made their money trading silver against gold."

As the Greeks say, *Akouse na deis*, "Listen to see." I will explain how the swapping worked. All of Europe underwent price waves when silver and gold began to flow in from wholly new sources in the Americas. The flood of silver, in particular, was destabilizing Turkish currency. For centuries Turkey had too little silver; suddenly it had too much. The Ottoman Turks never cared for finance; they left that to the Greeks, the Jews, and the Armenians. The Turks only cared about martial matters. So the Sultanate tried to fix the ratio of gold to silver by edict; it was the same peremptory instinct that caused Abdul Hamid II to ban electricity.

If the official ratio of gold to silver was fixed at 1:15, it meant one could buy one gold for fifteen silver, from official Turkish sources. Immediately, one could sell the one gold in another country for what it was really worth: say, thirty silver, now that there was so much silver around. Buy one gold at the pegged-rate of fifteen silver, and turn around and swiftly sell it for thirty silver. Here is where it gets interesting: Return swiftly to the official source in Turkey with the thirty silver and buy *two* gold coins. Sell those two gold coins in another country for sixty silver. Return with the sixty silver to the official source and buy *four* gold coins. And so on. One could swiftly spiral up a fortune. All you have ever expended is your original fifteen silver. Essentially, you are making money from the Sultan's delusion that he could control reality by fiat. All you needed, which the Symiots enjoyed, was sophistication about currency, fast boats, and the ability to fly freely among international ports.

Recall that Symiot boats could travel freely under the Ottoman flag, delivering urgent diplomatic messages from the Sublime Porte. They were simply doing the empire's business by delivering the mail; in the process they were playing their Turkish oppressors for fools. Symiot wealth rose on price waves, differences in currency, and Turkish obstinacy. Steve Katzaras recalled from his youth that the Turks seemed to "let the Greeks make money from them."

THEY LOVED THE BLUE DESERT

Symi was an oasis on the blue desert of the sea.

In love of sea routes and sea ventures, in architectural appearance, Symi was the Venice of the eastern Aegean. The Symiots were sophisticated and well traveled, cleverly working pressure gradients among currencies—their wide thinking arising out of their sea fever. The sea had brought the Symiots everything. With their wealth shrewdly gathered, the old Symiot families could invest in sponge fishing, chandlery, commerce, and resupplying sailing ships that made their way across the ancient trade routes of the Levant: Alexandria to Smyrna to Constantinople, Marseilles to Venice to Syria. They could dowry daughters with new homes, buy timber forests and grazing rights in Anatolia, build neoclassical mansions that whispered remembrances of Venice, and educate their children in Paris. The wealthy could buy resort homes along the coast of Asia Minor at Daccia—a name that is a dear cousin to the Russian *Dacha*, "summer cottage," of like meaning—to escape the blazing heat of Yialos in August.

In the age of sail, ship captains loved Symi, the sheer safety of her long-fingered harbors. No ship captain liked spending the night at sea. No harbors made captains feel more secure than the deep, protected harbors of Symi. They were like a momentary return to the womb.

Captains on the ancient trade routes often hailed from the seafaring islands of Symi, Kalymnos, or Kassos in the Dodecanese, or Chios in the Northern Aegean. Symiot mariners endlessly looped the sea routes, gone for two or three years at a time. They were engaged in cargo transportation, loading up and dropping off as entrepreurial occasion arose: perhaps delivering goods from Syria to Alexandria or from Smyrna to Odessa. Always they accepted the risk of life at sea; always they knew that the ocean has no pity, and the waves never weep.

Because of Symiot daring and deep harbors—because of the Poetics of Manhood—an island of twenty-six square miles, with little water, could support 26,000 people, and make possible a prosperous life on a land of hunger.

THE INHOSPITABLE SEA

Today, my great-uncles, George and Nikitas, would be 140 years old; but alas, they died young, drowned when a terrible storm blew up in the Black Sea. They had two brothers, Metrophanes the poet, and Michael, a seaman for whom I am named.

"The Black Sea had a nasty reputation, even with the ancient Greeks," Dr. Robert Ballard wrote in *National Geographic Magazine*. Ballard is the underwater explorer who found the *Titanic*. "They once called it *Axenos,* 'inhospitable,' for the ferocity of its storms and the hostility of the tribes that lived around it." But its nasty reputation never stopped Greek mariners from sailing through the Dardenelles, the Sea of Marmara, the Bosporus, past Constantinople, and into the Black Sea. In fact Greek communities dotted the shores of the Black Sea. That's how I ended up with two dead uncles preserved in poisoned muck at the bottom of the Black Sea.

Ballard reports that two American geologists, William Ryan and Walter Pitman, suggest in their book, *Noah's Flood,* that stories of a great deluge recorded in the Bible and elsewhere may have sprung out of a real cataclysmic event. They reason that melting glaciers raised sea levels, and 7,500 years ago caused the Mediterranean to burst through the Bosporus Valley and into the Black Sea basin, converting a freshwater lake into a saltwater sea.

"Water thundered over the breach with the force of 200 Niagara falls," Ballard writes, invoking Pitman's vivid description of the event. Ballard adds, "The denser salt water filled the bottom of the basin, leaving a layer of brackish water on top." Since the Black Sea does not have the temperature differences necessary to drive the circulation of the water, "oxygen from the atmosphere couldn't reach the sea bottom. Deadly hydrogen sulfide formed there and life suffocated."

Willard Bascom, another pioneer of the deep, Ballard reports, has "postulated that the Black Sea was rich in preserved shipwrecks because the anoxicity (lack of oxygen) meant an absence of wood borers such as teredo worms, mollusks that eat organic matter, and other marine life. Thus wood, canvas, cargoes such as grain and hides, and even human remains would theoretically be preserved." Ballard observes, "The fuller picture then is wonderfully bizarre: the possibility that every ship that sailed and perished in the Black Sea, from humankind's earliest wanderings to our own time—perhaps 50,000 separate wrecks—lies preserved in poison."

My great grandfather John Kalafatas sailed into the Black Sea with two ships he had inherited from his father Andreas. Andreas had owned ships and a shipyard. When he died, he left the ships to John and the shipyard to John's brother, Stamatis, who makes the dramatic appearance in Metrophanes' poem. A terrible storm blew up in the

Black Sea that sank the two ships and drowned John's sons George and Nikitas.

The reasoning of Ballard, Bascom, Pitman, and Ryan suggests that at the bottom of the Black Sea, buried in poison muck, are the remains of my two great-uncles, George and Nikitas, perfectly preserved in a tangle of canvas sails and broken ships.

My great grandfather John survived the catastrophe and walked back to Symi. The walk took a year or two. It is no surprise. The roads of Anatolia were so rutted that Turkish troops never bothered to practice marching in step; it had no real-world application.

SOCIALISM

"We had socialism here before there was socialism," one British-educated Kalymnian told me. His British tones evoked for me the British Fabian Society, which proposed the kind of socialism the Privileged Islands enjoyed long before the Fabians ever dreamed up their utopian model. This was the socialism not of Lenin but of the ameliorative variety. Still, who would have thought "utopia" might be found on a tiny sea-girded archipelago in the eastern Aegean? Recall that Utopia, according to the *American Heritage Dictionary*, was "an imaginary island" that served as the title and subject of a book by Sir Thomas More. It was described "as a seat of perfection in moral, social, and political life."

On the island of Symi, if you hike up the four hundred-step Kali Strata—well built, easily mounted despite its steepness, and lined with mansions—you come to the old town of Chorio. The Kali Strata is the "main street" of Yialos. There in Chorio you will find the Dimotikon Pharmakion, literally "the municipal pharmacy," a beautiful dispensary built in the neoclassical style in 1884.

The Privileged Islands—Symi, Kalymnos, Kastellorizo, and the others—all provided free medical care, free pharmeceuticals, and free schooling to children of the poor. From one to four doctors were paid for by the island senates, according to Dr. Skevos Zervos from the island of Kalymnos.

Physicians on the Privileged Islands were elected by an annual secret vote of the island. The duty of the elected physician was to "attend
gratis upon all islanders suffering illness." Zervos reports that the
choice invariably fell upon "the most industrious, steady, and skillful
practitioners." Drugs were dispensed at the public pharmacies free,
"however prolonged and chronic the ailment."

Cultural societies were also maintained, especially on Symi and Kalymnos; both islands boasted numerous physicians, professors, and
teachers. On Symi the Sophocles Society sponsored theater until the
Germans in World War II bombed the theater itself.

It was from such a "utopian island" that my grandfather emerged.
Amid her agony at the death and destruction brought by the diving
suit, Mother Symi "confesses" in "Winter Dream" her joy that "mercy
flows" in so many ways still on the island.

> *So call me joyful today*
> *and I'll sing other virtues.*
> *I have professors, doctors, drugs,*
> *and pharmacists who make them,*
> *a library and schools and girls*
> *in girl-schools with their teachers.*
> *So all poor parents educate*
> *their children without cost,*
> *and can be healed back from disease,*
> *medicine being free.*
> *I'm grateful to my offspring, I,*
> *their mother and their country,*
> *who treat each other with such grace.*
> *Who turn to wisdom with hot zeal*
> *whose love burns for more learning*

Kalymnos was called the "Little Paris." Symi in character was the
"Little Venice." In their history of Symi, Kostas Farmakidis and Agapi
Karakatsani wrote that, in the nineteenth century, the contact with the
"major centres such as Constantinople, Smyrna, Alexandria, Syros,
Genoa, Trieste, Paris, London, and Brussels, led to the introduction
of the European way of life to the upper classes of the island."

In *The Dodecanese: Diversity and Unity in Island Politics,* Roger Kasperson, a geographer, observed that, "Although Greeks generally have a high respect for intellectual achievements, the sponge-fishing islanders appear to place greater emphasis upon education and the arts than other Dodecanesians." Kasperson quotes I. M. Panagiotopoulou: "Deep in their hearts, the sponge-fishers nestle a love of art and a yearning for letters." The Sophocles society was founded in 1870 and a similar voluntary organization was established on Kalymnos. Kasperson reports that Kalymnians and Symiots seem to have greater knowledge of the outside world; in 1966, when he was in the Dodecanese, Kalymnos received a shipment of 500–600 Athenian newspapers every day. The Symiots and Kalymnians pride themselves on their "determined, vigorous, active character," he reported. In an evocation of the poetics of manhood, Kasperson mentions that children on other islands occasionally ask Kalymnians if they are *agrioi,* "wild men." One Kalymnian informant offered Kasperson this explanation for the origin of the Kalymnian character:

> The sea and mountains, especially in combination, make for rugged almost wild, energetic, independent men. The conquering of the sea and rough landscape makes the Kalymnian proud, unafraid to speak his mind.

When the Symiots, the Kalymnians, the Halkites, the Kastellorizians, the people of the Dodecanese—the people of the Aegean—went to sea, they set sail with sea fever and billowed out their sails with the great winds of the Levant. They loved the seaways and slipways. They loved life on the blue desert. They loved the wind that blows. Beyond the safety of known horizons, they found fortune, gold, sophistication, and wisdom: there, too, they found the way to themselves. Always the Greeks of the Aegean were restless until they left the secure horizon. They knew themselves best beyond sight of land.

Perhaps this is the great lesson of the Greek mariners and of the daring Greek divers of the Aegean. It stands as their message to the world: In the end, our most fearsome journey is the journey to ourselves.

THE MORFOMENI

In the Dodecanese, if you had been educated, you metamorphosed. You were transformed by your learning. The people of the Dodecanese believed so, and they gave it a name: the educated were called the *morfomeni*. They had been through a metamorphosis; they looked and sounded different. They were also *all* national patriots.

Nick Doumanis discusses the phenomenon in his book *Myth and Memory in the Mediterranean* in a chapter he calls "The Poetics of Patriotism." The *morfomeni* had cast off the local Dodecanese accent and instead spoke the "clean" *kathari* speech of Athens, he explains. They also had discarded the *vrakes*, the ballooned pants and black boots, and wore western clothing: "*pantalons*, laced shoes, jackets, and the *fedora* or a beret." They often "brilliantined" their hair, Doumanis points out. They had a modern look and symbolized social progress. The *morfomeni* were believed to be spiritually elevated and were treated preferentially, as Doumanis notes. Like Dr. Skevos Zervos who importuned Wilson, Lloyd George, and Clemenceau after World War I for union of the Dodecanese with Greece, they were national patriots. In photographs they often struck an aristocratic pose in their fine western suits, shirts, and ties; they projected a self-image that served to "accentuate their social superiority," in Doumanis' phrase, and that seemed somehow more appropriate to the salons of Western Europe. Metrophanes' three sons—my uncles John and George, and the youngest, my father, Nikitas—were all *morfomeni*. They were both patriots and expatriates; this is the reason they published "Winter Dream" in June of 1919 in Boston. Its publication was an expression of their love for their father occasioned by an important political event in the Dodecanese: Bloody Sunday 1919.

Collectively, the *morfomeni* of the Dodecanese shared the hope that one day Greece would again be worthy of its historical legacy, Doumanis observes, and the belief that one day the Dodecanese would be part of Greece. As educated patriots they could interpret Greek national values and, whether justified or not, set local uprisings in the context of the great Greek National Awakening. In the Dodecanese of the Italian Occupation, every "uprising" was given maximum political spin; interpreted by the *morfomeni* as part of the patriotic struggle to rid the islands of the foreign Italian oppressor. As an example, Doumanis points to the fact that the *morfomeni* of Kalymnos renamed the Rock War "the National-Religious Resistance." Such renaming turned the Rock War "into a myth about Kalymnian patriotism," thereby presenting the islanders as resisters. Doumanis reports that the *morfomeni* believed "that the function of history was to serve the state, to chart the forward progress of Hellenism, and to celebrate the exceptional qualities of the Greek people."

During the Italian occupation of the Dodecanese, Doumanis tells us, "numerous Dodecanesian *morfomeni* in the diaspora committed their anxious thoughts to paper in order to share their pathos with other *morfomeni*." Long, impassioned poems and other writings appeared that made use of classical and Byzantine motifs; such motifs suggested "timelessness" and "that the Dodecanese had always been a part of the Greek nation." Doumanis observes that the very "act of writing on patriotic themes was regarded as an important form of struggle." He writes that Dodecanesian expatriates

> ... from the safety of Athens, Alexandria and elsewhere, carried on the good fight throughout the occupation by composing poems and diatribes. Expatriates spilled much ink and went to great expense to publish their own works. Their expected audience, to be sure, was fellow expatriates, but the circulation of these works in the diaspora helped confirm the existence of a general will, as if the flame of Hellenism was kept alight.

" 'Showing' one's patriotism in print," he adds, "was considered a legitimate way of maintaining personal honour and reputation, for the more one 'showed' one's passion in print, the more one looked like a 'great patriot.' "

All of my grandfather's sons were *morfomeni* and Dodecanesian expatriates. In 1919, my father, attending the Greek marine engineering college in Piraeus, was soon to join his brothers in the United States. Metrophanes' sons published the poem in June 1919 because they loved and admired their father; but also because they had recently learned of the martyrdom of Dodecanesian patriots at the hands of their Italian occupiers.

BLOODY SUNDAY 1919

What is the phrase, "worlds collide"? I feel my "Irish upbringing" in South Boston colliding with my Greek roots in the Dodecanese. When I write of Bloody Sunday 1919 in the Dodecanese, it evokes for me the Easter Rising in Dublin in 1916 and the martyrdom of Irish patriots.

As Doumanis reports, in early 1919 there were rumors in the Dodecanese that Italian delegates at the Paris Peace Conference were misrepresenting Dodecanese opinion; the Italians were contending they had "declarations" from seventeen prominent Dodecanesians stating that they wanted Italian rule to become permanent. Dodecanese leaders responded by holding a plebiscite.* In resounding chorus the plebiscite told the world that the people of the Dodecanese desired unification with Greece. The plebiscite, organized for Easter Monday, April 20, 1919, was "orchestrated by the Church," Doumanis reports, and headed up by a vigorous, politically active young bishop, Apostolos Trifonos.

As expected, the vote was unanimous in favor of unification. Celebrations that ensued in the Dodecanese were kept under control, Doumanis reports—except in the village of Paradisi, Rhodes, where "ill-disciplined Italian troops opened fire on a crowd, killing a local priest and a young woman." In the Dodecanese the incident is remembered as *To Ematero Pascha tou 1919*, The Bloody Easter of 1919. The two dead, the priest and the young woman, were "immediately consecrated as martyrs," Doumanis writes, and Greek Prime Minister Eleftherios Venizelos was able to use the martyrdom to greater effect than the results of the plebiscite. Most of the Dodecanese islands were ceded to Greece. Given twists and turns in international events, however, union of the Dodecanese with Greece would have to await the years after World War II.

---

*When I was a child, my father never told me children's stories; instead he would tell me stories from Greek political history. My older brother Metrofanis told me breathtaking children's stories he invented out of thin air. My sister Roberta read me "The Little Engine That Could." My father would speak to me of the Dodecanese; I learned the word "plebiscite" at age seven. I was the only child at my elementary school who knew the word. Blessed is the flame that lights the candle.

Across the sea, in Boston, Massachusetts, inspired by Bloody Easter of 1919 on the island of Rhodes, my uncle John moved to have my grandfather's poem published, together with a valediction signed by the poet's three sons, John, George, and Nikitas. *Morfomeni* all. Perhaps John was remembering, as I do, Easter Monday in Ireland in 1916 and the fallen Irish patriots. Boston, after all, was the most Irish of American cities.

> The present poem, having been written at the end of the year 1903 by our ever-remembered father, Metrophanes I. Kalafatas, had remained unpublished at the sudden death of its composer on the 9th of March, 1904.
>
> Now that we, his sons, are men, and that the name of the Dodecanese is universally known for its freedom fight against the Italians, we have considered it our duty to print this book, both to acquaint the public with the life and customs of our island, and as eternal memorial to its composer's soul.
>
> We remain respectfully,
Ioannis, Georgios, Nikitas M. Kalafatas
Boston 7> 20th of June, 1919

Valediction

The peculiar dating of the valediction written by the poet's sons can be explained by the differences between the New Calendar and the Old Calendar of the Orthodox Christian Church. The valediction was submitted on the New Calendar date of June 7, which corresponds to the Old Calendar date of June 20. The symbol ">" in the English rendering of the poem and the symbol "⌐" in the original Greek serve to show the correspondence of the two dates. The thirteen days that separate the two June dates is the thirteen-day difference in the two calendars.

Below is a clarification of the Western calendar, the Old Orthodox Calendar, and the New Orthodox Calendar. The source is the website ⟨www.holidayfestival.com/Christianity.html⟩.

The Christian faith has three separate calendars: the Western, the Orthodox New Calendar, and the Orthodox Old Calendar.

The Western Calendar is that of the Roman Catholic and Protestant Churches.

The Orthodox New Calendar is the same as the Western Calendar for all fixed feasts but uses the old or Julian Calendar for moveable feasts such as Easter and is used primarily by the Greek and Cypriot Orthodox Churches.

The Orthodox Old Calendar is the Julian Calendar, at the time of writing 13 days behind the New Calendar, and is used by most other Orthodox churches and also by the Coptic church and most churches in the Middle East.

A dramatic example of the differences in the calendars can be found with Christmas Day, which is celebrated on December 25 on the New Calendar and on January 7 on the Old Calendar. The poet's sons were exercising diplomacy in citing both dates.

ENOSIS

On the island of Symi, along the waterfront, bolted to a large building, is a bronze plaque on which is inscribed, in Greek and in English:

The surrender of the Dodecanese to the Allies was signed in this house on May 5th 1945.

On April 1, 1947, a British military administration handed the Dodecanese over to a Greek one, and on March 7, 1948, the Dodecanese were incorporated into the Greek State: *Enosis*, union with Sweet Mother Greece at long last.

By Order of Victor Emmanuel: The Story of Michael Foreys ("Four-A's")

By conservative estimate I have spelled my name 25,000 times. Marjorie Schwartz, the receptionist in my office, when asked to spell my name, would say, "Kalafatas: All the vowels are A's, and it's 'K' as in kiss, 'l' as in love, 'f' as in fudge, 't' as in toffee, and 's' as in sugar." Somehow I never spelled it that way. In America the subtext of spelling an "ethnic" name is the act of an outsider trying to *spell* his way in. So it was a joy to arrive on Rhodes and Symi where the name brought instant recognition, if not fame. As a child I had listened, time and again, to my father say that the Kalafatas family was "one of the oldest, most aristocratic families in the Dodecanese islands." This from my father the leftist. (*Irony*, too, is a Greek word.) I lived in America, however, and knew the name was no advantage.

Not so in the Dodecanese. For six weeks I was on sabbatical from having to spell my name. On the island of Symi, Michael Foreys told me, "People *falsely* called themselves *Kalafatas* for the advantage." My dad would have loved it. "*Palio onoma*," they would say to me, "old name," as I introduced myself. I once heard George Stephanopoulos, President Clinton's communications director, describe his first trip to Greece: "I went to my father's village, and everyone was named *Stephanopoulos!*"

Michael Foreys was born Michael Kalafatas on the island of Symi in 1912. On this tiny island, smaller than Martha's Vineyard, he was one of four cousins who shared the name: Michael *Stamatis* Kalafatas, Michael *Georgios* Kalafatas, Michael *Theodoros* Kalafatas, and Michael *Nikitas* Kalafatas (my exact name). Italian authorities, who used the Latin alphabet, constantly confused the mail of the four cousins. So, Michael Stamatis Kalafatas changed his name to Michael Foreys ("Four-A's" since *Kalafatas* has four A's). In one brilliant, if eccentric, stroke, he eliminated the mix-up with his cousins and with a small number of people on the island named Kalafa*tis*. Kalafatas and Kalafatis are pronounced differently in Greek: Kahlahfah-tahs versus Kahlahfah-tis. To the Greek ear it makes a world of difference, but apparently not to the Italian ear.

Never again did Foreys have problems with mail. The name change required a royal decree, issued in 1940 by King Victor Emmanuel II of Italy. Most of all, the Foreys's name change reflects Michael's linguistic brilliance: he comfortably glides among five languages and loves the play and sound of words. His new name was a subtle joke, perceived only by those who knew English. In Greek naming tradition, if you follow the *Stamatis* of Michael's middle name back, you get to Stamatis Kalafatas who figures so prominently in the poem. He is Michael's great grandfather and my great granduncle. The two Michaels, chatting about the sponge trade in Michael's loft office over the carpentry shop in the summer of 1997, are third cousins, removed only by a great Ocean.

In talking with Michael, eighty-five, I recollect anew these lines: "One who learns from the old is like one who eats ripe grapes and drinks old wine."

eight

PEARLING IN AUSTRALIA

Of all the world's gems it is the pearl which has held the greatest fascination for humans. So powerful is the pearl's allure that for thousands of years people have risked their lives to wrest this perfect jewel from the ocean's depths.

—*Nova* (TV series), "The Perfect Pearl"

And I saw a new heaven...
And the twelve gates were twelve pearls...

—Revelation 21: 1, 21

For the Greek divers of the Aegean it was the allure of the sea that held the greatest fascination: Visiting the deep interiority of Mother Sea and "stealing away" her exotic treasures.

What could seem more like a visit to Mother Sea's deepest interiority, in search of her mysteries and her treasures, than to pry open an oyster and reach into her fleshy interior to steal away a beautiful South Sea pearl. The Greek pearl divers, like the Arab and Asian pearl divers who came before—like all of us—were mystified by the pearl's origin, entranced by its luster, and moved by its shape: a perfect circle. Splay open the shell and find the sun or the moon.

THE QUEEN OF GEMS

Before the triumph of the diamond, the pearl was the Queen of Gems, "passionately sought after by kings and queens, emperors, and maharajas," as the *Nova* program reported. Perfect pearls were a rarity until the development of the modern cultured pearl industry; their very possession seemed to "proclaim their owner's wealth and power," *Nova* added.

Gemologist Fred Ward, writing in "The Pearl," in *National Geographic,* informs us that "Pearls are among the oldest and most universal of gems, indicators of wealth in the Bible, the Talmud, and the Koran." So valuable were they in classical times, he reports, that "the Roman general Vitellius paid for an entire campaign by selling just one of his mother's earrings." Ward also describes the pearl craze in Rome, which peaked "at a remarkable banquet where Cleopatra is said to have wagered Marc Antony that she could give the most expensive dinner in history." Ward recounts,

> As the astonished foreigner watched, the queen sat before an empty plate and a goblet of wine (or vinegar). Removing one of her huge, matched-pearl earrings, she crushed and dissolved it in the liquid, then drank. When she offered Antony the remaining earring, the bet was declared won.

In *The Book of Pearls,* Joan Younger Dickinson tells us that in the Middle Ages Europeans used "a medicinal solution of powdered pearls, vinegar or lemon juice, sugar, and herbs," called *aqua perlata,* "to relieve melancholia, heart palpitations, and insanity." The drink came to be used in Japan and India as well.

READY-TO-WEAR

The pearl is the ultimate ready-to-wear adornment: open an oyster, find a pearl, and wear it.

It is likely that the first to use pearls as gems were oyster-eaters in India who came upon them while feeding on mollusks fetched along the shores of the Indian Ocean: the same sparkling Indian Ocean, the third largest ocean, that borders Australia and one day would make some Greek-Australians wealthy; nature's sea bounty once again delivered up to Greek daring.

According to the *Encyclopedia Brittanica,* the pearl is mentioned in

Hindu literature as known "before the influx of the Aryans" in 1500 B.C. While reading a book about pearls aboard a ship, I was approached by a crew member from India who pointed to the cover and said, "As a child, I bit into an oyster, and found a small pearl." The story itself seemed the gift of a small pearl.

For centuries pearls were formed only as an exquisite accident of nature and obtained from oysters gathered on the seafloor by free divers: Arabs in the Persian Gulf and Asians in the South Seas. In the Persian Gulf, like the Greeks, Arab free divers used a diving stone and towed net baskets to the seafloor into which they placed the oysters they collected. In his majestic *The Book of the Pearl*, written in 1908, George Frederick Kunz reported that typically they dove to seven or eight fathoms and remained under water for sixty seconds. The officially observed record was 109 seconds in seven fathoms of water. Like the Greeks, they dove only in "the season of good weather," from May until September. Throughout the writing of this book I have been struck at how so many seas of the world simply shut down for winter.

Pearl divers in the South Seas swam to the sea-bottom, according to Kunz. They dove feet first and flipped as gracefully as an otter at a depth of twelve or fifteen feet and swam to the oyster bed below.

THE CURRENCY OF ROMANCE

In *Nova*'s "The Perfect Pearl" a clip is run from a Hollywood film from the 1930s: a beautiful young woman and a dashing young man are in ever-so-close, face-to-face romantic dialogue. As *Nova* suggests, their conversation illustrates how pearls throughout history have been the "currency of romance."

————: I should love to have a man dive to twenty fathoms to bring me up a pearl.
————: And if I were that man, what then?
————: Then I might be . . . *very kind* to you.

While pearls can be found around the world, in freshwater and in saltwater, today's Australian South Sea pearls are the "Rolls Royce of Pearls": large in size, high in luster, beautiful, and durable. They come from the *Pinctada Maxima*, the world's largest oysters which produce the biggest and most expensive pearls. As *Nova* reports, the *Pinctada Maxima* "can live up to twenty years, growing to the size of a dinner plate." South Sea pearls possess high "orient," a term experts use to describe a pearl's "bright varicolored luster," its "iridescence," as Joan Younger Dickinson informs us.

In New York, I once stopped in at Tiffany's to admire a strand of huge white Australian pearls of dazzling price whose orient cast a silvery glow. A similar strand of gunmetal gray Tahitian pearls cast off a blue glow. The pearls seemed to be not of this planet.

In the 1950s "a string of pearls became the classic coming-of-age gift for a woman, their sensuality and beauty revered by men and women alike," *Nova* recalls. I think of my sister's Girls' Latin School graduation picture, taken in 1956 in Boston: a strand of luminous white pearls around her neck. And her ears adorned with a set of simple, elegant, white pearl earrings. On the cusp of womanhood, she evokes Vermeer's *Girl with a Pearl Earring*.

In the public sphere, of course, the women who illustrated the pearl's sensuality and beauty with a patrician edge were Grace Kelly, Audrey Hepburn, and Jacqueline Bouvier Kennedy, famous for their elegant pearls worn as perfect adornment. The first color plate in Kunz's *The Book of the Pearl* is of the Tsarina Alexandra, whose startling beauty is illumined by perfect pearls. My admiration for her made me feel, in Marxist parlance, like a counterrevolutionary: How can we rid Russia of the tsars if you love the Tsarina?

The woman who best represented the sheer sensuality of pearls, as *Nova* observes, was the erotic dancer Josephine Baker. An African-American and daughter of a St. Louis washerwoman, Baker's career reached its zenith in Paris in the 1920s, at the Follies Bergere. As she shimmied and danced, she often wore "nothing but" pearls: flamboyant costumes made entirely of pearls.

THE TEARS OF ANGELS

Before cultured pearls, pearls were so uncommon that some wealthy women wore their pearls to bed so they could awaken in the morning and realize instantly just how wealthy they were. The passage of pearls from rarity to the commonplace—to the everyday act of a woman's slipping on a string of pearls as she heads off to work—came to pass largely through the technical and marketing genius of Kokichi Mikimoto, the Japanese son of a noodle maker who invented and implemented a method for culturing pearls in the 1890s. It was Mikimoto who convinced the world that there was no difference between the natural and the cultured pearl: If it looks like a pearl and feels like a pearl, it is a pearl.

As I reverentially turned the pages of a luxurious volume of *The Book of the Pearl,* owned by the Wellesley College Library, I found in George Frederick Kunz's own hand, in elegantly aged ink, an inscription addressed to a woman: "Pearls are tears of angels shed to give mortals joy." The inscription was written in 1921, in the decade of the 1920s, when Mikimoto persuaded the world gem market that the natural pearl and the cultured pearl were synonyms. Ever after, "tears of angels" would bring wide joy.

Offering the world gem market a wide selection of fine quality larger Australian South Sea pearls came to pass largely through the intelligence, grit, and grace of three generations of Greek-Australians. First among them was the Paspaley family, whose origins were on the Dodecanese island of Kastellorizo, 4.5 square miles, a "tiny droplet of stone" as one guide book calls it, deep in the eastern Mediterranean.

ENDLESS COASTS

> How shall we find our livelihood roaming in some
> far land.

—Sophocles, *Oedipus at Colonus*

By and large the Greeks came to Australia in the twentieth century, and in especially large numbers after World War II. Australia was to Greece in the second half of the twentieth century what America was to Greece in the first half: a continental nation from sea to shining sea, a vast land of democratic vistas, where discipline and daring could send you swiftly up the ladder of success.

The Greeks came to Australia because of hard times at home—Nazi atrocities, civil war, and privation. The Greeks came because Australia wanted them, although some unions objected mightily, even as the United States turned the spigot of immigration to a trickle. The Greeks came because of demand for labor, especially in the maritime trades. Australia, after all, was the country of endless coasts.

WILD BEAUTY

Odysseus would have loved the coast of northwest Australia. It had everything Greek mariners loved: wild beauty, danger, terrible creatures in the deep, and the chance to "wrest from the sea" another item exotic and luxurious. Northwest Australia was the epicenter of pearl fishing in the Land Down Under.

Pearling began in western Australia when pearls were discovered in the *Pinctada Albina* oyster in the 1850s in Shark Bay. But the industry really took off after 1861 when beds of *Pinctada Maxima* oysters were discovered in Roebuck Bay in the Kimberly region of western Australia. By the early 1900s Broome had become Australia's largest pearling town, with a fleet of four hundred "pearl luggers"—pearl boats—and several thousand people involved in pearl fishing.

Since natural, perfect pearls are rare, the early pearling industry of Australia was the pearl-shell industry: the underwater search for mother-of-pearl. By the late nineteenth century, Australia was supplying 75 percent of the world's needs for mother-of-pearl, used in the manufacture of buttons, knife and gun handles, clock inlays, and the like. As Nick Paspaley, who presides today over a modern pearl culturing operation, writes at the Paspaley Pearling Company's website: "Pearls were not relied upon for income as they were extremely rare and the majority of natural pearls that were found were imperfect and therefore not very valuable. A valuable pearl was seen as a rare bonus." The Paspaley family would change all that.

Victoria Kyriakopoulos has written of the "Paspaley pearling dynasty" in *Odyssey* magazine ("The Oyster Is Their World"). In the heyday of the pearl-shell industry, she reports, "Divers, most of them Asian, scoured the coast for mother-of-pearl shells. . . ." But the invention of plastic buttons wiped out the pearl shell industry in the 1950s. The price for pearl shell plummeted; no longer could it support Australia's pearling fleet or the roistering life of the early pearling towns.

By and large, it was the drive and dreams of the Paspaley family that rescued Australia's pearling industry. The Paspaley family turned to culturing South Sea pearls, launching an industry that became a booming force in the Australian economy. Today, Australia produces high-quality cultured pearls by the many hundreds of thousands.

"The Paspaley name is to the pearling industry what De Beers is to diamonds—a mark of both exquisite quality and dominance," Kyriakopoulos observes. "But it wasn't always this way. It took the combined grit of three generations of Paspaleys to parlay a hardscrabble, low-margin diving operation into a seabed-to-showroom empire whose value is estimated at $350 million." But where did the Paspaley family hail from and how did they end up in Australia?

KASTELLORIZO

Kastellorizo, the smallest of the Dodecanese islands, is the easternmost extremity of Greece, seventy-two nautical miles southeast of Rhodes. Some may know it as the setting for the charming film *Mediterraneo*, in which a company of feckless Italian soldiers is left to guard a tiny Greek island, bereft of men, far from the center of the action. The Italians, in high archetype, are interested only in love, romance, and art.

Kastellorizo bears striking similarities to Symi although only one-fifth its size: it is rocky, lacking in water, and close to the Turkish coast—closer even than Symi, a mile and a half, as compared to Symi's four miles. Like Symi, Kastellorizo enjoyed soaring prosperity in the late nineteenth and early twentieth centuries; like Symi, it was strongly represented among the sponge-fishing fleets. It too was a great trading and bunkering port. And like Symi, beautiful mansions rose amphitheatrically from quayside. In 1910, nine thousand residents lived on tiny Kastellorizo, gathered close in a prosperous and sophisticated life.

But sadly, island fortunes changed. When steam-powered ships came along, capable of long-distance travel, Kastellorizo was simply bypassed. In 1913 it was occupied by the French, and in 1920 it came under Italian rule. Like Symi, Kastellorizo was cut from its natural ties to Anatolia. It was shelled from the mainland during World War I, and the island suffered terribly in World War II—Kastellorizo Town was burned and pillaged during the Allied occupation, with many beautiful homes and boats destroyed.

The island of Kastellorizo emptied out. Today, some pastel-colored, many-hued mansions remain—some ruined, some rebuilt—whispering of the island's bygone glory and awaiting the return of lost souls.

Only a few hundred year-round residents remain on Kastellorizo, mostly fishermen. The pride and tenacity of those who stayed behind is represented in the "Lady of Rho." Rho is an islet near Kastellorizo that, at one point, had one remaining resident, who bravely put up the Greek flag every morning. As a symbol of Greek independence, Kastellorizo is particularly poignant since, over its history, the island has been occupied by seven different nations before finally being "retroceded" to Greece in 1947.

Many Kastellorizians came to Darwin, Australia, the capital of the Northern Territory. In turn, many of their descendants moved to Perth in western Australia, where they live today as a vibrant Greek-Australian community. Mick Michaels, a past mayor of Perth, is of Kastellorizian lineage.

THE SMALL GREECE DOWN UNDER

Today, there are some 650,000 Greek-Australians, *Ellino-Australoi.* Close to half live in Melbourne. Among non–English-speaking groups in Australia, Greeks are third, after Italians and Vietnamese, as Demetra Egan informs us at her website on the Greek-Australian community. As she points out, Greek-Australians are an energetic, arrived force in Australian life. Like their Greek-American counterparts, the Greek-Australians are well-educated, affluent, and fully engaged in the public affairs of their country. In 1996, fourteen elected members of the Federal and state parliaments were of Greek descent.

While Greeks are found in every state in Australia—with Melbourne variously called the third or fourth largest "center of Hellenism" in the world—Darwin is the most Greek city in Australia. As such, it is a special cousin to Tarpon Springs, the most Greek city in an English-speaking nation of continental reach. While the first Greek immigrants to Darwin came mainly from Kastellorizo, today in Darwin one finds Greeks of Kalymnian and other origin as well. Among Greek-Australian families of especially high visibility in Darwin and in Australia as a whole is the Paspaley family.

DREAM FACTORY

Dream Factory is what Victoria Kyriakopoulos called the Paspaley family, because one family's dreams helped revolutionize Australia's pearling industry.

Theodosis Michael Paspalis, a tobacco merchant on Kastellorizo, migrated to Australia with his family in 1919. As we learn from the Paspaley Pearling Company's website, he settled at the ship's first port-of-call: Cossack in western Australia, a major port and base for the pearling fleet, located along the shores of the pristine Indian Ocean. The Paspalis family was among a handful of Europeans who lived amid thousands of Asians and Aboriginals. "Running water, electricity, shops, and government services were non-existent," his grandson Nick writes. Paspalis opened a grocery store and bought a share in a pearling lugger. Sadly, he died five years later.

His son Nicholas, born on Kastellorizo, continued on in the pearling industry, later changing his name to Paspaley. Paspaley bought his first lugger at age nineteen. "It had no engines and air was pumped to the divers by hand-pumps," writes Nick Paspaley. "When there was no wind to fill the sails, the lugger had to be rowed by hand."

In a remarkable tale of dream as prophecy, Kyriakopoulos recounts:

One night at sea, on his lugger off the coast of Western Australia, Nicholas had an ominous nightmare. The young Greek immigrant dreamed that after finding a rare and fabulous perfect pearl, he was murdered by his crew of Asian and Aboriginal pearl divers—a conceivable fate on the notorious lawless coast.

According to Kyriakopoulos, Paspaley insisted on opening the next day's pearl catch himself. "As he sliced open the very first shell, the pearl of his dreams was revealed," Kyriakopoulos writes. She tells us that Nicholas Paspaley hid the pearl in his glove and told the crew to drop him off at the nearest safe port, and to return home by sea. Over several days' time, he made his way home by cattle truck, Kyriakopoulos reports. When Paspaley arrived, she informs us, he learned that a cyclone had destroyed many luggers, and that hundreds of pearl divers had drowned.

"I SAW A DREAM"

In writing this book I have been haunted by dreams, not only by my own, but by those of others, including my grandfather's "Winter Dream," my father's deferred dream, and Nicholas Paspaley's dream as related by Kyriakopoulos.

Oddly, what impelled my father's dream—his attempt to find a place close to the people of the Dodecanese—is encapsulated in a book by Effy Alexakis and Leonard Janiszewski called *Images of Home*. The book contains photographs and stories of Greek-Australians who returned to their homeland, after being gone so long. Though my father never traveled to Australia, their words evoke his dilemma. "Once an individual has migrated, their identity and relationship with their country of origin can never be the same. Some have great difficulty deciding where to settle, uncomfortably spending their lives searching for an ideal between two countries."

I can speak only of the Dodecanese, but the islands beckon hauntingly to lost sons and daughters, to those who found prosperous new lives in Alexandria, Athens, Marseilles, London, New York, Boston, Darwin, Perth, and Melbourne, a siren call that drew many to that familiar and unfamiliar place for Greeks, between Scylla and Charybdis. Even though often immensely successful, never would they feel fully comfortable, or safe, between the land of their birth and the land of their prosperity.

I once heard anthropologist Charles Stewart speak of dreams as prophecy in Greece. Since Freud, he observed, dreams in Western culture are believed to be about the past. In the West we view dreams as gifts from our unconscious to our conscious mind: keys, if you will, that allow us to unlock our unconscious and free us of the dark burdens of our past. But we forget that Freud rejected earlier Western tradition. Before Freud, in the West, dreams were believed to be predictive, as many still believe in Greece today. Dream books are widely sold in Greece, to help people decode the symbols in their dreams and see into the future, even to alter that future dramatically.

According to Stewart, the differing views of dreams held in the West generally and in Greece specifically are reflected in our language. No surprise. We say, "I *had* a dream." In Greece they say, "I *saw* a dream," since the dreamers are seeing into the future. Before any might scoff, who among us would board an airplane anxiety-free after dreaming the plane had crashed? Our anxiety is an atavism from early Western tradition.

Stewart studied the mountain village of Koronos on the Aegean island of Naxos where people are famed for their dreams—"*oi oneirevamenoi,* 'those who see religious dreams.' " Stewart also "found that a variety of lively dreams concern objects buried in the earth." These are dreams of hidden icons, Cycladic statues, other artifacts from antiquity, and buried treasure "deposited by local residents or invaders beginning from the period of piracy in the Middle Ages down to the World War II occupation by the Germans and the Italians." According to Stewart, "Naxiote traditions often involve *dreams* as a means of learning about the treasure."

It would appear to be that such a dream of prophecy, a dream of hidden treasure and discovery, came to Paspaley. As described by Kyriakopoulos, Nicholas Paspaley's dream predicted discovery of treasure and allowed him to alter the future dramatically. For Charles Stewart, while Naxiote dreams of treasure appear to be about the future, they are really about the past. As he observes, in Greece "history is popularly viewed in highly reified ways—as an object that must be guarded for fear it might be stolen." The international furor over the "stealing" of the name *Macedonia* by one of the former republics of Yugoslavia is a case in point. In Greece, history itself is a treasure. On Naxos, many dreams of treasure are about valued items from the past, from Cycladic Civilization down through World War II. Stewart compares the Naxiote dreams of treasure to Durkheim's explanation of the frequency of our dreams about deceased ancestors: both are "ruminations on the continuity of society."

Is not Nicholas Paspaley's dream of finding a perfect pearl—so like the sun and moon we once worshipped—really a dream about our shared treasured past? Not only for the Greeks, but for us all, our history *is* our treasure.

According to Kyriakopoulos, Nicholas Paspaley's first pearl remained "his best pearl." Since valuable natural pearls are a rarity, Nicholas Paspaley would make his fortune largely by supplying mother-of-pearl to the world from the shells of the *Pinctada Maxima*. But as his son Nick writes at the company website, "it was known that the world's finest and most valuable pearls came from these shells, the most important and most beautiful pearl shells in the world."

The work of Mikimoto and of other Japanese in the cultured pearl industry nagged at the Australian pearlers. While the Japanese were culturing pearls using the smaller Akoya pearl shell, the Australians knew that the *Pinctada Maxima*, the pearl oyster the size of a dinner plate, was capable of producing a big, beautiful pearl. The critical question was how to get *P. Maxima* oysters to produce large, luminous round pearls in commercially viable quantities? Whoever could do that would become immensely wealthy.

In the *Nova* special, Nick Paspaley speaks movingly of his father and his father's generation of pearlers, and implicitly, of his relationship with his father.

> All my father ever did really, was live pearling, and so it was sort of a big part of my life. All my childhood experiences were out in luggers, and with my father at the shell sheds and down in the engine rooms, and things. I remember, as a little guy, the hours that my father and some of the other pearlers would stand around the verandah, with a couple of pearls in their hand, and I don't know what they spoke about, but they'd be there for hours discussing this particular pearl. And they just had a passion for pearls, and the industry, that's all they knew. And, to them, there was nothing else outside of that world.

The "golden age of pearling in Australia" was in the years leading up to World War I when four hundred pearl luggers and several thousand people were fishing for pearl shell in the waters off Broome, then the biggest pearling center in the world. A colorful array of stories exist from that time when Broome was a frontier town of booms and busts. The Great Depression hit Australian pearlers hard. Nicholas Paspaley survived it, only to see World War II entirely wipe out the pearling industry. Pearl luggers either were destroyed by the Australian army or sent south out of fear they might fall into Japanese hands. Beautiful Broome, in the heart of pearling country, was attacked from the air by Japanese Zeros, with loss of life and with boats and planes on the ground destroyed. In eerie echo of the internment of Japanese-Americans, Kyriakopoulos reports that, "In Broome, 500 Japanese divers are said to have been arrested and interned during the war." Some Japanese divers found their way back to Japan. They left behind in Broome a Japanese cemetery with the graves of nine hundred Japanese pearl divers who died from shark attacks, tangled or slashed air hoses, the bends, cyclones, or other disasters at sea. As the tally of nine hundred dead Japanese divers sinks into my mind, I am left to wonder about the poetics of manhood in Japan.

After the war, Nicholas Paspaley was among the first to reenter the pearling industry. But by the 1950s, as discussed, the invention of plastic buttons had sent the price of pearl shell into steep decline, to the point where it could no longer support the pearling fleet.

The 1950s was the age of plastic. As a child, I recall a small plastics factory's opening fifty yards from my home, the smell of melted plastic in my nostrils still. The only hope for the Australian pearling fleet was the cultivation of pearls in commercially viable quantities. Strong, tenacious, and full of dreams, Nicholas Paspaley became one of the first Australians to enter the pearl culturing business. In 1958 Paspaley formed a partnership with Japanese and American partners, *Nova* reports, and opened a pearl farm. It was an act of uncommon courage, not only because pearl culturing and farming was still a high-risk business, but also because Australian distrust of the Japanese ran high after World War II.

Egan reports that, after the war, the Australian government and the Australian people were "mistrustful of the Japanese divers who until then comprised the majority of the divers." The official "White Australia" policy of the era also precluded using other Asian divers. Divers were needed after World War II in order to dive for pearl shell when the price for mother-of-pearl was still high, and afterward to collect the wild oysters that were used in the cultivation of pearls.

According to Egan, given the need for divers, a group of Kalymnians from Sydney approached government officials with an idea: Why not bring in skilled divers from Kalymnos? After all, the Greeks had been involved in Australian pearling since the 1880s, and they had been diving for sponges in the Aegean since antiquity.

DIVERS FROM THE AEGEAN

The postwar years were difficult times on Kalymnos. The island was trying to reestablish its sponge-fishing industry after the war while the North African countries were setting high licensing fees or closing off whole areas to build up their own sponge-fishing industries. The invention of synthetic sponges had also cut into the lower end of the sponge market. Egan turns to the Australians Charmian Clift and George Johnston who, in their novel *The Sponge Divers*, captured that era on Kalymnos when many young Kalymnian men were desperate for work.

> All Kalymnos is unsettled, restless, drunk with these ridiculous hopes and expectations. . . . If it's handled right we'll all be able to go to Australia. . . . There'll be plenty of work for everyone, good money, nobody will go hungry.

Australian government officials could not believe their good fortune: here were Europeans who were trained divers. They also knew the Greeks to be law-abiding citizens who had integrated well into Australian society. Government officials asked pearl lugger operators in Broome what they thought of bringing in Kalymnian divers. According to Egan, George Haritos recollects the event as follows: "We were asked if anyone wanted Greek divers, Paspaley, Gonzales, Billy Sing, Curly Bell and ourselves. We decided to give the Kalymnian divers a try." And so, in 1952, the Australian government paid for the passage and handled travel arrangements to bring in two Kalymnian diving teams.

DISASTER

The experiment was a disaster. The Australian government sent one Kalymnian diving team to Broome, the other to Darwin. Despite their skill, the Kalymnians were "unaccustomed to the treacherous seas of the tropical north, with its extreme tides of seven or more metres, the dangerous sea life, the use of a half body suit and the industry's bad safety record," according to Egan. As regards the last, of course, the Kalymnians had their own island's bad safety record for which to account. Theo Halkitis nearly lost his life when he became entangled in the lugger's propeller shaft, Egan reports. The crew's chief diver, Hristos Kontoyiannis, was less fortunate: the propeller cut his air supply and he died of asphyxiation.

In *Images of Home* there is a black-and-white photograph of the Kalymnian crew of the pearl lugger *Postboy* paying their last respects at the gravesite of Kontoyiannis, which is piled high with flowers. In the caption, Alexakis and Janiszewski tell us "Mary Dakas (nee Paspalis), most probably Australia's only Greek female pearl lugger operator," is among the grieving. Mary Dakas and her brothers, Michael and Nicholas, the authors add, "would leave their mark on the Australian pearling industry."

Rumors persisted that Kontoyiannis' death "was not as accidental as it appears," Egan reports. Years later Kontoyiannis' son came to Australia to retrieve his father's bones and bring them back to Kalymnos. While in Australia, the son tried to find out the real story. Unconvinced of the coroner's report, he finally left for Greece with his father's bones: Hristos Kontoyiannis, one more Odysseus finally sailing home. According to Egan, the death of Kontoyiannis brought to the surface "ill feelings from the lugger operators who were unhappy about losing the cheap Japanese labor."

Other Kalymnian divers would follow those first crews to Australia to fetch wild pearl oysters from the sea. Their descendants can be found in Darwin today. Where once the Greeks in Darwin were preponderantly "Kazzies" from Kastellorizo, now the majority are from Kalymnos: so many Dodecanesians so far from home. Alas, my Dad would understand.

Among retired divers from the original community of Kalymnian divers, there remains a haunting feeling about the death of Hristos Kontoyiannis, according to Egan. To them his death remains an unresolved mystery.

I identify with their disquiet. To me the death of my grandfather remains an unresolved mystery. When my grandfather uttered as his last words, "They have killed me," was he referring to the ineptitude of the attending physician? It is entirely possible. In 1910 Abraham Flexner issued a report on the state of medical training in the United States, claiming that, before 1900, physicians killed more patients than they saved. Why would turn-of-the-century medicine be any better on a small island in the eastern Aegean?

But I thought *one* doctor attended to my grandfather, so who exactly were *They*? My brother remembers listening to my uncles John and George, and my father, Nikitas, discuss how their father, Metrophanes, died while being operated on for a mastoid infection. The physician scraped out the infection and poured acid into his ear.

In the chapel of my mind, I meditate on my grandfather's death. I cannot help but wonder whether the power elite of Symi, which included his own relatives, wanted no more opposition to sending diver after diver on perilous, profitable missions into the Deep Blue. These are people who wanted no abolition of the deep-diving equipment. I recall Michael Foreys's once saying, "The Symiots could be violent in their business dealings." I am aware that *paranoia* is a Greek word; still the words of Foreys ring in my ear, as my thoughts flood to the ghost of Hamlet's father:

> . . . Sleeping within my orchard,
> My custom always of the afternoon,
> Upon my secure hour thy uncle stole
> With juice of cursed hebona in a vial.
> And in the porches of my ears did pour
> The leprous distilment, whose effect
> Holds such an enmity with blood of man
> That swift as quicksilver it courses through
> The natural gates and alleys of the body
> . . . .

Thus was I sleeping by a brother's hand
Of life, of crown, of queen at once dispatched.
—Shakespeare, *Hamlet* (1.5.59–67, 74–75)

Scripture tells us, "The truth shall set you free." In this life the truth cannot always be known. I will never know the truth, nor will the friends of Hristos Kontoyiannis.

A HUMAN PASSION FOR PEARLS

Live pearling in Australia was a risky business, with an appalling death toll. Japanese, Greek, and divers of other lineage died ghastly deaths in the presence of the wild beauty of Australia's northwest coast. At their website on the history of pearling in Australia, Western Fisheries reports that four cyclones caught the pearling fleet at sea between 1908 and 1935—with more than one hundred boats lost and nearly three hundred men killed. On so reading, my American New England mind turns to *Moby Dick*:

> By vast odds, the most terrific of all mortal disasters have immemorially and indiscriminately befallen tens and hundreds of thousands of those who have gone upon the waters.... Panting and snorting like a mad battle steed that has lost its rider, the masterless ocean overruns the globe.

The masterless ocean surrounds Australia. Where else in the world would a Prime Minister have been eaten by a shark? Diving for pearl oysters took place first in shallow waters but, in depressing parallel to sponge fishing, the diving moved to deeper and deeper water as the oyster beds were vandalized. The diving suit came into use in pearling as in sponge fishing to send divers into deeper water and to boost productivity. As off the coast of Libya or Corsica, divers were sent too deep or kept down too long for their skill or tolerance; or sometimes the interval between dives was too brief or the ascent too hurried. This time, the risk was driven by a human passion for pearls. Below is dialogue from a second clip of the Thirties' era Hollywood film shown on *Nova's* "The Perfect Pearl."

————:   Are you still set on my bringing you a pearl from the depths of the Indian Ocean?

————:   Yes . . . a big pearl, a really big pearl.

It is fascination with the sea that has led the Greeks so often to seek work on, under, or around the sea. Australia's vast coasts provided boundless opportunity.

An almost casual fascination with the sea can be found in the words of Nick Paspaley, who presides over a modern pearl culturing operation. The same words appear at the Paspaley Pearling Company's website. The overlay of the words, the glow they cast, their "orient," is all about fascination with the sea, family continuity, and a shared, treasured past. The words ring of *The Odyssey* itself. In his introduction to Robert Fagles's translation of *The Odyssey*, Bernard Knox gives us Webster's definition of the English word "odyssey": "a series of adventurous journeys usually marked by many changes of fortune." Here, then, is Nick Paspaley:

> Although my life stories cannot compare with the adventures of my father's times, I have lived exciting times during my life in the pearl industry. There have been many life threatening experiences with cyclones, sharks, crocodiles, not to forget the wild men! There have also been tragedies.

PEARL MAKING

For millennia pearls occurred only as rare, exquisite accidents of nature. Oysters are sessile creatures. They sit, feed, and grow. They love places where there are plenty of algae, and currents that will bring them their daily portion. It is true that they are better off if they tumble a bit in the surf, and so toughen and are kept clean of barnacles and other marine growth. They filter water to get algae cells. Sometimes the currents carry an odd food particle like a tiny shrimp or perhaps a piece of shell, coral, or grit that enters the oyster's shell. Usually, the oyster expels the irritant, but not always. Should the irritant lodge in its soft flesh, the oyster will cloak it in a membrane called a pearl sack. The pearl sack secretes nacre, the substance that forms the smooth lining of the shell, which we call mother-of-pearl. With time the irritant is coated with layers of calcium carbonate, becoming smooth, no longer irritating to the oyster's flesh. The pearl grows larger each year, its color varying with the color of the shell and sometimes with the mineral salts in the water. Pearls around the globe come in many hues: silver-white, gold, pinks, peacock blue, green, endless shades of gray, and black. By this last sentence I am reminded that the globe itself is like a pearl: the water planet as a pearl.

Fred Ward teaches us in his *National Geographic* article that "a single oyster can create pearls of different hue." As *Nova* reports, "Some pearls grow into irregular and sometimes fantastic forms called baroques. A baroque is formed when an oyster is unable to turn the foreign object inside its shell, causing the nacre to build up unevenly." Sometimes a half-dome forms, growing against the shell; such pearls are called "mabes" and are used in the making of pins and rings. Rarely in nature does one find a perfectly round pearl, but it was perfect rounds that Mikimoto was after as he worked to "culture" pearls. His goal was to cause oysters to grow pearls on demand, no longer to await the rare and exquisite accidents of nature. It was the ideas of Mikimoto and of other Japanese researchers that produced the first successful method for culturing perfect rounds. Over the years Mikimoto had tried inserting many different substances into the oyster to engender the formation of a pearl; but in the end, it was a bead made from a freshwater U.S. mussel that produced the pearl he wanted. What actually worked was when that bead was inserted into the reproductive organs of the oyster, together with a tiny bit of mantle tissue from another oyster. It is that bit of mantle tissue from another oyster that causes the oyster to form a pearl sack around the irritant bead and produce a pearl.

Mikimoto also developed methods for "farming" pearls. The methods were first used in Japan. Mikimoto had divers gather up wild Akoya oysters from the coastal areas of Japan. These were then "nucleated" in an "operation" in which irritant bead and mantle tissue were inserted. The Akoya oysters were then were put into cages and suspended from rafts in the coastal bays of Japan. There they grew until harvested after four years. Mikimoto sold these gems to the world, having convinced the world that there was no difference between a natural and a cultured pearl. Doubtless, in her graduation picture, my sister is wearing a strand of Mikimoto pearls.

The Japanese closely guarded their method of culturing pearls. Japanese workers were sworn to secrecy. Countries wishing to culture pearls had to hire Japanese technicians. But, as *Nova* reports, "Japan's pearling industry expanded beyond its borders to other Pacific shores in search of larger South Sea oysters."

Nicholas Paspaley became a pioneer, establishing his pearl farm together with Japanese and American partners. According to *Nova*, oysters were gathered in the wild and "then transported to sheltered bays and used as raw stocks to cultivate pearls." Japanese technicians were used and Japanese farming techniques employed. Although larger than the Akoya shells, Australian oyster shells were more easily stressed, and mortality rates ran high. When Nicholas Paspaley's son, Nick Paspaley, graduated from university and joined the family's pearl culturing business in 1969, he was sent out to assess the problems and make recommendations. He developed wholly new systems better suited to the Australian shell.

As Nick Paspaley described to *Nova*, "When I was diving, picking up pearl shells, I could see the difference immediately between the health of those shells and their appearance and the shells in the pearl farm situation." His goal was to keep all pearl shells in the healthy condition in which they were found in the wild. After ten years of experiments, he developed a bold solution, *Nova* informs us: he took the entire pearl culturing operation out to sea, away from the harbor where water "was becoming less pristine and overcrowding was a growing concern." As *Nova* adds, "this floating enterprise is a high-tech solution to the threat of oyster mortality. But it is a solution few can afford."

Operations are done under hygienic conditions, with antiseptics used to reduce the chance of infection—using methods developed by Paspaley and his technicians, *Nova* reports. Everything is done to keep the oyster contented. Time out of the water is kept to a minimum. After nucleation, the oysters are stored in tanks and then transported to underwater farms to recover from the operation. Every two weeks they are cleaned to keep them clear of marine growths that might carry disease or parasites; cages are turned regularly so pearls can develop evenly as they are coated with nacre to increase the oyster's chances of producing "a perfect round." After recovery, the oysters are moved to one of the Paspaley pearl farms. *Nova* visited a pearl farm in Talbot Bay, "nestled among the ancient cliffs of the Kimberley Coast" that is "home to 100,000 nucleated oysters." The Paspaley Pearling Company owns several pearl farms on the coast of northwest Australia between Broome in western Australia and the Coburg Peninsula in the Northern Territory, north of Darwin. After two years of nurturing care, the oysters are taken from the water so that pearls can be harvested. If the oyster produces a good quality pearl, it is immediately nucleated again. An oyster can produce up to four pearls in its lifetime, producing larger pearls as the oyster itself grows in size over time.

The production of pearls from the Australian shell, in a controlled manner, has only been possible, as Nick Paspaley writes, "for the last 30 years, and only been commercially viable in meaningful quantities for the past 15 years." It came about, as he adds, by "a major change to the Japanese farming methods, which the Australian industry had until that time adopted. These changes were radical but I'm pleased to say that the new techniques allowed us to produce the pearls we had all dreamed of. Now, the entire Australian pearling industry uses similar systems to the ones we pioneered more than 15 years ago."

According to Kyriacopoulos, Nick Paspaley "commissioned the first purpose-built fiberglass ship, invested in marine biology research into the oysters' high mortality rates, and eventually redesigned the company's processes, developing the successful Paspaley formula." The *Paspaley III* was added to a company fleet of more than sixty vessels, she reports. "Paspaley's output increased from an average annual harvest of 30,000 pearls to 300,000 in the first five years after the *Paspaley III* was introduced; now, the annual harvest yields over 500,000 pearls—with massive increase in quality," according to Kyriacopoulos. She describes the *Paspaley III* as "virtually a mobile intensive care unit."

Other non-Greek and Greek-Australians, of course, helped develop Australian pearl cultivation. Among those of Greek descent who played active, crucial roles in the development of Australian pearl cultivation are Denis George, born in Constantinople, who came to Australia in 1948 and made pearl cultivation his life's work, and Michael G. Kailis. Kailis was from Kastellorizo; Alexakis and Janiszewski describe him as "Western Australia's prawn-fishing magnate," who became involved in pearl cultivation in the late 1970s.

As Nick Paspaley writes at the company website, "I realized my goal of creating strands of exceptional size, and have added to that goal the standard of exceptional quality. . . . As a result, Paspaley Pearl strands can truly be called the most beautiful in the world."

Modern pearling does not have the dangers that pearling had in the early years; it is safer, more controlled. But luckily for the Greeks, scions of Odysseus, there is the sea and there are the cyclones: still the masterless ocean, "panting and snorting like a mad battle steed that has lost its rider." The sea willingly provides the Greeks with ample opportunity to display the poetics of manhood: courage, improvisation, and personal stylistic.

At the end of the *Nova* special, there is a remarkable scene showing Nick Paspaley out on the sea. The narrator speaks of how Australia's cultured pearl industry "continues to benefit from the luxury of largely unpolluted waters."

In Australia's still remote northern coast, pearl farmers can collect wild shells, but only with permits and quotas imposed, a policy established to maintain Australia's wild oyster beds as a sustainable resource; no vandalizing of the sea-bottom is allowed. In words that would surely please Ecumenical Patriarch Bartholomew, the "Green" Patriarch and spiritual leader to millions of Orthodox Christians, Nick Paspaley speaks:

> You're talking to a man who has done well out of this beautiful natural resource. Over the years I've been involved in hatcheries, with people's ideas of cultivating pearls in great big factories in Japan with controlled environments and all that sort of—all those ideas.
>
> It's the arrogance of man that makes him think, well, I can create this in a factory. Well, I doubt it, you know the only reason we have success with these is because we've got nature creating this. . . . We couldn't do this if we tried. In fact, the only problems that we ever have in our industry are the problems that we've created.

To the Orthodox Church, humankind has a theological obligation to preserve and protect the waters of the world, for it is only humankind's carelessness that has stripped God's creation of its original splendor. Perhaps this is the place, tearfully, to end the story of the Greek divers of the Aegean and to remind us all from whence came their glory and their bounty. In the words of Genesis:

"And the spirit of God swept over the face of the water."

nine

MOUSMOULO

It is a beautiful night in Rhodes, as if every summer night were not so in the Dodecanese. We are out walking at about 10 o'clock in the evening with my cousin Nikitas *Michalis* Kalafatas, the inverse of my name, Michalis *Nikitas* Kalafatas.

In Greek naming tradition the parents give the firstborn son, as his first name, the first name of the *father's father* and then give to all sons as middle name the first name of the *father*. Thus, the father and the son of Nikitas Michalis Kalafatas are *Michalis Nikitas Kalafatas*—my very name. A small pool of names swiftly permeates an island and binds distant cousins together. It is one of the ways in which the Greeks in remote islands have survived indeterminacy and foreign rule. Through four hundred years of slavery under the Ottoman Turks and occupations before and since, the Greeks held on by family and in-group. Tonight I feel comfortable beside Nikitas, and close to him. He is my third cousin once removed.

A light sailor's breeze blows in as we stroll along Mandraki harbor. It blows in across the Straits of Marmara, sliding in off the mountains of southwest Anatolia that roll eastward and rise to become the Hindu Kush in Pakistan and eventually the Himalayas. This is the same moonlit harbor that entranced Lawrence Durrell in his *Reflections on a Marine Venus*, the memoir of his postwar days in Rhodes with the British Army. Durrell had been sent to Rhodes to publish a free and democratic newspaper after decades of Italian and Nazi occupation. "In Rhodes the days drop as softly as fruit from trees," Durrell wrote. And so it felt tonight, as we meandered past the beautiful Old City built by the Crusaders, lit by floodlight and the reflected glow of brightly lit cruise ship after cruise ship heading out into the Aegean dark. Day after day, tourists debouch from these ships for twelve hours to visit the stone stanchions where once rested the feet of the Colossus of Rhodes as he stood astride Mandraki harbor, the Acropolis at Lindos, the Old City, or, of course—pleasing to my cousin the merchant—the shops of Rhodes that cater to the sunseekers of northern Europe. On the breast of the Colossus, I recall, was a mirror so large and bright that the distant approach of ships from Egypt was made visible to the inhabitants of Rhodes.

We are walking past a brace of sleek sailboats when Nikitas stops and says, "This is my boat." I didn't even know that he sailed, modest and reserved as he is. He confesses that he was the 1996 Dodecanese sailing champion and that two weeks ago he had won the Rhodes to Symi regatta. "I love your grandfather's poem, and I've read it three times," he says. "So, after I sailed into Symi harbor—and after all the other boats had arrived and assembled—I took the microphone and recite the last sixteen lines of the poem":

Oh beloved and renowned mother Symi,
  if only you were blessed with vineyards and fresh waters.
Though graced with boulders, you rejoice,
  full of good men of generous upbringing.
If only you had fruitful trees and land to cultivate,
  olive-groves to tend to in abundance.
You've never been empty or abandoned
  by those who emigrate to bitter lands.

A bell-of-stone, a net, the tools
of those aboard your boats.
Such is the trade of young and old
that Symiot men inherit.
We found no fields to cultivate.
In the sea's waves and depths we dive,
in sea we found our olive-groves
our gardens and our vineyards.
In eons to come this is our trade.

On his way to winning the Rhodes to Symi regatta, Nikitas Kalafatas (the name also of my father, son of the poet) had followed the identical course, Rhodes to Symi, that my grandfather Metrophanes Kalafatas had sailed in 1902 and that opens the Prologue to "Winter Dream." In the harbor of Symi, my grandfather's homeland, Nikitas—the victor—declaims the last sixteen lines of the poem. All of this happening five thousand miles from the hamlet outside Boston where my odyssey began.

Nikitas calls his sweet twenty-six-foot sailboat *Mousmoulo*, after a small yellow fruit that has the taste of a sweet peach. The stories in the Dodecanese, like the days, drop as softly as fruit from the trees.

MOTHER LIGHT

In early summer 1998 I received a call from organizers of Symi Festival '98 inviting me to speak at "Symiots of the Diaspora," a symposium of first-, second-, and *third*-generation Symiots living abroad. They would be returning to Symi to share, reconnect, and reenergize. "Another gift from my grandfather," I thought, "like the poem." The symposium would be one of sixty-five cultural events in music, theater, dance, poetry, and the like, at the Festival that was fast turning Symi into a summer arts magnet. Symi Festival had, in fact, just been placed among the *Kaleidoscope* cultural programs of the European Union— alongside Freiberg and Florence.

As I sat in the Old Dimarchion, where the symposium took place, I sensed deeply the world of arts and letters from which my grandfather emerged. Under the stars and amid the ghostly beauty of Symi's neoclassical architecture, I listened to the Greek Music State Orchestra perform a new composition by Stavros Xarchakos, inspired by the Aegean. I loved that the concert took place at Kampos, once a famed shipyard in the days when Symi craftsmen slipped five hundred new boats into the Aegean each year.

In that setting, with the ghost of my grandfather nearby, I realized something that should be of interest to Greeks everywhere in the diaspora—indeed that should be of interest to anyone of any ethnic group in diaspora. In any diaspora, those who return are often seen as returning to refuel and to reconnect to a lost past. They are seen as there to *take* something, not to give something. They might be seen as a source of political, financial, or emotional support. But I realized something quite different. When the Greeks left for America and Australia, when the Jews left Eastern Europe, when any group anywhere leaves for diaspora life, they leave with language, with culture, and most important, *with stories*. They leave with important history and stories that are part of the patrimony of their homeland, a patrimony that might be lost forever to their homeland. And so, often, they have history to give back, providing missing tiles in the mosaic. In returning to Symi with my grandfather's poem, I was returning part of the island's lost history, part of its patrimony. While there for the Festival, I spoke with my cousin on Rhodes, Nikitas Kalafatas, and my cousin on Symi, Michael Foreys, eighty-seven, a brilliant man who has lived virtually his entire life on Symi. I was able to tell both, with certitude, the name of their great great grandfather. And I gave them an important story to go with the name of the one person who joined us all, third cousins as we are. They lacked the name and the story despite their being scions of an old, distinguished family of the Dodecanese. *They* didn't know the name or story, *but I did*: I, a child of the diaspora, had a lost past to give back. It's important for Greeks in the diaspora— for everyone in diaspora—to know that sometimes they have a lost past to give back. They have history, too.

I learned something else. It's about *who is Greek*. George Papandreou, the Greek Foreign Minister, on Symi for a conference of Balkan ministers, graciously stopped by the Symposium to welcome us and to speak eloquently of his vision of Hellenism as a galaxy, with Greece just a somewhat larger star in that galaxy. But for me, "epiphany" came later, when an effervescent twenty-year-old student, Alexandros Baralis, a second-generation Symiakos from Marseilles, rose to say, to huge applause, *"If you feel Greek, you are Greek!"* That includes a third-generation Symiakos like me, living near Boston, and, of course, philhellenes everywhere.

In Greek, *Metrophanes* means "He who shines light on his mother." *"He who reveals his mother."* I am blessed to have the gift of this poem and to have my grandfather reveal to me—and now to others—his mother Symi and the largely lost world in which he lived.

ten

THE PURLOINED LETTER

*Purloin, v. Forms: 5-6 perloyn(e, 5-7 purloyn(e, (5 pourloigne), 7 purloine, 6-
purloin, 6. [a. AF. purloigner = OF. porloigner, -lognier, -lunier, purloigner,
-luignier, -luinier, later pourloign(i)er, -longnier, f. por-, pur-: -L. pro + loing,
loin: -L. longe far; hence, "to put far off or far away, to put away, do away
with." The sense "make away with, steal" appears to be of English development.*

—*Oxford English Dictionary*

What follows is a letter that I imagine Anastasia, wife of the poet and
my grandmother, wrote to my older brother Metrofanis on the night
she died. Anastasia, "the Resurrection," was born on the island of
Rhodes in 1868; she died on a cold, rain-swept night in the winter of
1941 at my parent's home in Cambridge, Massachusetts, nine years
after emigrating to the United States.

For reasons made clear in the letter, Anastasia had an especially
close relationship with my brother, who was four when she died. I was
born in 1943 and never knew my grandmother.

To my mind the letter is so real that it must have existed: It clarifies
all I desired so passionately to know. In the Latin and French meaning
of the word, it was purloined: it was "put far off, put far away, done
away with." It was removed from our midst. The following is an explanation of what I believe happened to the letter.

A harried Greek physician, Dr. Speare, arrived at my parents' home
that night as my grandmother's condition worsened. Shortly after his
arrival, Dr. Speare pronounced Anastasia dead, at age seventy-two, of
Bright's Disease. With calls still to make, other Greek immigrant

homes to visit, the doctor gathered up his bag and belongings and rushed out into the Cambridge night. Inadvertently, he had picked up my grandmother's letter. As he neared his car, the letter fell away from his hands and onto the soaked street. In the driving rain the ink was washed away, and with it my grandmother's final words to the world.

January 9, 1941

Beloved Metrofani,

Where does the flame go when the candle is blown out?

Within hours I will find out. Death is near, the end upon me. I have learned not to fear death because, if you do not fear your own death, you fear nothing at all. When I die, Metrofani, know that I will not be far. The dead are not gone. They are just invisible. That's why they come to you so easily in dream and thought.

I cried when you left tonight because I could not read to you— as I do every night. The pain was too great. Forgive me. The pain is less, and so I write of your grandfather. When you are older, you will read this letter and know the glory of the name you carry.

For me Metrophanes is forever young. He died at thirty-eight.

He had a steady friendship with the friendship of beauty and an intractable hatred toward self-gain. He was an authentic philopatrist—a man who loved his country—and good person. His works were exceptional works of praise as are the works of the Holy Script and the Holy Bible.

To him the hand of the stranger was the hand of God. He dressed the naked, ministered to the ill, took in the foreigners and gave them blessings. When he was hungry, his eye did not turn; when he was thirsty, his aim was steady. He lent to God each day without tiring, and after all this he gave his soul back to the One who made it.

When we met, I was just a girl from Embona, a village on the roof-top of Rhodes—a place of cool sea breezes and beautiful vineyards, famous for the folk-dancing of its beautiful girls in colorful costumes—embroidered, silk-finished dresses, bright sashes, and red brocade head-scarfs tied so that the shape of a rose appeared at the side of your head. I was one of those girls. If you want to know how I looked then, look at your cousin Anastasia, my granddaughter, who has my name. In her beautiful fine features I see myself as a girl. Bright eyes I had—brown and gold, with flecks of green, and your grandfather fell in love with me. Two souls, one heart.

I loved to learn; and your grandfather pulled back a curtain, and there I saw a world I never knew, of books and poems and passion. Though he died young, we were wed for eternity by our love and by the power of The Word. "In the beginning was The Word," the Bible says, but so it is in the end. The Word joins us all, as my soul shall be joined to yours, Metrofani, for all-time through the stories that I read to you.

The world of the past is gone now, but I see it still even as the White Wings of Death are about to scatter my days. Your grandfather was born on Symi—from ancient times a place of sails and flashing oars. The Symiots were great travelers and traders; the main harbor of Symi a babel of languages—Greek, Turkish, Italian, Arabic, Persian, French, Russian, and English.

The Kalafatas family was an old Symiot family. Metrophanes' father John, brother to Stamatis—Mayor of Symi—took two great sailing ships into the Black Sea with sons George and Nikitas on board. A storm broke both ships and sank them. George and Nikitas drowned. John and a few others survived, swimming twenty-four hours to the coast of Bulgaria. So much time passed before they returned to Symi that all were believed dead. The sea that feeds the Symiots also eats them.

John's wife promised God that, should her husband survive, their next-born son would serve the Church. They named him Metrophanes, after the first Patriarch of Contantinople—one of the great names in Orthodox Christianity. As a young man, they sent him to the seminary on the island of Patmos, where Saint John heard the word of God and wrote the Book of the Apocalypse. They expected your grandfather to become a priest and a Church leader.

But Metrophanes never found God in the seminary. He found God in the eyes of the children he taught, in the hand of the stranger, in the Power of the Word. He found God when he sailed, in the timeless winds of the Aegean and Mediterranean— in the Levanter, the Meltemi, and the Sirocco. Your grandfather was poetry-in-sail, Metrofani, as he was in Word. To me he has been Forever Young.

Your grandfather climbed out a window of the seminary and fled, abandoning the Church forever. He became a teacher, school principal, and poet. He loved the writers of antiquity and of the Cretan renaissance, like Vitzentzos Kornaros, who wrote "Erotocritos," a great love poem that I hope, Metrofani, you will one day read. Poetry was so loved in the Aegean that it was sold there on the streets of the islands.

Your grandfather was right to leave the Church. Too many lead the life expected of them. It is better to follow the light of your own nature. Listen to your heart always; it knows all things. In your heart, truly, you will find a lantern that can light the way.

I know that I worried too much over you. But I was an old woman who had lost her husband Metrophanes when he was young and your little cousin Metrofanis, his namesake, when he was five. That's why I fussed so over you. I know that you will grow to be great and strong. I so loved holding my Metrofani. Holding a child is a second encounter with God. Your cousin died before I came to this country, but I loved him nonetheless. When I die, as I asked, I will be buried in the same grave with little Metrofani; our names on the gravestone together, Anastasia and Metrofanis, a familiar coupling of names to me, again at long last.

There is an Arab saying: "God created the desert so that man could appreciate the date trees." And so it is that God created death so that life itself will be more precious.

When you feel the gentle summer breeze on your cheeks, Metrofani, it will be my kisses. When the snow falls softly on your shoulders, it will be the loving touch of your grandfather. We will try to help you in your life. The dead are not altogether powerless.

I see still through the mists of memory: the blue-green sea, the dapple of the sun, children napping in the heat of the afternoon, cool in our little home in Lahania; your grandfather sitting, writing his poems at the table by the open window—the curtain blown by the sea-winds that were his muses. On them the spicy smell of wild herbs and the wood forests of Anatolia, and always the song of the cicadas.

Kiss your little sister, Fotini, for me, and all of your cousins: Nicholas, Anastasia, Vasiliki, Panagiotis, and Demetra. Tell them that, for all time, their yiayia and papou will inhabit the air around them.

God calls us one by one to the Eternal Shore.

Me Agapi,

Your Yiayia, Anastasia

eleven

"WINTER DREAM"

by
Metrophanes I. Kalafatas

Rendered into English by the poet Olga Broumas

PART A

Prologue

I, the composer of this poem, Metrophanes I. Kalafatas, having arrived by sea to Lahanas of Rhodes, returning to my homeland Symi in my small boat around the twentieth of April of the year 1902, found myself outside the cafe of Xenophon A. Lourtesi. Well-docked, and fatigued from seafaring, I sat for a small rest upon the stern. I could also see my compatriots traversing the promontory on the shore.

Watching all this time, I saw many of them whisper, both on the street and in the cafe. These whispers communicated certain common concerns which, I surmised after listening, praised God. I approached some friends and, with great surprise, learned the reason for their praises. I heard that these whispers rose from certain news announcing the abolition of the deep sea diving gear—the helmet, body suit, and tank. And so my soul overflowed with joy, hearing this information from my friends. And when, after precise inquiry and with a boiling wish to have the news confirmed, I was unable to discover its foundation and source, I felt an ineffable sorrow in my deepest innerfold and tasted indescribable bitterness; and I remained, all that day as well as the next, sorrowful, grim and thoughtful.

Suffering this position and troubled by thoughts until nightfall, I plunged into sleep wherein a woman appeared to me in dream who clarified all I desired so passionately to know.

And, wanting to manifest all this, I composed the following versification, by which I both proclaim the state of my country and broadcast the failings of the deep sea diving gear. Due to the large range of the dream, I called this poem Winter Dream.

WINTER DREAM

Which syllables today resound
　　frequently praising God in my ears?
What source, what cause
　　of constant whispers in cafes?
So many people here and there
　　repeating conversations, why?
I thought that it must be great news
　　which I prepared to seek.
I stood and thought and, wondering,
　　I could not learn the reason.
My brow was dark, my friends,
　　night came. I lay down brooding,
my head leaned on my arm.
　　Tired, I touched my pillow
and barely asleep saw in my dream
　　a woman, easy to look upon,
upright in mourning,
　　handsome, vibrant, good, robust,
and older.
　　I greeted her and brought a stool.
Please sit I said, dear lady.
　　Who are you, where from, what do you seek,

coming to visit? Are you a traveler?
  Or lost and seeking guidance
or my help?
  Please sit and tell me. If I can help
you'll find me ready.
  Immediately her eyes released
rivers of tears.
  Disturbed, weeping and whispering,
she starts to speak:
  I'm neither lost nor passing by,
I am your mother Symi.
  I know your joy in serving your land,
how you detest connivance.
  I see you praise me in your poems,
call me the Muses' mother,
  so I appear with a message
by which your questions will be solved.
  My message concerns serving your land,
the common life of divers.
  Be careful, listen well
to what I say and make it known.
  The diving gear is old and soon will cease,
the divers will again be strong,
  the time has come, the end is near,
the diving stone will rule once more.
  The diving gear has weakened,
the naked dive will bloom again,
  our forefathers' art will flower.
Long live the first technique!
  The murderous gear wounds my liver.
I hate it, the disgusting thing,
  as much as the devil's legions,
as much as the head of Gorgon and Medusa,
  the venomous viper's hiss.
The gear's repulsive shape
  brings frigid horror to my limbs.
Once they were turned to stone by Medusa,

now by the ugly Helmet!
It took my children by drowning,
    and sent vigorous youths to Hades,
it stole the offspring and the mates
    of young mothers and fathers
who grieve until today.
    Besides the ones it sent
so early to their grave,
    many unburied dead survive
to walk the markets,
    poisoned by the helmet's drink.
Lame, frightened, miserable,
    the poor suffer its tyranny,
orphans beg in the streets.
    The diving bosses broke the law,
their gear causes this torment,
    this scourging poverty.
The diving gear broke down the guilds,
    replaced by ragged paupers.
House painters idle, tailors too,
    the European dress now reigns,
our forefathers' abolished.
    Miserable families in droves
have gone to live in exile.
    Counting the lame, the dead, the émigrés,
the city mourns a third of its people.
    Harm to the spirit and the flesh
without one act
    of charity or grace.
Our people destroyed
    by its ways,
honor and pride are lost,
    self-interest glories in their place.
There are no ethics, arrogance rules,
    pouring out of those Helmets.
The diving bosses are the cause
    of this barbaric shamelessness.

My own eyes saw a merchant
    frequent these villains, sit with them
at dominoes and cards,
    blacken his honor and his name
to gain advantage for his gear,
    till frequency turned to arrogance
and arrogance became habit.
    These are the virtues of the suit
and this its common anguish.
    Beware its ruthless crudity,
its heartless willful evil.
    They hound and grieve me as I watch
my citizens' indifference.
    In times of idolatry
when kings were harsh
    and forced the faithful to worship
idols and violent gods,
    our holy martyrs suffered death
to shore the faith and witness the true god.
    Eager and resolute, they spilled their blood,
established true religion,
    and greatly shamed idolatry.
Thus they prevailed against the flowing blood
    and gave us centuries of calm.
I never hoped new trials would return.
    The pious then were butchered for the Church,
the faith and true religion,
    not for vile earnings and for greed
as now for suits and helmets.
    Many die without justice
and many walk the markets lame.
    Our merchants seeing them turn deaf,
scramble to their cashiers
    to earn high yields on their returns.
They are the bitter enemies of their true duty.
    With triple usury they loan,
and seal their ears if people perish.

With all their powers they should try
to cast off the gear's existence,
   to see it as a guillotine
and stone it down,
   united with widows and orphans.
But while others seek to throw it out,
   our merchants try to shore it.
Seeking to better their accounts
   they shamelessly crowd graveyards.
And finally, my child, I say
   the suits and helmets douse my soul
with rivers of snake venom.
   So let me tell you an account
of all they poured upon my head.

φ

One time the people tried to break the gear
before its strength gained on the land,
   before its atrocities prevailed,
its wings spread like today.
   President of the senate then
was Stamatis Kalafatas,
   old in age,
a wise man faithful to the senate.
   He governed fairly,
suffered for his land and was imprisoned.
   He stood up for the common good,
suffered the prisons of Rhodes and Kos,
   yet returned to public office.
The crowd had gathered of one mind,
   men, women, children in agreement,
swarming the shore like angry bees,
   roads full of men and boys.
A roar was heard in the cafes,
   let's break the gear in storage!
They came to Kalafatas for permission

to break the gear and rescue
their true livelihood.
Blessed be his name, he tried to make them pause
and counseled them to change their minds.
He said, this action is not good,
the senate will pay the cost.
They were unyielding, very wild,
railing against the gear like rabid wolves.
The horde didn't listen to the wise
counsel of old Kalafatas,
but lashed out and took him in their hands,
and carried him to the storehouse in mid-air.
Set next to helmets and to suits
against his will, he touched the gear.
And then the throng descended,
and in five minutes
destroyed breathing tubes and suits.
The people meant no crime.
They only meant to break the gear
and pay for it, but not buy more.
Indeed, the common bank did pay,
but owners did the opposite.
They took the gold for better gear,
a new invention more refined.
And ever since they flogged the town,
and fanned the flame beneath it,
became destroyers of the land,
took wages from the devil.
And I was found between the dire
Scylla and Charybdis,
so take note my child and clearly proclaim,
of all I've narrated leave nothing unsaid,
detail it in your verse.
Wishing to quench the fire in my soul,
again I tell my story.
It's proper that I praise and bless.
It is a pressing duty

to support
    all those distinguished in their country's noble acts,
whose rest is their benevolence.
    I narrated all the grief
of good and ill repute.
    You heard how the gear has saddened me
and even now I dress in black.
    I cannot bear disgraceful acts
nor silence about charities.
    And now I'll tell the joyous
and be the owner of true bliss.
    Gifted with priceless goods I was,
and wealthy in all I needed.
    I am surrounded by safe ports
and greatly praised by sailors.
    To the northeast of my island
Pedi and Aigialos rule over all.
    All boats are harbored there,
others are moored ashore.
    From Kampos and Aigialos ships sail
perfected by shipbuilders.
    Another winter port to the southwest
has always been famous for its length.
    The Panormitis monastery
holds its feast to high praise here.
    To my north, St. Aimilianos, another safe port,
surrounded by piers and a domed church
    for fishermen and carpenters, a serene place.
As for religion
    I boast of many beautiful
large churches endowed by patriots
    and richly ornamented
with precious vessels, silver lamps,
    silver and gold plated icons.
Fourteen large parishes I am
    and just as many churches.
Small monasteries populate the peaks

full of the monks to rule them.
Often and tirelessly they work
   to build cells and arenas,
and many orchards do they tend,
   rejoicing their viewers.
Enchanted views becalm my ills—
   the monastery-studded hills
existing full of joy
   please me and give me power to speak on:
For every church
   I have a preacher who can preach
Theology on Sundays,
   who goes in turn to parishes
and floods their gentle hearts with gifts.
   Who irrigates all thirsting hearts
with God and feeds the hungry
   with sky's own bread.
The barren fields he tries to till
   the fruitless trees to berry.
I tell no lie—God's honor seeds
   and fruits good deeds.
Goodness abounds and is made act,
   the sky's grape pressed to wine.
Their pleasure in God so sweetens me
   because above all mercy flows.
So call me joyful today
   and I'll sing other virtues.
I have professors, doctors, drugs,
   and pharmacists who make them,
a library and schools and girls
   in girl-schools with their teachers.
So all poor parents educate
   their children without cost,
and can be healed back from disease,
   medicine being free.
I'm grateful to my offspring, I,
   their mother and their country,

who treat each other with such grace.
   Who turn to wisdom with hot zeal
whose love burns for more learning,
   whose luck brought them a great man,
a scholar, learned as he could be,
   Schoolmaster Peridis now deceased
whose forty years taught and nursed
   my children with the spirits'
higher milk. Who spread the lights of learning
   forty times, the value of virtue and good will,
who aptly raised the social core,
   whose trusted friend was mercy.
After his life fulfilled each post
   by pleasing God, his blissful soul
rose to the sky, and as it did
   the senate richly honored him
in funeral and graveside—
   great praises and tall tombstone rose.
Today without a doubt he drinks in Paradise
   unspoiled beauty,
joyful with grace. I leave him there
   the teacher George Peridis,
and come now to his eminence,
   Michael Petrides.
I say the deeds of this late man,
   true patriot, good citizen,
were masterpieces I must praise,
   deeds of the Gospel and the Holy Scripts.
   The hungry he did not ignore
nor did he miss the thirsty—
   in short, to any need he came across
he never answered "no."
   He dressed the nude, consoled the ill,
gathered and almed the stranger,
   he helped to wed the young and poor,
the girls orphaned of fathers,

was firm in friendship to all good,
and fiercely loathed the stingy.
  He lent himself to God each day and then,
his soul was the Creator's.
  He tasted all the earthly goods
now he partakes of Heaven.
  And many buildings are now known
commonly as Petridia:
  the clock, the school, the modern roads,
erected and funded by his kin
  to please the souls of everyone,
his memory eternal.
  The goodness of these citizens I spoke of
somewhat briefly.
  I spoke in truth without a lie
I should say more but time goes by—
  I turn to the bloodthirsty gear,
its abolition and its death,
  the detailed cause of whispered talk
in the cafes—the syllables
  that echoed in your ears,
uttered by your compatriots in praise
  of God.
Be careful now to keep my words,
  engrave them in your heart:
what evil weighs upon our necks
  flows from our crimes and sins,
as now the helmet on our heads
  is God's punishing whip.
But, forced on us against the law
  and all the Sultan's orders,
even God the all-merciful
  began so to despise it
that, as his angel, sent a man
  guileless and full of spirit,
Flegel by name and Russian-born,

in whom I recognized a kind,
masterful benefactor.

Blessed more than once he reached our shores,
studied and learned our torments,

and was so moved by the machine's
criminal miserable results,

he undertook himself the task
to practice good and undo harm.

He gave it all his power,
spent without mercy his own funds,

coming and going first to France
and Italy in tandem,

and then to Crete to meet success
and leave again for Cyprus,

where he found England willingly
coming to our defense.

From there to Egypt without rest
where he delayed Mandroucha.

He wastes no time in laziness,
from there he sails to Samos,

who also swore to ban the gear,
hating its very sight.

And part of Syria stayed free,
Karman, and Asia Minor.

May god of Goodness will him grace,
and generous Flegel feel it,

and reach Constantinopolis
to smite the rabid tiger.

I too was grateful for his deeds,
brave acts, and wealth of virtues.

No gift too large to honor him,
a statue I must raise,

bearing the sign: MAN OF GREAT FAME
FLEGEL WHO FREED our homeland SYMI.

But my daughter, the Elders' Senate, too
suffers from penury,

worn down by debt, she cannot pay
her own clerks' wage.
   They met in public to decide .
what actions might relieve her
   or what inventions raise receipts
and as one body turned their eyes
   toward Attaleia first.
Enough my child, what I've portrayed
   so far of rights and wrongs,
make them well-known to young and old,
   and waking, forget nothing.
And I believe that from now on
   my torments will be stilled.
And all at once invisible
   she vanished from my side.
I woke at dawn, shrouded in sleep
   and sunk into broad thought.
I thought I shouldn't waste my time
   And took up pen and paper.
At Mother Symi's fierce command,
   I speak to all our land.
So did you hear, listen well,
   good citizens, brave fishermen, and divers,
about our faithful friend
   and all his work,
traveling with such zeal?
   Let us be grateful, Symiots,
honor him as an earthly God,
   and to God also raise a hymn
of praise and celebration
   at our rebirth,
and mark God's coming to our aid
   with gratitude let's shout:
Long life to our rebirth!

Continuation of the previous, to the second
abolition of the gear in the year
1903 by our ruler
Sultan Abdul Hamid Han the Second.

We praise his Highness our Ruler with pure hearts,
with hymns and adorations,
    his good will abolished the machines
and sent them from our land.
    Untouched they stayed, idle from work,
in Turkey's seas and shores.
    Long life we wish our Ruler's Heart,
Sultan Abdul Hamid,
    inspired by God to ban the gear
and punish all its murders.
    In 1903 he did decree
against such gear in Turkey,
    and sent them as far as Spain.
We pray God grace our honored Flegel
    with health and a long life,
and all in turn should honor,
    respect, and thank him.
He never rests, ceaselessly tries,
    his mortal end pursues him.
He made it his goal to shut down Hades,
    revenge Ajax and Minos,
who took the murdered souls
    the slimy gear had threshed.
He went as on a holy trail,
    returning mercy when his gut was stung.
He ran to Athens to convince
    the Greeks to join against them.
We hope with God that he'll succeed,
    and wait for his good news.
He bravely fought against the gear,
    Islanders, sing his praises.
He humbled the gear

and proved their captains shameless,
though some quick minds with energy
were able to conceive
of ways to heal the helmet's wounds.
They did not profit from the gear,
and they deserve our praise.

END OF PART A

PART B

Prologue

Word having spread in the year 1883, that the Ottoman empire had
issued a decree to ban the machine-diving trade, their owners and
middlemen conspired by bribery to keep it secret, and thus avoid a
stoppage in their work.
The wretched divers, who worked hard fighting the tides and storms,
would fail due to the gear, which to this day exists. They cursed their
fate that granted them this trade, to daily risk their lives for just their
bread.
And here, to make this story more substantial, I animate the boat,
which was named by our ancestors "vessel"; and which, seeing their
daily trials, begins to console them as follows.

Dialogue of Divers and Vessel in the Year 1883

The Vessel to the Divers

What's wrong, my men, what is your gloom,
your brooks of bubbling tears,
what sorrow took your reasoning,

I know the cause but where to start,
what speech use to console you?
  Incurable your suffering,
no herbs can soothe your wound.
  Divers, your fate has worn you out,
swabbers are now mechanics.

The Divers

Who gave you mind to speak to us,
  inanimate, deaf thing, try to console us?
On you the suits, on you the tubes,
  the bronze shoes on your decks,
who speak with us and ask us now
  to share in our disaster.

The Vessel

If as you say inanimate, how can I ask them questions
  after they mount my engine?
Speechless, inanimate, but by God's care
  I too was built by Helias on the field,
God blessed and charged me always
  to be with you sponge-divers.
What profit do I see from them,
  I can't bear more, my very bow
they turn to a latrine.
  They stink my guts, festoon my sides,
torture me by steam-engines.
  My tears flow to pierce my breast,
my innards boil and spark.
  Once I had only ablest young
craftsmen to use and run me.
  They'd rise at dawn to spread my sails,
I was a sea-bird trailing
  my belly proud, skimming the waves

with bold, bright, many-colored paints,
   adorned like a true bride.
Now forced by engine, my life drains,
   I cannot even breathe.
They too paint colors on my skin,
   then overload my body.
Instead of food for seven souls,
   they weigh me down with twenty,
and cram my deck with furnishings:
   upon my breast a pivot with great wheels
turns me a frightful sight.
   My swiftness cut, my power lost,
I suffer my life's end.
   Instead of stripping when they work,
they don waterproof dress,
   one suit entire shaped like man,
impermeable to water.
   Astride a chair they dress him up,
with screws they seal his body,
   lead on his shoulders, heavy shoes,
upon his head the helmet.
   A ladder's tied from gutter to the sea
to aid in his descent.
   Soon as he's dressed, two strong young lads
begin to turn the wheel.
   And through its axis turning hard
a long tube called markoutsi
   conveys air to the man who walks
a long time picking sponges.
   Those who would dive inside the suits
are labeled the Mechanics,
   and carry on with unheard pride
when first donning the helmet,
   as if it were an olive wreath.
They put on airs, look down their nose—
   look close: they piss their trousers.
They come on two legs, leave on three,

all strength loosened by water.
Wild olive-limbs they turn to legs—
    it seems their own won't do.
This is their profit and their growth,
    and when they die their alms
are the cost of burial.
    They stroll in rich pants, velvet vests,
then leave them to be auctioned.
    But now they're fixed, the swine-herd thieves,
the tricksters, the hen-roosters.
    Thanks to their pride, their stealing's stopped,
their trickery diminished.
    No hen would roost inside her coop,
no rooster crow at daybreak.
    They too have peace now, and the poor
pigs can rejoice:
    their meat is sold at five per weight,
or hawked in the street for four,
    where once they demanded and they got
six piasters as a favor—
    the thieves had so thinned out the herds.
Now they dress Western like the Franks,
    they even wear gold chains.
They want their wives addressed Madame,
    no thought that it's all foreign.
Then their poor widows tear their hair,
    forget the new, put on the old,
and start to stitch sad dirges
    to rip apart the very heart
of anyone who hears.
    Morning and night you hear them weep
until your entrails seethe.

Widows' Laments

All eyes are dry yet mine still flow,
    tears pierce my breast and drench my heart.

Where is my precious hyacinth, my flower of March?
   The diving gear devoured it.
I turn and look toward the door,
   expect you to appear,
open our wooden chest, put on a shirt.
   In Hades you lie, in Haros' gardens,
and I still ask if you've been seen
   down near the cafes.

☩

(continuation of vessel's narration)

But many beautiful young men are lost,
   hale and strong as lions.
They end up beggars, impotent,
   miserable, awful, they walk the streets.
Happy the dead,
   who suffer no more trouble.
Happier even if buried on land,
   their funeral in order.
Many who die upon my deck
   are happy to rest in soil.
So many corpses piled with rocks,
   some thrown to sea unwilling.
Now, they all say, all this will stop,
   ordered by Constantinople.
On this November all will cease,
   fire will melt their bronze and lead.
You too rejoice, no more grief—
   pour wine, embrace, get drunk.
Enjoy well our freedom's grace,
   because it's true and doubtless.

The Divers to the Vessel

My little boat of human speech,
   and beautifully painted,

crafted by Zaharias' Yannios
    to bear well the North wind,
where did you learn the great good news
    you tell as if just coming
back from the King?
    If this is true, the gear will cease,
your nails turn gold and silver,
    your sails to silk, your ropes to steel,
no engine nor its shame.
Flag on your mast, sign on your prow,
    forget, my boat, your sorrow.
Joyful inscriptions will announce
"God give the Sultan years."
    We'll write *Aphrodite* at your eyes.
Seeing the words the gear will freak.

Vessel

Enough, be still, you wretched ones,
    I don't want more expenses.
Stop bringing me human remains
    to carry down to Hades.
I don't want their groans, their cries, their tears,
    their piss staining their clothes,
their stinking cave beneath my prow,
    their bodies rubbed with camphor.
The captains turn to murderers:
    In known bad waters
they order them to dive.
    Though orders came to us last March,
they've been kept under cover,
    so that the Symiots might sail,
their diving not prevented.
    But five or six spongers heard of it
and argued with the captains,
    and all the women of the town

rushed to the shore with wooden clubs,
    as if possessed by demons.
They rushed the town hall at Kaimak
    and stood on the stairs demanding reasons,
and forced Benyamin and Katrion,
    along with other merchants,
back to their house.
No water would they let them drink
    till they produced the orders
in plain for all to see.
Violent and patient they stood firm,
    exposed the scheming secrets
and Kaimak-bey promised them
    at last, to earn their quiet,
to quit the machines and so they left,
    and wait unto this day
demanding that the diving cease.

Coda: On the Divers' Sponge-Gathering Craft and Their Manner of Work

A lot of people want to learn
how divers dive into the deep,
    and ask with great desire
to know about sponge harvests.
    First they'll decide to go to sea,
then the best five are chosen,
    these five then choose another two,
making the boat's crew seven.
    They then stock up on rope and food,
and sail where God instructs them.
    And having sailed, seen off by God,
reach an agreed-on spot.
    There, they prepare the sponging gear,
tools they will use in common.
    Our old ancestors, to sink deep

beneath the waves and currents,
    a stone invented, white, oblique,
tied to a thin rope through its core.
    The Bellstone, as today it's known,
by which to plumb the deep.
Hugging it tightly divers sink,
    steering by underwater leaps,
alighting where they want.
    Having prepared exactly so,
and ready now to venture,
    they wake at dawn, their bedding store
along the ship's sharp corners,
    and wash their face and cross themselves,
call God their only helper,
    who instantly heals the open wound,
protects from any danger.
    After this call they sit at stern,
dipping their bread in coffee.
    Then they set out to tack their sails,
coursing toward their work.
    Finding a rock ledge they decide
to drop the iron anchor—
    when iron holds to rock it needs
men of strong will and courage.
    Having decided they disrobe,
call again God most highest,
    God omnipresent, God of all,
save, guard the human race,
    protect your hands' creation,
who bow beneath your feet.
    And naked now he grips the stone,
his sack hung round his chest.
    His sack is strong, webbed of tough string
to wood or iron ring,
    hung from his neck, tied to his waist,
for the uprooted crop:

Adriatic sponge and light-winged sponge.
This sack we know as Snare.
   He draws his inbreath with command,
and plunges like a sea-bird,
   the bellstone firmly in his hands
until he touches rock.
   His left hand leans the bellstone by
and, crouching, feels for sponges.
   He leaves the bellstone if he finds
good cutting place, uprooting
   as many as will fill his sack.
Two guards stand ready on the prow,
   tied to him by long rope.
His inbreath gone, he tugs the rope,
   and feeling it they raise him—
these guards are known as Oars.
   If either Oar suffers a lapse
of his complete attention,
   the diver suffers too.
And if the lapse becomes too long,
   he bids his health farewell.
But the two Oarsmen keep their heads
   and stand with full attention.
The divers tangle in wild plants,
   suffering pain and damage
as piercing rocks puncture deep wounds.
   They feel no pain at seafloor.
They feel it when they plunge back up
   and wipe dry with their sheet—
harrowing pain, unbearable
   throbbing the heart's own branches
Of all the damage there is one
   that causes great misfortune,
they call it Filth. It has its root
   sunk deep under some sponges.
If it's uprooted whole, intact,

it's harmless but if crushed
and touched or badly handled,
　　not even linseed oil and flax
will offer easy cure.
The diver needs razors, a strict fast,
　　in pain and tears for his health.
Wanting to give my listeners
　　details about the craft
and all the divers' obstacles,
　　I'm forced to write its perils
from which they suffer from the start:
　　When they set out to first undress,
They must shield from the sun.
　　Then in the spot they call the works,　.
they hazard a few dives
　　until they come up with a sponge.
First sponge in hand, they make a cross
　　upon the ship, this custom
they call Crossing.
　　Then raise a flag atop the mast,
reach for some food and drink,
　　and bless the work to start.
The days are full of trials.
　　Throughout the heat exhausts them,
then the cold
　　from which there is no pause.
They burn in sun, shiver in wind,
　　have headache every day,
and helpless in the summer sun,
　　their whole skin sears and burns.
Blisters fill up and then they break,
　　incurable if left exposed,
and they can't bear even a shirt,
　　nor touch their backs to mattress,
nor can they lie down on their side,
　　but only on the belly

earn precious comfort and some rest.
 Each dive gambles their ears,
which ring with pain and often burst,
 leaving them with insomnia
amidst the pain and torture.
 To guard against this they have found
small ways to ease misfortune:
 They hold their nose for their descent,
two three four times then sink.
 If they don't know about this trick,
they come back up midway,
 spit blood and some are scared
so much they leave the trade
 until their membranes heal.
Before they learn the craft,
 all aspects of their being
suffer such pain.
 These are the Passions of the dive,
the Symiots' craft and symptoms.
 They leave the island late
in April, some in May,
 and through September suffer,
constant as martyrs of the Lord.
Oh beloved and renowned mother Symi,
 if only you were blessed with vineyards and fresh waters.
Though graced with boulders, you rejoice,
 full of good men of generous upbringing.
If only you had fruitful trees and land to cultivate,
 olive-groves to tend to in abundance.
You've never been empty or abandoned
 by those who emigrate to bitter lands.
A bell-of-stone, a net, the tools
 of those aboard your boats.
Such is the trade of young and old
 that Symiot men inherit.
We found no fields to cultivate.

In the sea's waves and depths we dive,
in sea we found our olive-groves
our gardens and our vineyards.
In eons to come this is our trade.

THE END

The present poem, having been written at the end of the year 1903 by our ever-remembered father, Metrophanes I. Kalafatas, had remained unpublished at the sudden death of its composer on the 9th of March, 1904.

Now that we, his sons, are men, and that the name of the Dodecanese is universally known for its freedom fight against the Italians, we have considered it our duty to print this book, both to acquaint the public with the life and customs of our island, and as eternal memorial to its composer's soul.

We remain respectfully,
Ioannis, Georgios, Nikitas M. Kalafatas

Boston 7> 20th of June, 1919

twelve

KHEIMERINOS ONEIROS

ΜΗΤΡΟΦΑΝΟΥΣ Ι. ΚΑΛΑΦΑΤΑ
ΕΚ ΣΥΜΗΣ   1903

ΧΕΙΜΕΡΙΝΟΣ
ΟΝΕΙΡΟΣ

ΗΤΟΙ

ΣΚΗΝΑΙ ΑΠΟ ΤΑ ΔΩΔΕΚΑΝΗΣΑ

ΜΕΡΟΣ Α

ΑΙ ΠΡΟΣΠΑΘΕΙΑΙ ΠΡΟΣ
ΚΑΤΑΡΓΗΣΙΝ ΤΩΝ ΣΚΑΦΑΝΔΡΩΝ

(*Εἶδος ἐπικινδύνου σπογγαλιευτικοῦ πλοίου*)

ΜΕΡΟΣ Β

ΠΩΣ ΕΡΓΑΖΟΝΤΑΙ ΕΙΣ ΤΗΝ ΣΠΟΓΓΟΑΛΙΕΙΑΝ

ΥΠΟ ΤΗΝ ΘΑΛΑΣΣΑΝ

ΟΛΟΚΛΗΡΟΣ ΙΣΤΟΡΙΑ ΕΙΣ ΕΝ ΠΟΙΗΜΑ

ΕΚΔΟΤΑΙ
ΙΩΑΝΝΗΣ ΚΑΙ ΓΕΩΡΓΙΟΣ Μ. ΚΑΛΑΦΑΤΑ
BOSTON· MASS· U· S· A·
1919

ΠΡΟΛΟΓΟΣ

Ὁ τοῦ παρόντος πονηματίου συντάκτης, Μητροφάνης Ι.
Καλαφατᾶς, κατὰ τὴν 20ην Ἀπριλίου τοῦ ἔτους 1902 ἀφικόμε-
νος ἐκ τοῦ ἐκ Λαχανιᾶς (Ρόδου) πλοός μου εἰς τὴν πατρίδα μου
Σύμην, διὰ τῆς μικρᾶς λέμβου μου, ἣν ἔξωθεν τοῦ καφενείου
Ξενοφῶντος Δ. Κουρτέση καλῶς προσορμήσας, κεκοπιακὼς ἐκ
τῆς θαλασσοπλοΐας, ἐκάθησα πρὸς μικρὰν ἀνάπαυσιν ἐπὶ τῆς
πρύμνης. Ἐθεώρουν δὲ καὶ τοὺς ἐκ τῆς προκυμαίας τοῦ Αἰγιαλοῦ
μας συγχνοδιαβαίνοντας πατριώτας μου.

Ἐν τῷ διαστήματι τούτῳ ἀτενήσας εἶδον πολλοὺς καὶ ἐκ
τῶν διαβαινόντων, καὶ ἐκ τῶν ἐντὸς τοῦ καφενείου ψιθυριζόν-
των. Οἱ ψιθυρισμοὶ δὲ τούτων ἐγνωστοποίουν κοινά τινα συμφέροντα, συμπεράνας τοῦτο ἐκ τοῦ ὅτι ἤκουον νὰ δοξολογῶσι
τὸν Θεόν. Μετὰ μεγάλης μου ἐκπλήξεως πλησιάσας τινὰς τῶν
φίλων μου, καὶ πυνθανόμενος τὴν αἰτίαν δι' ἣν ἐδόξαζον τὸν
Θεόν, ἤκουσα παρ' αὐτῶν ὅτι οἱ ψιθυρισμοὶ οὗτοι πηγάζουσιν
ἀπὸ νέα τινὰ ἄτινα κοινονιολογοῦσι τὴν κατάργησιν τῶν σκα-
φάνδρων· διὸ καὶ ἐνέπλησε χαρᾶς τὴν ψυχήν μου ἡ πληροφορία
αὕτη τῶν φίλων μου. Λύπην δὲ ἄφατον ἐνδομύχως ἠσθάνθην
καὶ πικρίας ἀπεριγράπτου ἐγεύθην, ἀφοῦ μετὰ τὴν ἀκριβῆ ἔρευ-
ναν, καὶ ἀναβράζουσαν τῆς ψυχῆς μου ἐπιθυμίαν, ἐστάθη οὐχὶ
δυνατὸν ν' ἀνακαλύψω τὴν βάσιν καὶ πηγὴν τῆς εἰδήσεως ταύτης
καὶ ἔμενον καθ' ὅλην τὴν ἡμέραν ἐκείνην καθὼς καὶ τὴν ἐπιοῦ-
σαν, σκυθρωπός, περίλυπος καὶ σκεπτόμενος.

Τῇ δὲ θέσει ἐκείνῃ διάγων καὶ μέχρι τῆς ἑσπέρας ὑπὸ
διαφόρων λογισμῶν ἐνοχλούμενος, βυθισθεὶς εἰς ὕπνον, ἐνεφα-
νίσθη μοι γυνή τις κατ' ὄναρ, ἥτις καὶ διεσαφήνισέ μοι ἅπαντα
ὅσα ὡς διψῶσα ἔλαφος ἐπεθύμουν νὰ μάθω.

Διὸ καὶ πασίδηλα θέλων ταῦτα ποιῆσαι, συνέταξα τὴν
ἀκόλουθον στιχουργίαν, δι' ἧς καὶ τὴν θέσιν τῆς πατρίδος
διακηρύττω καὶ τὰ τῶν σκαφάνδρων ἐξασθενήματα ἐκπομπεύω.
Ἕνεκα δὲ τῆς μεγάλης ἐκτάσεως τοῦ ὀνείρου ὠνόμασα αὐτὴν
"ΧΕΙΜΕΡΙΝΟΝ ΟΝΕΙΡΟΝ"

ΧΕΙΜΕΡΙΝΟΣ ΟΝΕΙΡΟΣ

Τίνες οἱ φθόγγοι οἵτινες σήμερον ἀντηχοῦσι
συχνάκις εἰς τὰ ὦτα μου καὶ τὸν Θεὸν ὑμνοῦσι;
Τίς ἄραγε ἡ ἀφορμὴ καὶ πόθεν ἡ αἰτία
τῶν συνεχῶν ψιθιρισμῶν τῶν εἰς τὰ καφενεῖα;

Καὶ διατὶ οἱ ἄνθρωποι τόσας συνομιλίας
ἱστάμενοι ἐδῶ κ' ἐκεῖ τὰς ἐλλεπαλληλίας;
'Εδῶ ὑπάρχει ἔλεγον εἴδησίς τις σπουδαία
καὶ ἂς προθυμοποιηθῶ νὰ συζητῶ τὰ νέα

Συλλογισμένος ἔστεχον καὶ σκυθρωπὸς ἠπόρουν
τὸ αἴτιον ὦ φίλοι μου νὰ μάθω δὲν εἰμπόρουν
'Ενύκτωσε κ' ἐπλάγιασα κατασυλλογισμένος
κ' ἐπάνω εἰς τὸ χέρι μου εἴμουν ἀκουμβισμένος

Καὶ κουρασθεὶς ἠκούμβησα εἰς τὸ προσκέφαλόν μου
καὶ μόλις ὅτε ὕπνωσα εἶδον εἰς τ' ὄνειρόν μου
Μίαν γυναῖκα εὐηδῆ ὄρθιον ἱσταμένην
μὲ πένθιμα φορέματα ὅλην ἐνδεδυμένην

Εὔρωστον δὲ καὶ ζωηρὰν καλὴν καὶ ρωμαλέαν
καὶ εἰς τὴ ἡλικίαν της ὀλίγον γηραλέαν
'Αφοῦ τὴν ἐχαιρέτησα ἔφερον καὶ σκαμνία
τῆς εἶπον σᾶς παρακαλῶ καθήσατε κυρία

Τίς εἶσαι πόθεν ἔρχεσαι τίνα ζητεῖς τί κάμνεις;
κ' ἦλθες νὰ μᾶς ἐπισκεφθῆς; Διαβάτρια τυγχάνεις;
Τὸν δρόμον ἄραγ' ἔχασες καὶ θέλεις ὁδηγίαν
καὶ τὴν ἐμὴν βοήθειαν ζητεῖς ὡς προστασίαν;

Καθήσατε παρακαλῶ νὰ μοὶ ἐξηγηθῆτε
κ' ἂν ἐξαρτᾶται ἀπό μὲ πρόθυμον θὰ μὲ βρεῖτε
'Αμέσως τότε ἄρχισαν τὰ μάτια της νὰ τρέχουν
καὶ δάκρυα ποταμηδὸν τὴν ὄψιν της νὰ βρέχουν

Μὲ δακρυρρόους ὀφθαλμοὺς καὶ σιγανομιλοῦσα
ἀρχίζει νὰ μοὶ ὁμιλῆ ὅλως ἀνησυχοῦσα:
Οὔτε τὸν δρόμον ἔχασα οὔτε διαβάτις εἶμαι
'Η Σύμη ἡ μητέρα σου καὶ ἡ Πατρίς σου εἶμαι

Γνωρίζω ὅτι χαίρεσαι εἰς τὰς πατραγαθίας
καὶ ἀποστρέφεσαι πολὺ τὰς μηχανορραφίας
Σ' ὅλα σου τὰ ποιήματα εἶδον νὰ μ' ἐκθειάζης
καὶ ὡς μητέραν τῶν μουσῶν νὰ μὲ ἐγκωμιάζης

Κ' ἐνεφανίσθην εἰς ἐσὲ φέρουσα ἀγγελίαν
δι' ἧς θὰ λύσης ἀκριβῶς ἣν ἔχεις ἀπορίαν
'Η εἴδησίς μου πρόκειται περὶ πατραγαθίας
περὶ συμφέροντος κοινοῦ τῆς σπογγαλιείας

Κι' ἐπιμελήθητι καλῶς νὰ διασαφηνίσης
ὅσα θὰ σοὶ διηγηθῶ νὰ τὰ κοινολογήσης

Αἱ μηχαναὶ παρήχμασαν καὶ πρόχειται νὰ παύσουν
οἱ δύται πάλιν στὸ ἑξῆς πιστεύω θὰ ἀχμάσουν

Ἡ προθεσμία ἔληξε τὸ τέλος πλησιάζει
καὶ ἡ καμπανελλόπετρα θ' ἀρχίση νὰ ἀχμάζη

Ἐξήνθησεν ἡ μηχανὴ τὸ βοῦττος θὰ βλαστήση
χ' ἡ τέχνη τῶν προγόνων μας θέλει τελεσφορήση

Τὸ πρῶτον ἐπιτήδευμα νὰ ζήση! μὲ ζωώννει
ἡ δολοφόνος μηχανὴ τὸ ἧπαρ μου πληγώνει

Τόσον τὴν ἀποστρέφομαι ὡς συγχαμένον πρᾶγμα
παρ' ὅσον ἀποστρέφομαι τὸ τῶν δαιμόνων τάγμα

Ὡς ἡ μορφὴ τῆς χεφαλῆς Γοργόνος τῆς Μεδούσης
χ' ὡς σύριγμα φαρμαχερᾶς ἐχίδνης συριζούσης

Θανάτου φρίχην παγεράν στὰ μέλη μου παρέχει
ἡ ἀποτρόπαιος μορφὴ τῆς μηχανῆς ἣν ἔχει

Τοὺς τότε ἀπελίθωνεν ἡ τῆς μεδούσης θέα
τοὺς νῦν ἀπολιθώνει τους ἡ Π ε ρ ι χ ε φ α λ α ί α !

Ἠφάνησε τὰ τέχνα μου ἔπνιξε πλειοτάτους
χαὶ εἰς τὸν ἅδην ἔστειλε νέους ἀνδρειωτάτους

Νέας πολλὰς ἐχήρευσεν ἠτέχνωσε μητέρας
χαὶ βλέπω ἕως σήμερον πενθοῦντας τοὺς πατέρας

Κ' ἐχτὸς τῶν ὅσων ἔστειλεν ἀώρως εἰς τὸν τάφον
βλέπω χαὶ εἰς τὴν ἀγορὰν πλῆθος νεκρῶν ἀτάφων

Ἐχ τοῦ ποτοῦ τῆς μηχανῆς δηλητηριασμένους
χουτσοὺς χαὶ τρομηχιάριδες χαὶ χαχομοιργιασμένους

Καὶ ὑποφέρουν οἱ πτωχοὶ μεγάλην τυραννίαν
χαὶ εἰς τὰ οἰχονομιχὰ ἄμετρον δυστυχίαν

Βλέπ' ὀρφαν' ἀπροστάτευτα ἐπαίτας εἰς τὸν δρόμον
ἡ μηχανοξεχινηταὶ παρέβησαν τὸν νόμον

Ἡ μηχανὴ 'ναι αἴτιος ὅλης τῆς δυστυχίας
χαὶ τῆς εἰς τὸν χοινὸν λαὸν δεινῆς ἀναργυρίας

Ἡ μηχανὴ χατήργησε συνάφια χαὶ τεχνίτας
χαὶ τοὺς ἀποχατέστησε πτωχοὺς χαὶ ραχενδύτας

Τοὺς βογιατζίδες θὰ εἰπῶ χαὶ τοὺς ραπτοβραχάδες
χαθυστεροῦνται χαὶ αὐτοὶ τώρα αἱ φουχαράδες

Τὴν Εὐρωπαϊχὴν στολὴν ἠσπάσθησαν ἐν γένει
ἡ δὲ τῶν προπατόρων μας μένει χατηργημένη

Καὶ πλῆθος οἰχογενειῶν ἀπὸ τὴν δυστυχίαν
μετώχησαν νὰ ζήσωσιν εἰς τὴν ἀποδημίαν

Χωλούς, μετοίχους χαὶ νεχροὺς ἐὰν ἀπαριθμῆτε
τὸ τρίτον τῶν χατοίχων της ἡ πόλις ὑστερεῖται

Καὶ ἠθιχῶς χαὶ ὑλιχῶς ἐπέφερε ζημίας
χαὶ δὲν ὑπάρχει ἀγαθὸν οὐδὲν χρηστοηθείας

Κατέστρεφε χ' ἠφάνησε τὸ γένος τῶν ἀνθρώπων

καὶ τραύματ' ἀναρίθμητα ἐπέφερε στὸν τόπον

Ἐχάθη ἡ ὑπόληψις καὶ ἡ φιλοτιμία
καὶ ἀντ' αὐτῶν ἐρρίζωσεν ἡ ἀφιλοτιμία

Ἐξέλειψεν ἡ ἠθικὴ τὸ ἀγέρωχον ἀκμάζει
ὅπερ ἀπὸ τὰς μηχανὰς τὴν σήμερον πηγάζει

Σ' ὅλην τὴν βαρβαρότητα καὶ τὴν ἀναισχυντίαν
οἱ μηχανοξεκινηταὶ διέδωκαν αἰτίαν

Ἔβλεπον ὀφθαλμοφανῶς ἕνα ἀπ' τοὺς ἐμπόρους
ὅστις συνανεστρέφετο τοὺς κακοήθης ὅλους

Τοὺς ἔβλεπον κατάσκαλα εἰς τὸ αὐτὸ τραπέζι
τὴν πρέφαν καὶ τὸ ντόμινον μαζύ των νὰ συμπαίζῃ

Ἡμαύρωνε καὶ τὴν τιμὴν καὶ τὴν ὑπόληψίν του
χάριν τῶν συμφερόντων του διὰ τὴν μηχανήν του

Ὥστε τὸ θάρρος τὸ πολὺ καὶ ἡ μεγάλη σχέσις
ἐπέφερεν ἐγωϊσμὸν καὶ ἔκτοτ' ἔγιν' ἕξις

Ἰδοὺ λοιπὸν τῆς μηχανῆς τὰ προτερήματά της
καὶ ὑποφέρουσι κοινῶς τὰ κακουργήματά της

Βαβαί! τῆς ἀσπλαγχνίας των ὦ τῆς θηριωδίας!
φεῦ! τῆς ἀσυμπαθείας των καὶ ἐθελοκακίας

Αὐτὰ μὲ κατατρύχουσι καὶ μὲ στενοχωροῦσι
βλέπουσα τοὺς πολίτας μου νὰ ἀδιαφοροῦσι

Εἰς τὸν καιρὸν καὶ ἐποχὴν τῆς εἰδολολατρείας
ὅτε ὑπῆρχον βασιλεῖς σκληροὶ τῆς ἀσεβείας

Καὶ παρεκίνουν τοὺς πιστοὺς διὰ νὰ προσκηνήσουν
τὰ εἴδωλα καὶ τοὺς θεοὺς βιαίως νὰ τιμήσουν

Οἱ ἅγιοί μας μάρτυρες δια νὰ ἐνισχύσουν
τὴν ἱερὰν θρησκείαν μας καὶ πίστιν νὰ στηρίξουν

Ἐτιμωροῦντο αὐστηρῶς καὶ σκληροτελευτοῦντες
οἱ τὸν ἀληθινὸν Θεὸν πιστῶς ὁμολογοῦντες

Ἔμενον δὲ ἀκλόνητοι καὶ μετὰ προθυμίας
διὰ τὴν πίστιν ἔτρεχον στὰς αἱματοχυσίας

Καὶ οὕτως ἐστερέωσαν τὴν ἀληθῆ θρησκείαν
μεγάλως δὲ κατήσχυναν τὴν εἰδωλολατρείαν

Καὶ ἴσχυσαν νὰ παύσωσι τὴν αἱματοχυσίαν
κ' ἐπὶ αἰῶνας ἱκανοὺς ἤγομεν ἡσυχίαν

Ἀλλὰ δὲν ἤλπιζον ποτὲ πῶς θὰ ἐπαναφέρουν
ἄλλα καινὰ μαρτύρια ἅτινα ὑποφέρουν

Οἱ εὐσεβεῖς ἐσφάζοντο διὰ τὴν ἐκκλησίαν
καὶ διὰ νὰ στηρίξωσι τὴν πίστιν καὶ θρησκείαν

Ὄχι δι' αἰσχροκέρδειαν ἢ χρηματοδοσίαν
ὅπως τώρα ἀπόλλυνται στὴν σκαφανδροεργίαν

Καὶ βλέπω σήμερον πολλοὺς ἀδικοθανατοῦντας
καὶ πλείστους εἰς τὴν ἀγορὰν χωλοὺς περιπατοῦντας

Οἱ ἔμποροί μας βλέποντες ὅλα αὐτὰ κωφεύουν
τῶν χρηματοταμείων των τὴν εἴσοδον θηρεύουν

Καὶ διὰ νὰ τοκίζωσι σ' αὐτοὺς τὰ χρήματά των
γίνονται ἄσπονδοι ἐχθροὶ εἰς τὰ καθήκοντά των

Μὲ τόκον τρισυπέρογκον δίδουν τὰ δάνειά των
καὶ ἂν χάνετ' ὁ λαὸς ταππώνουσι τ' αὐτιά των

Τὴν τῶν σκαφάνδρων ὕπαρξιν πρέπει νὰ προσπαθήσουν
μὲ ὅλας τὰς δυνάμεις των μακρὰν νὰ ἀπορρρίψουν

Καὶ λαιμητόμον μηχανὴν αὐτὴν νὰ θεωρήσουν
αἱ χῆραι καὶ τὰ ὀρφανὰ νὰ τὴν λιθοβολήσουν

Κ' ἐνῶ οἱ ἄλλοι τρέχουσι νὰ τὴν ἐκσφενδονίσουν
οἱ ἔμποροί μας προσπαθοῦν νὰ τὴν ἐπιστηρίξουν

Διὰ νὰ ὠφελήσωσι τὰ ἑαυτῶν ταμεῖα
ἐφοδιάζουν ἀφειδῶς τὰ τῶν νεκρῶν μνημεῖα

Καὶ τέλος πάντων νὰ εἰπῶ αἱ μηχαναὶ παιδί μου
μὲ τὸ φαρμάκι τοῦ φειδιοῦ ραντίζουν τὴν ψυχήν μου

Καὶ ἄκουσον νὰ σοῦ εἰπῶ μίαν διήγησίν μου
πόσα κακὰ ἐπέφερεν αὕτη στὴν κεφαλήν μου

Ἠθέλησαν μίαν φορὰν τὰς μηχανὰς νὰ σπάσουν
προτοῦ νὰ δυναμώσωσι στὸν τόπον νὰ ἀκμάσουν

Πρὶν νὰ ὑπερισχύσωσι τὰ κακουργήματά των
ὅπως σήμερον φαίνωνται 'πλωμένα τὰ πτερά των

Ἦτο δὲ τότε πρόεδρος στὴν Δημογεροντίαν
Σταμάτης ὁ Καλαφατᾶς γέρων τὴν ἡλικίαν

Ἀνὴρ δὲ σώφρων καὶ πιστὸς στὴν Δημογεροντίαν
καὶ ἐδιοίκει τὸν λαὸν μὲ ἀμεροληψίαν

Ὑπὲρ πατρίδος ἔπαθε καὶ φυλακὰς ὑπέστη
διὰ συμφέροντα κοινὰ στοὺς διωγμοὺς ἀντέστη

Στὰς φυλακὰς Ρόδου καὶ Κῶ ἔπασχεν ὑποφέρων
καὶ πάλιν στὸ προκείμενον ἔτυχε δημογέρων

Τὸ πλῆθος ἐσυνάχθηκεν πάντες ὁμονοοῦντες
ἄδρες γυναῖκες καὶ παιδιὰ ἦσαν ὁμοφρονοῦντες

Ἔβλεπες τὸν αἰγιαλὸν ὡς σμήνη μελισσίων
ὅλοι οἱ δρόμοι ἔγεμον ἀνδρῶν τε καὶ παιδίων

Μία βοὴ ἠκούετο ἀπὸ τὰ καφενεῖα
τὰς μηχανὰς νὰ σπάσωμεν τὰς εἰς τὰ μαγαζεῖα

Ἦλθον εἰς τὸν Καλαφατᾶν τὴν ἄδειαν νὰ δώσῃ
τὰς μηχανὰς νὰ σπάσωσι τὸ ἔργον νὰ γλυτώσῃ

Τοῦ μακαρίτου ὁ σκοπὸς ἀπέβλεπε νὰ παύσουν
καὶ συνεβούλευεν αὐτοὺς τὴν γνώμην των ν' ἀλλάξουν

Δὲν εἶναι ἔλεγε καλὴ αὐτὴ ἡ χειρονομία
καὶ ἔξοδα θὰ ὑποστῇ ἡ Δημογεροντία

Ἄκαμπτοι οὗτοι ἔμενον καὶ ἐξηγριωμένοι

μαχόμενοι τῶν μηχανῶν ὡς λύκοι λυσσασμένοι

Τὰς συμβουλὰς τοῦ γέροντος Καλαφατᾶ Σταμάτη
ὁ ὄχλος δὲν ὑπήκουσεν ἀλλὰ παρεξετράπη

Στὰς χεῖρας των τὸν ἥρπασαν καὶ εἰς τὸ μαγαζεῖον
μετέωρον τὸν ἔφερον στὰς μηχανὰς πλησίον

Ἑκὼν καὶ ἄκων ἔθηκε στὰς μηχανὰς τὸ χέρι
καί κατ᾽ αὐτῶν ἐπέπεσε τὸ πλῆθος καὶ τ᾽ ἀσκέρι

Πέντε λεπτῶν διάστημα τὰς ἐκαταχάλασαν
μαρκοῦτσι καὶ φορέματα τὰ κατεχομματιάσαν

Καὶ τοῦ λαοῦ τὸ φρόνημα δὲν ἦτο ἐναντίον
οὐδὲ ἀνοσιούργημα οὐδόλως καὶ ἀχρεῖον

Ἀπέβλεπέ μεν ὁ σκοπὸς τὰς μηχανὰς νὰ σπάσουν
νὰ τὰς ἀντιπληρώσωσιν ἄλλας νὰ μὴ ᾽γοράσουν

Ὅπως καὶ τὰς ἐπλήρωσε τὸ γενικὸν ταμεῖον
οἱ κάτοχοι ὅμως αὐτῶν ἔπραξαν τ᾽ οὐναντίον

Ἔλαβον τὰ ἀργύρια κ᾽ ἔφερον καλυτέρας
τῆς νέας ἐφευρέσεως ἔτι ἱκανοτέρας

Καὶ ἀπὸ τότε ἤρχισαν τὴν πόλιν νὰ μαστίζουν
καὶ τὴν πυρὰν ἣν ἥναψαν νὰ τὴν ἀναρριπίζουν

Καὶ ἔγιναν καταστροφεῖς φθορεῖς τοῦ τόπου ὅλου
λήψονται δὲ καὶ τὸν μισθὸν παρὰ τοῦ διαβόλου

Κ᾽ ἐγὼ εὑρέθην μεταξὺ Χαρίβδεως καὶ Σκύλλης
καὶ πρόσεξον ὦ τέκνον μου σαφῶς νὰ ἀναγγείλης

Εἰς ὅσα διηγήθηκα τίποτε μὴν ἀφίσης
στὸ ποίημά σου ἐκτενῶς νὰ τὰ τακτοποιήσης

Καὶ πάλιν ἐπεκτείνομαι εἰς τὴν διήγησίν μου
θέλουσα σβέσαι τὴν πυρὰν ἣν ἔχω στὴν ψυχήν μου

Πρέπον εἶνε νὰ ἐπαινῶ καὶ νὰ τοὺς μακαρίζω
καθῆκον ἀπαραίτητον νὰ τοὺς ὑποστηρίζω

Ὅλους τοὺς διαπρέψαντας εἰς τὰς πατραγαθίας
καὶ ἔχουν ὑποστήριγμα τὰς ἀγαθοεργίας

Σοὶ διηγήθην ἀκριβῶς τὰ περὶ δυστυχίας
τὰ περὶ ὑπολήψεως καὶ ἀνυπολήψίας

Ἤκουσας πῶς αἱ μηχαναὶ μ᾽ ἔχουν καταθλιμμένην
καὶ μ᾽ ἔχουν ἕως σήμερον στὰ μαῦρα ἐνδεδυμένην

Δὲν ὑπαφέρω τὰ αἰσχρὰ διόλου νὰ κρατήσω
ἀλλ᾽ οὔτε καὶ τὰ ἀγαθὰ νὰ ἀποσιωπήσω

Καὶ διηγοῦμαι στὸ ἑξῆς τὰ περὶ εὐτυχίας
καὶ κάτοχος τῆς ἀληθοῦς εἰμὶ εὐδαιμονίας

Μὲ ἀνεκτίμητ᾽ ἀγαθὰ εὑρέθην προικισμένη
εἰς ὅλα τὰ συντείνοντα καλῶς πεπλουτισμένη

Ὑπὸ λιμένων ἀσφαλῶν πρῶτον περικυκλοῦμαι
καὶ παρὰ τῶν θαλασσινῶν μεγάλως ἐπαινοῦμαι

Βορειονατολικῶς τῆς νήσου μου ὑπάρχουν
τὸ Πέδι κι᾿ ὁ Αἰγιαλὸς πάντων τῶν ἄλλων ἄρχουν

῝Ολα τὰ πλοῖα εἰς αὐτοὺς εἶνε λιμενισμένα
καὶ ἄλλα ἔξω στὴν ξηρὰν ὑπάρχουν τραβιγμένα

῾Ο Κάμπος στὸν Αἰγιαλὸν ἔνθα καὶ ναυπηγοῦνται
πλοῖα παρὰ τῶν ναυπηγῶν καὶ τελειοποιοῦνται

῎Αλλος λιμὴν χειμωνικὸς λίαν ἐκτεταμένος
εἰς τὸ νοτιοδυτικὸν πάντοθεν φημισμένος

Τοῦ Πανορμίτου τῆς μονῆς ἔνθα τελετουργεῖται
ἡ ἱερὰ πανήγυρις καὶ λίαν ἐπαινεῖται

῞Αγιος Αἰμιλιανὸς στὸ βόριόν μου μέρος
καὶ οὗτος ἀσφαλὴς λιμὴν κὰι περιτειχισμένος

Μὲ προχυμαίαν καὶ ναὸν καὶ θόλον ἐκτισμένον
δι᾿ ἁλιεῖς καὶ ξυλουργοὺς μέρος ἡσυχασμένον

Προβαίνουσα στὸ ζήτημα᾿ τὸ περὶ τῆς θρησκείας
καύχημα μέγα θεωρῶ πῶς ἔχω ἐκκλησίας

Πολλὰς μεγάλας καὶ καλὰς πλουσίως στολισμένας
δυνάμει τῶν πατριωτῶν καλῶς πεπλουτισμένας

῞Ολαι μὲ σκεύη πλούσια κανδήλας ἀσημένας
καὶ τὰς εἰκόνας ἔχουσιν ἀργυροχρυσομένας

Καὶ ἀπὸ δεκατέσσαρας μεγάλας ἐνορίας
σύγκειμαι ὅλη ἡ πατρὶς ἐξ᾿ ἴσου κ᾿ ἐκκλησίας

Καὶ πληθισμὸς μικρῶν μονῶν εἰς τὰ βουνὰ ὑπάρχουν
ὅλαι δὲ αὗται ἔχουσι κατόχους καὶ τὰς ἄρχουν

Συχνὰ δὲ καταγίνονται ἀόκνως κ᾿ ἐνεργοῦσι
κελλία καὶ περιοχὰς στὸ νὰ οἰκοδομοῦσι

Δενδροφυτείας τακτικῶς σ᾿ αὐτὰς τοποθετοῦσι
καὶ τέρψιν εἰς τοὺς θεατὰς μεγάλην προξενοῦσι

Θέα δὲ γοητευτικὴ πραΰνει τὰ δεινά μου
ἐστολισμένα τῶν μονῶν βλέπουσα τὰ βουνά μου

Πλήρης χαρᾶς ὑπάρχουσα πολὺ εὐχαριστοῦμαι
καὶ τὸν τῆς συνεχείας μου λόγον ἐκδιηγοῦμαι

῎Εχω ῾Ιεροκήρυκα ὃς τὴν Θεολογίαν
κηρύττει τας Κυριακὰς εἰς πᾶσαν ἐκκλησίαν

Καὶ μεταβαίνων ἐναλλὰξ σ᾿ ὅλας τὰς ἐνορίας
τὰ νάματά του πλημμυρεῖ στὰς εὐγενεῖς καρδίας

᾿Αρδεύει πάντων τὰς ψυχὰς τὰς τὸν Θεὸν διψόντων
καὶ τρέφει μὲ οὐράνιον ἄρτον τὰς τῶν πεινώντων

Τὰς χέρσους γέας προσπαθεῖ νὰ τὰς καλλιεργήσῃ
καὶ δένδρα ἀκαρπόφορα νὰ τὰ καρποφορήσῃ

Κι᾿ ἀψευδῶς ἐκφράζομαι ὁ τῆς θεοσεβείας
σπόρος ἐκαρποφόρησε στὰς ἀγαθοεργίας

Κυκλοφορεῖ ἡ ἀρετὴ καὶ τελεσιουργεῖται

καὶ γλεῦκος τὸ οὐράνιον βλέπω ληνοπατεῖται

Ἡ πρὸς τὰ θεῖα τέρψις τῶν μεγάλως μὲ ἡδύνει
πρὸ πάντων ὅτι πλημμυρεῖ ἡ ἐλεημοσύνη

Καὶ διὰ τοῦτο εὐτυχὴς τὴν σήμερον καλοῦμαι
καὶ διὰ ἄλλα ἀγαθὰ ἀκόμη διηγοῦμαι

Ἔχω τοὺς διδασκάλους μου ἔχω τοὺς ἰατρούς μου
ἔχω τὸ φαρμακεῖον μου τοὺς φαρμακοποιούς μου

Εἶνε ἀναγνωστήριον ὑπάρχουν καὶ σχολεῖα
εἰσὶ καὶ διδασκάλισσαι καὶ παρθεναγωγεῖα

Ἕκαστος ἄπορος γονεὺς δύναται ν᾽ ἀναπτύξῃ
τὰ τέκνα του καὶ ὀβολὸν χωρὶς νὰ δαπανήσῃ

Δύναται νὰ ἰατρευθῇ ὁπόταν ἀσθενήσῃ
κ᾽ ἔξοδον εἰς τὰ ἰατρικὰ οὐδόλως νὰ προκύψῃ

Εὐγνωμονῶ στὰ τέκνα μου ἡ μήτηρ καὶ πατρίς των
διότι φέρονται καλῶς πρὸς τοὺς ὁμογενεῖς των

Τρέφουσι ζῆλον ἔνθερμον στὴν ἀληθῆ σοφίαν
καὶ ἔρωτα διακαῆ ν᾽ αὐξήσῃ ἡ παιδεία

Ἐπέτυχον δὲ εὐτυχῶς καὶ ἄνθρωπον σπουδαῖον
διδάσκαλον εἰδήμονα ἐφ᾽ ὅσον ἦτο δέον

Τὸν κύριον διδάσκαλον Περίδην τὸν σχολάρχην
ἀπουσιάζει δὲ τὸ νῦν τοῦ ζῆν καὶ τοῦ ὑπάρχειν

Καὶ ἔτη τεσσαράκοντα ὁλόκληρα διδάξας
καὶ τὴν πνευματικὴν τροφὴν στὰ τέκνα μου θηλάσας

Ἥπλωσε τετραγωνικῶς τὰ φῶτα τῆς παιδείας
τὰ ἀγαθὰ τῆς ἀρετῆς καὶ τῆς εὐδαιμονίας

Καὶ ἱκανῶς ἀνέπτυξεν ὅλην τὴν κοινωνίαν
καὶ εἶχε φίλην του πιστὴν τὴν ἀγαθοεργίαν

Ἀφοῦ εἰς πᾶν θεάρεστον τὸν βίον του διῆλθεν
ἡ μακαρία του ψυχὴ στοὺς οὐρανοὺς ἀνῆλθεν

Καὶ ἐξελθούσης τῆς ψυχῆς ἡ Δημογεροντία
πλουσίως συνετέλεσεν εἰς τὴν αὐτοῦ κηδείαν

Μετὰ μεγάλων θειασμῶν ἔγεινεν ἡ ταφή του
καὶ μέγαν τύμβον ἤγειραν εἰσέτι πρὸς τιμήν του

Ἀναμφιβόλως σήμερον χαίρεται καὶ ἀγάλλει
τοῦ παραδείσου τ᾽ ἄφθαρτα ἀπολαμβάνει κάλλη

Ἀφίνω τὸν διδάσκαλον Γεώργιον Περίδην
στὸν Μιχαῆλον ἔρχομαι τὸν κύριον Πετρίδην

Αἱ πράξεις λέγω τοῦ ἀνδρὸς τούτου τοῦ μακαρίτου
γνησίου φιλοπάτριδος καὶ ἀγαθοῦ πολίτου

Ἦσαν ἀριστουργήματα ἄξια ἐγκωμίου
ἔργα τῶν ἱερῶν γραφῶν καὶ τοῦ Εὐαγγελίου

Πεινῶντας δὲν παρέβλεπε διψῶντας δὲν ἡστόχει
κοινῶς εἰς πάντα ἐνδεῆ δὲν ἤξευρε τὸ ὄχι

Τοὺς δὲ γυμνοὺς ἐνέδυε νοσοῦντας διηκόνει
τοὺς ξένους περιέθαλπε καὶ τοὺς ἐλεημώνει

Εἰς συνοικέσια πτωχῶν καὶ ὀρφανῶν ἐνήργει
καὶ εἰς ἀποκατάστασιν κορασιῶν συνήργει

Φιλίαν εἶχε σταθερὰν μὲ τὴν φιλοκαλίαν
καὶ μῖσος ἀδιάλλακτον μὲ τὴν φιλαργυρίαν

Καὶ τὸν Θεὸν ἐδάνειζεν ἀόκνως καθ' ἑκάστην
καὶ μετὰ ταῦτα τὴν ψυχὴν παρέδωκε στὸν Πλάστην

Ἀπήλαυσε τὰ ἀγαθὰ ὅλων τῶν ἐπιγείων
καὶ πάλιν τώρα μέτοχος σκηνῶν τῶν Οὐρανίων

Εἶναι καὶ ἀναστήματα κοινῶς Πετριδεῖα
ἅτινα οἱ Πετρίδιδες δαπάνῃ τῶν ἰδίᾳ

Ἤγειραν πρὸς καλλωπισμὸν ὅλης τῆς κοινωνίας
καὶ πρὸς ὠφέλειαν ψυχῆς καὶ μνήμης αἰωνίας

Εἶνε τὸ Ὡρολόγιον ὑπάρχει καὶ σχολεῖον
καὶ δρόμοι Εὐρωπαϊκοὶ εἰς τὸ ἐπιτελεῖον

Τὰ ἀγαθὰ τῶν πολιτῶν εἶπον εἰς συντομίαν
εὕρηκα δὲ ἀλήθειαν χωρὶς ψευδολογίαν

Ἔπρεπεν ἔτι νὰ εἰπῶ ἀλλὰ περνᾶ ἡ ὥρα
στὴν αἱμοβόρον μηχανὴν ἔρχομαι πάλι τώρα

Ἤδη θὰ σοὶ διηγηθῶ περὶ τῆς παρακμῆς της
περὶ τῆς καταργήσεως καὶ τέλους τῆς ζωῆς της

Θὰ μάθῃς δὲ λεπτομερῶς ἅπασαν τὴν αἰτίαν
τῶν συνεχῶν ψιθυρισμῶν τῶν εἰς τὰ καφενεῖα

Τοὺς φθόγγους τῶν πατριωτῶν οἵτινες ἀντηχοῦσαν
συχνάκις εἰς τὰ ὦτα σου καὶ τὸν θεὸν ὑμνοῦσαν

Τὰς ἐντολάς μου πρόσεξον ὅμως νὰ τὰς φυλάξῃς
στὴν πλάκα τῆς καρδίας σου αὐτὰς νὰ ἐγχαράξῃς

Ὅσα κακὰ προέρχονται αἴφνης εἰς τὸν λαιμόν μας
πηγάζουν ἐξ ἀνομιῶν καὶ ἐξ ἁμαρτιῶν μας

Ὅπως καὶ τὰ τῆς μηχανῆς τώρα στὴν κεφαλήν μας
μάστιξ ἐστὶν ἀπ' τὸν Θεὸν καὶ ῥάβδος πρὸς ποινήν μας

Πράξασα δὲ παράνομα παρ' ὅσον διετάχθη
καὶ ὁ Πανάγαθος Θεὸς πάλιν τὴν ἐσυγχάνθη

Κι' ὡς ἄγγελλος παρὰ Θεοῦ ἐφάνη ἐσταλμένος
ἄνθρωπος καλοκάγαθος ἀνὴρ ἐμψυχομένος

Φλέγερ ὀνομαζόμενος καὶ Ρῶσσος τὴν πατρίδα
τοῦτον φιλευεργέτην μου καὶ κύριόν μου οἶδα

Οὗτος ὁ τρισμακάριστος φθάσας στὰ χώματά μας
ἐξήτασε καὶ ἔμαθε τὰ δυστυχήματά μας

Μαθὼν δὲ καὶ τῆς μηχανῆς τὰ κακουργήματά της
τ' ἄθλια καὶ ἐλεηνὰ ἀποτελέσματά της

Συνεκινήθη κι' ἔλαβεν ὁ ἴδιος τὴν εὐθύνην

νὰ ἀποσύρῃ τὸ κακὸν νὰ πράξῃ καλωσύνην

Κατέβαλεν ὁ ἄνθρωπος ὅλα τὰ δυνατά του
διέφθειρεν ἀνηλεῶς ὡς καὶ τὰ χρήματά του

Ἔνθεν κ'ἀκεῖθεν ἔτρεξε πρῶτον εἰς τὴν Γαλλίαν
συνάμα δὲ ἐνήργησε καὶ εἰς τὴν Ἰταλίαν

Ἀναχωρήσας ἀπ' ἐκεῖ στὴν Κρήτην πρῶτον ἦλθε
τῶν ζητημάτων ἔτυχεν ἄπρακτος δὲν ἀπῆλθεν

Εὐθὺς στὴν Κύπρον ἔτρεξεν δι' αὐτὴν τὴν αἰτίαν
πρόθυμον ὑπερασπιστὴν εὗρε καὶ τὴν Ἀγγλίαν

Ἐπέρασε στὴν Αἴγυπτον χωρὶς ν' ἀργοπορήσῃ
καὶ τὴν Μανδρούγαν ἴσχυσε νὰ τὴν καθυστερήσῃ

Δὲν ἀναβάλλει τὸν καιρὸν οὐδόλως νὰ ὀκνεύσῃ
ἐκεῖθεν ἀπεφάσισε στὴν Σάμον ν' ἀποπλεύσῃ

Καὶ αὔτη συνεφώνησεν εἰς τὴν κατάργησίν των
μὴ ὑποφέρουσα ὁρᾶν ποσῶς τὴν ὑπαρξιν των

Ἔμεινε δὲ ἐλεύθερον τὸ μέρος τῆς Συρίας
ὅλον τό τῆς Καραμανιᾶς καὶ τῆς Μικρᾶς Ἀσίας

Ἀλλ' εἴθε ὁ Πανάγαθος Θεὸς νὰ εὐδοκήσῃ
ἢ καὶ ὁ γενναιόδωρος Φλέγερ νὰ ἐνεργήσῃ

Εἰς τὴν Κωνσταντινούπολιν κι ἐκεῖ νὰ εἰσχωρήσῃ
καὶ τὴν λυσσῶσαν τίγριδα μακρὰν νὰ ἀποπτήσῃ

Εὐγνωμονοῦσα καὶ ἐγὼ στὰ κατωρθώματά του
εἰς τὰς γενναίας πράξεις του καὶ πλούσια καλά του

Μεγάλα δῶρα ἥρμωζον διὰ ἀνταμοιβὴν του
καὶ ἀνδριάντα ἔπρεπε νὰ στείσω εἰς τιμήν του

Νὰ φέρῃ καὶ ἐπιγραφὴν: ΑΝΗΡ ΜΕΓΑΛΗΣ ΦΗΜΗΣ
ΦΛΕΓΕΡ Ο ΕΛΕΥΘΕΡΩΤΗΣ πατρίδος μας τῆς ΣΥΜΗΣ

Ἀλλὰ καὶ ἡ θυγάτηρ μου ἡ Δημογεροντία
πάσχει κι ἐκείνη δυστυχῶς ἀπὸ ἀναργυρίαν

Τὸ χρέος τὴν κατέβαλεν ἔχει λειφοδοσίας
χρέος στοὺς ὑπαλλήλους της περὶ ἀντιμισθίας

Ἔγινε καὶ συνέλευσις διὰ ν' ἀποφασίσουν
τί ἔπρεπε νὰ πράξωσι νὰ τὴν ἀνακουφίσουν

Τί μέσα νὰ ἐφεύρωσι πρὸς εἴσπραξιν χρημάτων
κ' εἰς τὴν Ἀττάλειαν ἔρριψαν πρῶτον τὰ βλέμματά των

Ἀρκοῦσι τώρα τέκνον μου ὅσα σοὶ διηγήθην
περὶ κακῶν καὶ ἀγαθῶν μεγάλως ἐξηγγίθην

Αὐτὰ εἰς ὅλον τὸν λαὸν νὰ τὰ κοινολογήσῃς
μὴ λυσμονήσῃς τίποτε ὁπόταν ἐξυπνήσῃς

Κ' ἐγὼ πιστεύω στὸ ἑξῆς θὰ παύσουν τὰ δεινά μου
καὶ ἀφανὴς ἐγένετο εὐθὺς ἀπὸ κοντά μου

Ἐξύπνησα ἀπὸ τὸ πρωὶ τοῦ ὕπνου σκοτισμένος
καὶ εἰς μεγάλην ἔκτασιν εὑρέθην βυθισμένος

Ἐσκέφθην πῶς δὲν ἔπρεπε νὰ χάνω τὸν καιρόν μου

κ' ἔπιασα πένναν καὶ χαρτὶ νὰ γράψω τ' ὄνειρόν μου

   Κατὰ παραγγελίαν δὲ τῆς Σύμης τῆς μητρός μας
κηρύττω τοῦτο σήμερον ν' ἀκούσῃ ὁ λαός μας

   Ἠκούσατε λοιπὸν καλῶς ὦ ἀγαθοὶ πολῖται
ὦ ἄνδρες καγχαβάζιδες καὶ σεῖς γενναῖοι δύται;

   Τὰς ἐνεργείας τοῦ ἀνδρὸς καὶ τοῦ πιστοῦ μας φίλου
πῶς ἔτρεξεν ἐδῶ κ' ἐκεῖ μετὰ μεγάλου ζήλου;

   Ἄνδρες Συμαῖοι ὅλοι μας ἂς τὸν εὐγνωμωνῶμεν
καὶ ὡς ἐπίγειον Θεὸν ὅλοι ἂς τὸν τιμῶμεν

   Καὶ τῷ Θεῷ προσοίσωμεν ὕμνον δοξολογίας
εἰς ἑορτὴν χαρμόσυνον τῆς παλιγγενεσίας

   Καὶ ἂς πανηγυρίσωμεν ὅλοι μας ἡνωμένοι
Θεοῦ τὴν συγκατάβασιν δοξάζοντες ἐν γένει

   Καὶ μὴ ἀγνωμωνήσωμεν ἐν τῇ εὐεργεσίᾳ
καὶ ζήτω ἂς φωνάξωμεν ἡ παλιγγενεσία

—————

   Συνέχεια τῆς προηγουμένης, εἰς τὴν δευτέραν
κατάργησιν τῶν Σκαφάνδρων κατὰ
τὸ ἔτος 1903 παρὰ τοῦ Ἄνακτος
ἡμῶν Σουλτᾶν, Ἀβδοὺλ
Χαμὶτ Χὰν τοῦ Β'.

   Ἂς τὸν δοξολογήσωμεν μὲ ἀγαθὰς καρδίας
τὸν ὕψιστον Παντάνακτα μὲ ὕμνους καὶ λατρείας

   Ηὐδόκησεν αἱ μηχαναὶ ἵνα καταργηθῶσι
καὶ τῆς πατρίδος μας μακρὰν αὗται νὰ μεταβῶσι

   Ἔμενον ἀνενόχλητοι κ' ἐλεύθερ' ἐργασίας
τῶν θαλασσῶν καὶ τῶν μερῶν τοῦ κράτους τῆς Τουρκίας

   Εἰς τὴν τοῦ Ἄνακτος Σουλτὰν Ἀβδοὺλ Χαμὶτ, καρδίαν
εἰς ὃν καὶ ἐπευχόμεθα πάντες μακροζωΐαν

   Ἐνέπνευσεν ὁ ὕψιστος ἵνα τὰς καταργήσῃ
καὶ τὰς δολοφονίας των αἰσχρῶς νὰ τιμωρήσῃ

   Καὶ ἐξέδωκε διάταγμα ἐν τῇ χρονολογίᾳ
Χίλια ἐννεακόσια κατὰ τὸ ἔτος τρία

   Νὰ μὴ ὑπάρχουν μηχαναὶ στὸ κράτος τῆς Τουρκίας
αἵτινες φυγαδεύουσι μέχρι τῆς Ἱσπανίας

   Εὐξόμεθα καὶ τῷ Θεῷ ἵνα μακροζωΐαν
τῷ μεγατίμῳ Φλέγερ μας χαρίσῃ καὶ ὑγείαν

   Καὶ ὅλοι διαδοχικῶς πρέπει νὰ τὸν τιμῶμεν
νὰ τὸν ὑποληπτόμεθα νὰ τὸν εὐγνωμονῶμεν

   Ἀκαταπαύστως προσπαθεῖ ποτὲ δὲν ἡσυχάζει
ὁ τῶν ἀνθρώπων ἄωρος θάνατος τὸν βιάζει

   Καθῆκον ἐθεώρησε τὸν Ἅδην νὰ κλειδώσῃ
τὸν Αἰακὸν καὶ Μίνωα νὰ ἀποζημιώσῃ

   Διότι δέχονται ψυχὰς ἀδικοφονευμένων

ἐκ τῆς βδελυρομηχανῆς κακῶς ξεψυχουμένων

Καὶ ὡς ἱεραπόστολος ἔνθεν κακεῖθεν τρέχει
τὰ σπλάγχνα ἐκκεντώμενος τὸ ἔλεος παρέχει

Εἰς τὰς Ἀθήνας ἔτρεξε κ' ἐκεῖ νὰ ἐνεργήσῃ
στὴν καταδίωξιν αὐτῶν τοὺς Ἕλληνας νὰ πείσῃ

Καὶ σὺν Θεῶ ἐλπίζωμεν ὅπως τὸ κατορθώσῃ
καὶ νέας περιμένομεν εἰδήσεις νὰ μᾶς δώσῃ

Οὗτος διὰ τὰς μηχανὰς γενναίως ἠγωνίσθη
καὶ παρὰ τῶν νησιωτῶν ἀξίως εὐφημίσθη

Αὐτὰς μὲν ἐταπείνωσε τοὺς δὲ σεμνυνομένους
πλοιάρχους των ἀπέδειξε τώρα κατησχυμμένους

Ἐκ τούτων ὅμως μερικοὶ δραστήριοι φανέντες
καὶ ἐκ τῆς ὀξυνοίας των καλῶς ὠφεληθέντες

Δύνανται ὅ,τι βουληθοῦν διὰ νὰ κατωρθώσουν
καὶ τὴν πληγὴν τῶν μηχανῶν εὐκόλως νὰ οὐλώσουν

Καὶ ὀβολοῦ οὐ χρήζουσιν αἱ μηχαναὶ εἰς τούτους
διὸ καὶ βραβευσόμεθα ἁρμόζει τοὺς τοιούτους

ΤΕΛΟΣ ΤΟΥ Α΄ ΜΕΡΟΥΣ

ΧΕΙΜΕΡΙΝΟΣ ΟΝΕΙΡΟΣ
ΜΕΡΟΣ Β
ΠΡΟΛΟΓΟΣ

Διασπαρεὶς λόγος κατὰ τὸ 1883 ἔτος, ὅτι παρὰ τῆς Ὀθωμα-νικῆς Κυβερνήσεως, ἐξῆλθε διάταγμα δι' οὗ ἀπαγορεύεται τὸ Σκαφανδρικὸν ἐπιτήδευμα, οἱ κάτοχοι καὶ οἱ ξεκινηταὶ τούτων, πρὸς ἀποφυγὴν τοῦ ἐμποδίου τῆς ἐργασίας κατόρθωσαν διὰ δωροδοκιῶν νὰ φυλαχθῇ τοῦτο μυστικῶς.

Οἱ δυστυχεῖς δύται κοπιῶντες πολὺ καὶ μοχθῶντες καὶ κατὰ τῶν τρικυμιῶν καὶ παλιρροιῶν (ρευμάτων) παλαίοντες ἀπετύγ-χανον ἕνεκα τῶν μηχανῶν, αἵτινες μέχρι σήμερον ὑπάρχουσι καταστρεπτικὰ ὄργανα τοῦ εἴδους τούτου ἀνεθεμάτιζον τὴν ἡ-μαρμένην ἀποδίδοντες εἰς αὐτὴν τὸ αἴτιον καθότι ἐπροίκισεν αὐτοὺς διὰ τοῦ ἐπιτηδεύματος τούτου, νὰ δοκιμάζωσι καθ' ἑκάσ-την κινδύνους ζωῆς δι' αὐτὸν καὶ μόνον τὸν ἐπιούσιον ἄρτον·

Καὶ ἐνταῦθα ἵνα οὐσιωδεστέραν τὴν διήγησιν σχηματίσω παριστάνω ὡς ἔμψυχον ὑποκείμενον τὸ ἴδιον πλοῖον, ἐκ τοῦ πάλαι παρὰ τῶν προγόνων μας "σκάφην" ὀνομασθεῖσαν, ἥτις καὶ βλέπουσα καθ' ἑκάστην τὰς δυσκολίας αὐτῶν, ἀρχίζει νὰ τοὺς παρηγορῇ κατὰ τὸν ἀκόλουθον τρόπον.

ΕΝ ΕΤΕΙ ΧΙΛΙΟΣΤΩ ΟΚΤΑΚΟΣΙΩΣΤΩ ΟΓΔΟΗΚΟΣΤΩ ΤΡΙΤΩ

ΔΙΑΛΟΓΟΣ ΔΥΤΩΝ ΚΑΙ ΣΚΑΦΗΣ

Η ΣΚΑΦΗ ΠΡΟΣ ΤΟΥΣ ΔΥΤΑΣ

Τί ἔχετε ὦ ἄνθρωποι τίς ἡ κατήφειά σας
κ᾿ ὡς ἀναβλύζουσαι πηγαὶ τρέχουν τὰ δάκρυά σας;

Τίς θλίψις ἐκυρίευσε λέγω τὸ λογικόν σας
κ᾿ εἰς σκυθρωπότητα πολλὴν βλέπω τὸ πρόσωπόν σας;

Γνωρίζω τὴν αἰτίαν σας πλὴν πόθεν νὰ ἀρχίσω
τί ὁμιλίαν νὰ σᾶς πῶ νὰ σᾶς παρηγορήσω;

Βλέπω ὅτι κατήντησεν ἀνίατον τὸ πάθος
καὶ δὲν χωροῦν τὰ βότανα εἰς τῆς πληγῆς τὸ βάθος

Ἡ τύχη σᾶς κατέτρεξεν ὅλους τοὺς σπογγαράδες
καὶ ἔγιναν μηχανικοὶ πολλοὶ πατσαβουράδες

ΟΙ ΔΥΤΑΙ

Τίς σ᾿ οὔδωσε τὸ λογικὸν διὰ νὰ ὁμιλήσῃς
ἄψυχον πρᾶγμα καὶ κωφὸν νὰ μᾶς παρηγορήσῃς;

Εἰς σὲ καὶ τὰ φορέματα εἰς σὲ καὶ τὰ μαρκοῦτσα
πάνω στὴν πλώρην σου πατᾷ ἡ προὔντζενη παποῦτσα

Μᾶς διαπραγματεύεσαι τώρα καὶ ἐρωτᾷς μας
καὶ γίνεσαι συμμέτοχος καὶ σὺ τῆς συμφορᾶς μας;

Η ΣΚΑΦΗ

Καθὼς μὲ λέγετ᾿ ἄψυχον πῶς νὰ τοὺς ἐρωτήσω
ἀφοῦ μοῦ βάλλουν μηχανὴν πῶς νὰ τῶν ὁμιλήσω

Ἄψυχος εἶμαι κι᾿ ἄλαλος πλὴν ἐκ θεοῦ προνοίας
κ᾿ ἐμὲ μὲ κατεσκεύασεν στὸν κάμπον ὁ Ἡλίας

Ἀλλ᾿ ὁ Θεός μου ἔδωκεν εὐχὴν καὶ εὐλογίαν
νὰ εἶμαι πάντοτε μὲ σᾶς στὴν σπογγοαλιείαν

Τί κέρδος ἔχω ἀπ᾿ αὐτούς; Δὲν ὑποφέρω πλέον
διότι καὶ τὴν πλώρην μου τὴν κάμνουν ἀναγκαῖον

Μέσα μὲ κάμνουν νὰ βρωμῶ ἀπέξω μὲ στολίζουν
εἰς τὰς ἀτιμομηχανὰς πολὺ μὲ βασανίζουν

Τὰ δάκρυά μου τρέχουσι τὸ στῆθός μου τρυποῦσι
τὰ μέσα μ᾿ ἀναβράζουσι καὶ σπυνθηροβολοῦσι

Διότι τότε ἔβλεπον νέους ἀξιοτάτους
τεχνίτας νὰ μὲ διοικοῦν στὸν νοῦν ἐμπειροτάτους

Νὰ συχωθοῦν ἀπ᾿ τὴν αὐγὴν ν᾿ ἁπλώσουν τὰ πανιά μου
σὰν πάπια εἰς τὴν θάλασσαν νὰ σύρνω τὴν κοιλιάν μου

Καὶ μὲ ποικίλα χρώματα ἤμην χρωματισμένη
καὶ ἐφαινόμην ἀληθῶς ὡς νύμφη στολισμένη

Τώρα μοῦ βάλλουν μηχανὴν καὶ φθείρουν τὴν ζωήν μου
οὔτε νὰ πάρω δὲν μπορῶ καὶ τὴν ἀναπνοήν μου

Ἂν καὶ αὐτοὶ μὲ χρώματα τὴν ὄψιν μου στολίζουν
φορτία δὲ δυσβάστακτα τὸ σῶμα μου γεμίζουν

Ἀντὶ ἑπτὰ ψυχῶν τροφὰς εἴκοσι μοῦ σηκώνουν
καὶ μ' ἔπιπλα διάφορα τὴν πλώρην μου φορτώνουν

Στὸ στῆθος μου μοὶ βάλλουσιν ἄξονα μὲ ταῖς ρόδαις
καὶ γίνομαι ἐλεηνὸν θέαμα καὶ φρικῶδες

Κόπτεται καὶ ὁ δρόμος μου φεύγει κ' ἡ δύναμίς μου
καὶ ὑποφέρω βάσανα στὸ τέλος τῆς ζωῆς μου

Καὶ ὅταν θὰ ἐργάζονται ἀντὶ νὰ ἐκδυθῶσι
φορέματ' ἀδιάβροχα πρέπει νὰ ἐνδυθῶσιν

Ἓν φόρεμα ὁλόκληρον ὡς σχῆμα τοῦ ἀνθρώπου
ἀδιαπέραστον νεροῦ κ' ἐπιτηδείου τρόπου

Εἰς τὴν καρέκλαν καθιστὸν στὴν πλώρην τὸν ἐνδύουν
τὸ σῶμα του 'τὸ φόρεμα μὲ βίδες περικλείουν

Μολύβια εἰς τοὺς ὤμους του παπούτσια βαρέα
στὴν κεφαλήν του βάλλουσι τὴν περικεφαλαίαν

Κλίμαξ τις στὸν πανόσταζον εὑρίσκεται δεμένη
καὶ μέσα εἰς τὴν θάλασσαν ὑπάρχει κρεμμασμένη

Ὡς μέσον βοηθητικὸν διὰ νὰ κατεβαίνη
διὰ τῆς κλίμακος αὐτῆς στὴν θάλασσαν ἐμβαίνη

Σὰν τὸν ἐνδύσουν τακτικῶς ἀμέσως τότ' ἀρχίζουν
δυὸ παλληκάρια δυνατὰ τὴν ρόδαν νὰ γυρίζουν

Καὶ δι' αὐτοῦ τοῦ ἄξωνος βιαίως στρεφομένου
διὰ σωλῆνος δὲ μακροῦ μαρκούτσου καλουμένου

Ἀέρα διαδίδουσι σ' ἐκεῖνον ποῦ ὁδεύει
καὶ κάμνει ὥραν ἀρκετὴν καὶ σπόγγους ἁλιεύει

Μηχανικοὺς ὠνόμασαν αὐτοὺς ποῦ κατεβάζουν
καὶ φαντασμὸν ἀνήκουστον ἐπάνω των βαστάζουν

Ὅταν πρωτοφορέσωσι τὴν περικεφαλαίαν
νομίζουν πῶς τοὺς ἔστεφαν κλάδον ἀπὸ ἐλαίαν

Μεγάλως δὲ φαντάζονται καὶ ὑψηλοφρονοῦσι
ἂν ἐξετάσῃς ἀκριβῶς πάνω των κατουροῦσι

Μὲ δύο πόδια ἔρχονται καλῶς σταυρισμένοι
μὲ τρία ὅμως φεύγουσι νερὰ χαλαρισμένοι

Πόδας κατασκευάζουσιν ἀπ' ἀργολιᾶς κλωνάρια
φαίνεται δὲν τῶν ρέσκουσι τὰ ἴδια τῶν ποδάρια

Αὐτὸ εἶνε τὸ κέρδος των καὶ ἡ διαφορά των
κι' ὅταν ποθάνουν ψυχικὸν δίδουν τὰ θαυτικά των

Μὲ σαλουβάργια περπατοῦν γελέκια βελουδένα
κι' ἔπειτα τὰ δημοπρατοῦν καὶ φεύγουν μαζωμένα

Ἀλλὰ καὶ διωρθώθησαν ὅλ' οἱ κλεπτοχοιράδες

καὶ κατεργάρηδες πολλοὶ καὶ πετεινορνιθάδες

Χάριν τῆς φαντασίας των ἔπαυσαν τῆς κλεψιαῖς των
ἐμετριάσασι πολὺ καὶ τῆς κατεργαριαῖς των
Ὄρνιθα δὲν ἐφαίνετο στὴν κοίτην νὰ κοιτάση
οὔτε ἀλέκτωρ νἀκουσθῇ τὴν νύκτα νὰ φωνάξῃ

Τώρα ὅμως εὑρήκασι καὶ ταῦτα ἡσυχίαν
τὰ κακομοιρογούρουνα χαίρουσιν εὐτυχίαν

Γρόσια πέντε τὴν ὀκᾶν τὸ κρέας των ζυγίζουν
ἐνίοτε καὶ τέσσαρα στοὺς δρόμους τὸ γυρίζουν

Ἐνῶ ἐπώλουν πρότερον ἕξη καὶ μὲ χατῆρι
διότι κατεστρέφοντο ὑπὸ κλεπτῶν οἱ χοῖροι

Τώρα φραγκοφορέσασιν ὑπάρχει καὶ καθένα
καὶ δὲν τὸ συλλογίζονται πῶς εἶνε ὅλα ξένα

Θέλουν καὶ τὰς συζύγους των νὰ λέγωσι κυρίας
τὰ λοῦσα ἐξακολουθοῦν καὶ τὰς πολυτελείας

Ἔπειτα σὰν χηρεύσουσι τραβοῦσι τὰ μαλλιά των
ξεχάνουν καὶ τὰ λοῦσα των καὶ πιάνουν τὰ παληά των

Καὶ μοιρολόγια θλιβερὰ ἀρχίζουν νὰ τεργιάζουν
καὶ τοὺς ἀκούοντας αὐτὰς κατάκαρδα τοὺς σφάζουν

Καὶ θλιβερῶς πρωΐ βραδὺ ἀκούονται νὰ κλαίουν
καὶ μέσα τὰ ἐντόσθια τῶν ἀκουόντων καίουν

ΜΟΙΡΟΛΟΓΙΑ ΧΗΡΕΥΟΥΣΩΝ

Ὅλα τὰ μάτια 'ναι στεγνὰ καὶ τὰ δικά μου τρέχουν
τὸ στῆθός μου κατατρυποῦν καὶ τὴν καρδιάν μου βρέχουν

Ποῦνε τὸ ζημπουλλάκι μου τὸ μαρτολούλουδό μου;
ἡ μηχανὴ μοῦ τῶφαγε καὶ δὲν τὸ βλέπω πκήον μου

Ὅλο γυρίζω καὶ θωρῶ στὴν πόρταν ν' ἀνεφάνῃς
νἀνοίξῃς τὴν κασέλλαν μας πουκάμισον νὰ βάλῃς

Κάτω στὸν Ἅδην βρίσκεσαι στοῦ χάρου τοὺς μπαξέδες
κ' ἐγὼ ρωτῶ ἂν σ' ἔδασι μέσα στοὺς καφενέδες

———————

Χαθῆκαν ὅμως καὶ πολλοὶ κ' ὡραῖα παλληκάρια
γεροὶ καὶ χειροδύναμοι ὡσὰν τὰ λεοντάρια

Ἐπαῖται καὶ ἀνίκανοι ἕταιροι καταντοῦσι
ἄθλιοι καὶ ἐλεηνοὶ στοὺς δρόμους περπατοῦσι

Εἶναι δὲ μόνοι εὐτυχεῖς ἐκεῖνοι ποῦ ποθαίνουν
διότι ἄλλα βάσανα πλέον δὲν ὑποφέρουν

Μάλιστα εὐτυχέστατοι εἰς πόλι ἂν τοὺς 'θάψουν
καὶ τὴν ἀκολουθίαν των ἐν τάξει ἂν περάσουν

Πολλοὶ δὲ μέσ' στὸ σκάφος μου ἐὰν καὶ τελειώσουν
εἶνε κ' ἐκεῖνοι εὐτυχεῖς εἰς χῶμα ἂν τοὺς χώσουν

Πολλῶν ὅμως τὰ πτώματα πέτραι ξηραὶ καλύπτουν
καὶ μερικοὺς στὴν θάλασσαν μὴ θέλοντες τοὺς ρίπτουν

Τώρα ὅμως θὰ παύσωσι καθὼς τὸ λέγουν ὅλοι

διότ᾽ ἦλθε διάταγμα πὸ μέσα πὸ τὴν Πόλιν

Τὸν μῆνα τὸν Νοέμβριον ἐξάπαντος θὰ παύσουν
τοὺς προύντζους καὶ μολύβια των εἰς τὴν φωτιὰν θὰ καύσουν

Χαρῆτε τόρα καὶ ἐσεῖς καὶ μὴ λυπεῖσθε πλέον
βάλτε κρασάκι σφίξατε πῆτε ὑπὲρ τὸ δέον

Διασκεδάσατε καλὰ χάριν ἐλευθερίας
διότι εἶνε βέβαιον ἄνευ ἀμφιβολίας

ΟΙ ΔΥΤΑΙ ΠΡΟΣ ΤΗΝ ΣΚΑΦΗΝ

Σκαφάκι μ᾽ ἀνθρωπόλαλο ᾽μωρφοζωγραφισμένον
ἀπ᾽ τὸ Γιανιὸ τοῦ Ζαχαριᾶ καλοβιαρισμένον

Ποῦ ἔμαθες τὴν εἴδησιν τὴν ἔντερπνον κ᾽ ὡραίαν
καὶ ὁμιλεῖς σὰν ν᾽ ἄρχεσαι τώρ᾽ ἀπ᾽ τὸν Βασιλέα ;

Ἀν εἶνε βέβαιον αὐτὸ αἱ μηχαναὶ νὰ παύσουν
μ᾽ ἀσῆμι καὶ μὲ μάλαμα θὰ γίνουν τὰ καρφιά σου

Τὰ δὲ πανιὰ μεταξωτὰ καὶ τὰ σχοινιὰ ᾽πὸ σῦρμα
νὰ μὴ σοῦ βάλουν μηχανὴν κ᾽ εἶνε μεγάλον κρῖμα

Σημαίαν στὴν μειζάναν σου σηνιάλον στὸ πινόν σου
νὰ λησμονήσῃς στὸ ἐξῆς ὦ Σκάφη τὸν καϊμόν σου

Χωροποιὰς ἐπιγραφὰς θὰ φέρωσιν ἐπάνω
" Θεέ μου πολυχρόνιον ποίησον τὸν Σουλτᾶνον "

Στὸν Ἀἰνὲν θὰ γράψωμεν ὄνομα Ἀφροδίτη
ὁρῶσα τὰς ἐπιγραφὰς ἡ μηχανὴ νὰ φρίττῃ

ΣΚΑΦΗ

Ἀς παύσωσιν αἱ ἄθλιαι καὶ ἔξοδα δὲν θέλω
νὰ μὴ μοῦ φέρουν λείψανα στὸν ἄδην νὰ τὰ στέλλω

Ἀς μὴ γρικῶ γκουμαχισμοὺς φωνὰς καὶ κλάμματά των
καὶ νὰ τῶν φεύγουν πάνω των τὰ κατουρήματάτων

Ἀς μὴ τὴν κάμνουν νὰ βρωμᾷ τὴν πλώρην μ᾽ ἀπὸ κάτω
μὲ τοὺς καμφούρους καὶ λοιπὰ ποῦ τρίβουν τὰ κορμιά των

Καὶ δήμιοι οἱ πλοίαρχοι οἱ ἴδιοι καταντῶσι
διότ᾽ εἰς ἔκτακτα νερὰ τοὺς φέρουν καὶ βουττῶσι

Ἀλλὰ τὰ διατάγματα εὑρίσκονται φθασμένα
στὴν Σύμην ἀπ᾽ τὸν Μάρτιον καὶ τᾶχουν φυλαγμένα

Ἐκρύβησαν δὲ μυστικῶς διὰ νὰ ξεκινήσουν
διὰ νὰ μὴ ἐμποδισθοῦν καὶ φέτος νὰ βουτήσουν

Πλὴν τὸ ἐμοιρισθήκασι πεντέξη σπογγαράδες
καὶ ἐλογομαχήσασι μὲ τοὺς ξεκινητάδες

Καὶ αἱ γυναῖκες τοῦ χωριοῦ μὲ ξύλα ὁπλισμέναι
ἦλθον εἰς τὸν Αἰγιαλὸν ὡσὰν δαιμονισμέναι

Εἰς τὸ χονάκι ἔτρεξαν στὴν Καϊμακαμίαν
καὶ εἰς τὴν σκάλαν ἔς-εχον νὰ μάθουν τὴν αἰτίαν

Βενιαμὶν καὶ Κατριὸν καὶ μερικοὺς ἐμπόρους
τοὺς ἐπεριωρίσασιν εἰς τὸ χονάκι ὅλους

Νερὸ δὲν τοὺς ἀφίνασι νὰ βγοῦν διὰ νὰ πιοῦσι
ἂν πρῶτα τὸ διάταγμα δὲν φέρουν νὰ τὸ δοῦσι
Μὲ βίαν καὶ ὑπομονὴν ἐστέχοντο νὰ λύσουν
τὰ μυστικῶς κρυπτόμενα νὰ τὰ ἀνακαλύψουν
Ὁ δὲ Καϊμακάμβεης διὰ νὰ ἡσυχάσουν
ὑπόσχεσιν τοὺς ἔδωκεν αἱ μηχαναὶ νὰ παύσουν
Αἱ δὲ γυναῖκες ἔφυγον καὶ ἔτι περιμένουν
αἱ μηχαναὶ νὰ παύσωσι μεγάλως ἐπιμένουν

ΣΥΜΠΩΜΑΤΑ ΤΟΥ ΥΠΟ ΤΩΝ ΔΥΤΩΝ ΣΠΟΓΓΟΑΛΙΕΥΤΙΚΟΥ ΕΠΙΤΗΔΕΥΜΑΤΟΣ ΚΑΙ ΤΙΝΙ ΤΡΟΠΩι ΕΡΓΑΖΟΝΤΑΙ.

Ὑπάρχουν ἄνθρωποι πολλοὶ οἵτινες ἀποροῦσιν
εἰς τὸν πυθμένα τοῦ βυθοῦ οἱ δύται πῶς βυθοῦσι
Διὰ νὰ μάθουν ἐρωτοῦν κ' ἔχουν ἐπιθυμίαν
οἱ δύται πῶς ἐργάζονται εἰς τὴν σπογγαλιείαν
Πρῶτον θ' ἀποφασίσωσι νὰ ναυτολογηθῶσι
καὶ ἄνδρες δέον ἱκανοὶ πέντε νὰ ἐκλεχθῶσι
Οἱ πέντε θὰ ἐκλέξωσιν ἀκόμη ἄλλους δύο
ὅλον τὸ πλήρωμα ἑπτὰ ἔσονται εἰς τὸ πλοῖον
Ἀπὸ σχοινιὰ καὶ τρόφιμα θὰ ἐφοδιασθῶσι
κ' ἀναχωροῦν παρὰ θεοῦ ἔνθα θὰ φωτισθῶσι
Πλεύσαντες δὲ καὶ σὺν θεῷ ἀφοῦ εὐοδοθῶσι
στὸ μέρος ὃ ἐνέκριναν διὰ νὰ ἐργασθῶσι
Τότε θὰ ἐτοιμάσωσι τὰ σπογγοαλιεῖα
ὅλα τὰ χρησιμεύοντα κοινῶς ὡς ἐργαλεῖα
Οἱ πάλαι τῶν προγόνων μας διὰ νὰ δυνηθῶσι
στὰ τῆς θαλάσσης κύματα καὶ βύθη νὰ βυθῶσι
Πέτραν λευκὴν ὑπόμακρον ἐπὶ λεπτοῦ σχοινίου
ἐφεῦρον ἵνα δένωσι πρὸς χρῆσιν ἐργαλείου
Ταύτην 'Καμπανελλόπετραν' τὴν σήμερον καλοῦσι
δι' ἧς οἱ δύται δύνανται στὰ βύθη νὰ βυθοῦσι
Πάνω σαὐτὴν θὰ κρεμασθῇ ὁπόταν θὰ βουτήσῃ
καὶ πηδαλιουχούμενος φθάνει ὅπου θελήσει
Ἀφοῦ θὰ κάμουν ἀκριβῶς τὴν προετοιμασίαν
καὶ εἶνε πλέον ἕτοιμοι διὰ τὴν ἐργασίαν
Ξυπνῶσιν ἀπὸ τὸ πρωὶ καὶ τὰς αὐτῶν στρωσίας
ἀφοῦ τοποθετήσωσι στοῦ πλοίου τὰς γωνίας
Τὸ πρόσωπόν των νίπτουσι καὶ κάμνουν τὸν σταυρόν των
κ' ἐπικαλοῦνται τὸν θεὸν τὸν μόνον βοηθὸν των
Ὅστις τὰ πάθη τῶν πληγῶν ἀμέσως θεραπεύει
καὶ ἀπὸ πάντα κίνδυνον καθένα προστατεύει
Μετὰ τὴν ἐπικάλεσιν στὴν πρύμνην θὰ καθίσουν
λίγον ψωμὶ εἰς τὸν καφὲ θὰ βάλουν νὰ μασήσουν

Κ' ἔπειτα θὰ σαλπάρωσι νὰ κάμουν τὰ πανιά των
διὰ νὰ ἀρμενίσουσι νὰ πάγουν στὴν δουλιά των

Μέρος πετρῶδες θὰ εὑροῦν κ' ἐκεῖ θ' ἀποφασίσουν
τὸ σίδερον νὰ ρίψωσι διὰ νὰ κολυμβήσουν

Ἀφοῦ πιάσῃ τὸ σίδερον ἐπάνω εἰς τὴν πέτραν
χρηάζονται οἱ ἄνθρωποι μὲ φρένας καὶ μὲ νέφρα

Ἀφοῦ θ' ἀποφασίσωσι διὰ νὰ ἐκδυθῶσι
πάλιν τὸν ὕψιστον Θεὸν θὰ ἐπικαλεσθῶσι

Θεὲ ὁ πανταγοῦ παρὼν καὶ ὢν εἰς πάντα τόπον
σῶζε καὶ διαφύλαττε τὸ γένος τῶν ἀνθρώπων

Φρούρει καὶ περισκέπαζε τὸ πλᾶσμα τῶν χειρῶν σου
νὰ προσκυνῶμεν πάντοτε τὸ ὑποπόδιόν σου

Καὶ ἔπειτα θὰ ἐκλιθῇ τὴν πέτραν του θὰ πιάσῃ
ἀφοῦ στὸ στῆθος πρότερον τὸν σάκκον του κρεμάσῃ

Ὁ σάκκος εἶνε δυνατὸς ἐκ μύτου πεπλεγμένος
καὶ εἰς στεφάνι σιδηροῦν ἢ ξύλινον ραμμένος

Εἰς τὸν λαιμὸν του τὸν κρεμᾷ τὸν δίνει κι' εἰς τὴν μέση
στοὺς ἐκριζομένους του καρποὺς νὰ διὰ χρησιμεύσῃ

Σπόγγους τσιμούχας καὶ φιλὰ σ' αὐτὸν τοποθετοῦσι
τοῦτον τὸν σάκκον σήμερον Ἀπόχην τὸν καλοῦσι

Τὴν εἰσπνοήν του ἀκριβῶς ἀφοῦ περιορίσῃ
τότε ὡς θαλασσόπτηνον στὸ ὕδωρ θὰ πηδήσῃ

Καὶ στερεῶς τὰ χέρια του ἔχων ἐστηριγμένα
μὲ τὴν χαμπανελλόπετραν φθάνει εἰς τὸν πυθμένα

Κουμβᾷ τὴν πέτραν στὸ πλευρὸ μὲ τὸ ζερβὸν του χέρι
καὶ ἐσκυμμένος ψηλαφᾷ σπόγγους δια νὰ εὑρῇ

Ἄν εὑρῃ μέρος κοπτερὸν τὴν πέτραν του θ' ἀφίσῃ
θὰ ξεριζώσ' ὅσους μπορεῖ τὸν σάκκον νὰ γεμίσῃ

Φύλακες δύο στέκονται στὴν κουπαστὴν τοῦ πλοίου
καὶ διοικοῦν τὸν ἄνθρωπον διὰ μακροῦ σχοινίου

Ἀφοῦ σωθεῖ ἡ εἰσπνοὴ τραβάει τὸ σχοινίον
καὶ ἐννοοῦν οἱ ἄνθρωποι ποῦ στέκονται στὸ πλοῖον

Ἀφοῦ νοιώσουν τὸ τράβιγμα πάνω τὸν ἀνεβάζουν
αὐτοὺς τοὺς δύο φύλακας Κουπάδες ὀνομάζουν

Ἐαν συμβῇ εἰς τὸν κουπᾶν ἀκούσιόν τι λάθος
θὰ ὑποφέρ' ὁ ἄνθρωπος στὸ τῆς θαλάσσης βάθος

Ἐὰν ὅμως τὸ λάθος του ὑπὲρ τὸ μέτρον γείνῃ
ὑγείαν καὶ χερετισμοὺς ὁ ἄνθρωπος τ' ἀφίνῃ

Ἔχουσιν ὅμως πάντοτε τὸν νοῦν στὴν κεφαλήν των
ὄρθιοι στέκονται κ' οἱ δυὸ μ' ὅλην τὴν προσοχήν των

Ἄγρια χόρτα ἀπαντοῦν ἅτινα ἐπιφέρουν
ζημίας στοὺς κολυμβητὰς καὶ πόνους ὑποφέρουν

Ἐπίσης πέτραι κεντρωταὶ αἵτινες τοὺς πληγώνουν

ἀλλὰ κάτω στὴν θάλασσαν τοὺς πόνους δὲν τοὺς νοιώνουν

Τοὺς πόνους τοὺς αἰσθάνονται ὅταν θὰ ξενερίσουν
ὅταν μὲ τὴν σινδῶνα των τὸ σῶμα θὰ σπογγίσουν

Πόνους αἰσθάνονται δρυμεῖς κτύπους ἀνυποφόρους
οἵτινες τοὺς διαπεροῦν εἰς τῆς καρδιᾶς τοὺς κλώνους

Ἐκ τούτων ὅσα βλάπτουσιν, ἔχει ἓν εἶδος ἄλλο
καὶ προξενεῖ στὸν ἄνθρωπον δυστύχημα μεγάλο

Βρώμην τὴν ὀνομάζουσι καὶ εἶνε ριζωμένη
εἰς μερικὰ σπογγάρια, στοὺς πάτους κολλημένη

Ἐὰν ἐκριζωθῇ γερή χωρὶς ποσῶς νὰ σπάσῃ
εἶνε ἀνιπόψιαστος ἀπὸ τοῦ νὰ τὸν βλάψῃ

Ἂν δυστυχῶς δὲ συντριβῇ κ' ἐπάνω του ἐγγίσῃ
καὶ μὲ ἐγχείρησιν κακήν, ἂν τὴν κακοφορμήσῃ

Ξανθὴ καὶ λιναρόσπορον ἀνάγκη νὰ ζητήσῃ
καὶ θεραπείαν δύσκολον, πάλιν θὰ ἀπαντήσῃ

Ξυράφια ναὔρῃ κοπτερά, ἐπίσημον νηστείαν
μὲ πόνους καὶ μὲ δάκρυα νὰ λάβῃ τὴν ὑγείαν

Θέλων εἰς τοὺς ἀκροατὰς δοῦναι πληροφορίας
τῆς τέχνης, ἃς ὑφίστανται οἱ δύται δισκολίας

Νὰ γράψω ἀναγκάζομαί τὰ δυστηχγήματά της
ἅτινα ὑποφέρουσιν εἰς τὰ προοίμιά της

Ὅταν θὰ κάμωσιν ἀρχὴν διὰ νὰ ἐκδιθῶσι
πρῶτον ἀπὸ τὸν ἥλιον πρέπει νὰ φυλαχθῶσι

Εἰς τὸν λεγόμενον "σεφτὲν" βουτιαῖς ὀλίγαις κάμνουν
ἕως ὅτου νὰ εὕρωσι σπόγγον νὰ τὸν ἐκβάλουν

Τὸν σπόγγον τὸν πρωτοφανῆ στὸ χέρι του τὸν ποιάνει
καὶ εἰς τὸ πλοῖον μὲ αὐτὸν Σταυροῦ σημεῖον κάμνει

Εἶνε καὶ τοῦτο ἔθιμον σταύρωμα ὀνομάζουν
καὶ τὴν σημαίαν στὸν ἱστὸν πάραυτα ἀνεβάζουν

Καὶ ἔπειτα θ' ἀρπάξουσι νὰ φάγουν καὶ νὰ πιοῦσι
καὶ καλορρίζικος σεφτὲς ὅλοι θὰ εὐχηθοῦσι

Τὰς ἐπιούσας πάσχουσι ἀπὸ ταλαιπορίας
καθ' ὅλον τὸ διάστημα αὐτῆς τῆς ἐργασίας

Τὴν ζέστην δὲν τὴν δέχονται ἀλλ' οὔτε καὶ τὸ κρύο
πάσχουσι δὲ οἱ δυστυχεῖς δεινῶς καὶ ἀπὸ τὰ δύο

Καίονται εἰς τὸν ἥλιον τρέμουν εἰς τὸν ἀέρα
καὶ ἀπὸ πονοκέφαλον πάσχουν κάθε ἡμέρα

Ἕνεκα δὲ τοῦ καύσωνος καὶ ἀπροφυλαξίας
ὅλον τὸ δέρμα καταντᾷ εἰς ἄκρας δυστυχίας

Φούσκας σηκώνει τὸ κορμὴ καὶ ἔπειτα θὰ σπάσουν
καὶ καταντοῦν ἀνίατοι ἂν δὲν τὰς προφυλάξουν

Πουκάμισον δὲν δέχονται ἐπάνω τους νὰ ἐγκίσῃ
ἀλλ' οὔτε καὶ τὴν ράχιν τους στὸ στρῶμα ν' ἀκουμβήσῃ

Μὲ τὸ πλευρὸν δὲν δέχεται ἀλλὰ μὲ τὴν κοιλίαν
ἔτσι εὑρίσκει ἄνεσιν κἄπως καὶ ἡσυχίαν

Τ᾽ αὐτιὰ των κινδυνεύουσιν ὁπόταν θὰ βυθῶσι
καὶ ὑποφέρουσι δεινῶς ἐνίοτε καὶ σπῶσι

Καὶ τότε δοκιμάζουσι νέας ταλαιπορίας
μεγάλα δυστυχήματα ἐπίσης κ᾽ ἀγρυπνίας

Μέσα δὲ βοηθητικὰ διὰ νὰ προφυλάξουν
τοὺς πόνους τῶν αὐτίων των μικρὸν νὰ ἡσυχάσουν

Τὴν μύτην ἐπενόησαν ὅταν βουττοῦν νὰ πιάνουν
δυὸ-τρεῖς φορὰς καὶ τέσσαρας καὶ οὕτω κάτω φθάνουν

Πολλοὶ δὲ μὴ γνωρίζοντες τὴν μύτην τῶν νὰ πιάνουν
οἱ δυστυχεῖς τὸν γῦρον των στὰ μεσαχὰ τὸν κάμνουν

Αἵματα πτύουσι συχνὰ καί τινες δειλιοῦσι
ἕνεκα τούτου δὲ πολλοὶ τὴν τέχνην παραιτοῦσι

Ὅσον νὰ ξεμυξάσωσιν νὰ στρώσῃ ἡ δουλειά των
μεγάλως ὑποφέρουσι μὲ ὅλα τὰ σοστά των

Αὐτᾶναι τὰ συμπτώματα τῶν σπογγοαλιέων
ἡ τέχνη καὶ τὰ βάσανα καὶ πάθη τῶν Συμαίων

Ἀπὸ τὴν Σύμην φεύγουσι στὰ τέλη Ἀπριλίου
καὶ ἄλλοι ὑστερώτερα εἰς τὰς ἀρχὰς Μαΐου

Καὶ δυστυχίας τρομερὰς ὡς τέλη Σεπτεμβρίου
τὰς ὑποφέρουν σταθερῶς ὡς μάρτυρες Κυρίου

Ὦ! ἐρασμία μου πατρὶς Σύμη ἐξακουσμένη
μὲ γῆν ἀμπέλους καὶ νερὰ ἃς ἤσουν προικισμένη

Μὲ βράχους σὲ ἐπροίκισε πλὴν χαίρεις εὐτυχίαν
ὡς γέμουσα ἀνδρῶν καλῶν ἐχόντων τὴν παιδείαν

Ἄς εἶχες δένδρα κάρπιμα καὶ γῆν νὰ γεωργῶμεν
καὶ ἐλαιῶνας ἀρκετοὺς νὰ τοὺς καλλιεργῶμεν

Δὲν ἔμεινες ποτὲ κενὴ καὶ ἔρημος ἀνθρώπων
οἵτινες ξενιτεύωνται ἐπὶ ἀγρίων τόπων

Μία καμπανελλόπετρα εἶνε τὸ ἐργαλεῖον
καὶ μιὰν ἀπόχην ἕκαστος ὅσ᾽ εἶναι εἰς τὸ πλοῖον

Αὐτὴν τὴν τέχνην κάμνουσι καὶ γέροντες καὶ νέοι
αὐτὴν ἐκληρονόμησαν οἱ ἄνδρες οἱ Συμαῖοι

Χωράφια δὲν εὑρήκαμεν νὰ τὰ καλλιεργῶμεν
στὰ τῆς θαλάσσης κύματα καὶ βάθη θὰ βυθῶμεν

Στὴν θάλασσαν εὑρήκαμεν ἀμπέλους κι᾽ ἐλαιῶνας
αὐτὴ εἶναι ἡ τέχνη μας εἰς πάντας τοὺς αἰῶνας

ΤΕΛΟΣ

Τὸ παρὸν ἔργον συνταχθὲν περὶ

τὰ τέλη τοῦ ἔτους 1903 ὑπὸ τοῦ δειμνήστου πατρὸς ἡμῶν Μητροφάνους 1. Καλαφατᾶ, ἔμεινεν ἀνέκδοτον, ἔνεκεν αἰφνιδίου θανάτου τοῦ συντάκτου, ἐπισυμβάντα τὴν 9 Μαρτίου 1904

Ἤδη ὅτε οἱ υἱοὶ αὐτοῦ ἠνδρώθημεν, τὸ δὲ ὄνομα τῶν Δωδεκανήσων, ἔγεινε πασίγνωστον ἀνὰ τὴν ὑφήλιον, διὰ τὸν ὑπὲρ ἐλευθερίας ἀγῶνα των κατὰ τῶν Ἰταλῶν, ἐθεωρήσαμεν καθῆκον ἡμῶν, τὴν ἐκτύπωσιν τοῦ βιβλίου τούτου, καὶ διὰ τὸ κοινὸν ὅπερ δύναται νὰ λάβῃ γνῶσιν τῆς ζωῆς καὶ ἐθίμων τῶν νήσων μας, καὶ διὰ τὴν ψυχὴν τοῦ συντάκτου εἰς αἰώνιον μνημόσυνον.

Διατελοῦμεν μεθ᾽ ὑπολήψεως

Ἰωάννης, Γεώργιος, Νικήτας Μ. Καλαφατᾶ.

Ἐν Βοστώνῃ τῇ 7]20ῃ Ἰουνίου 1919.

EPILOGUE: *WINDFLOWER*

I saw a dream, or at least I hope I did. If I did, it means that dream is prophecy; it means one day I will see my grandfather. It means that many prayers will have been answered.

In dream I see my grandfather sailing the Timeless Seas. Only now and again does he put in for a small rest at some port city on the Shores of Eternity: Jerusalem, Alexandria, Byzantium, Troy itself. He is at the tiller of his swift *skaphos*, the *Windflower*; its White Wings of sail billow and urge the boat ever on. His way is lit by Eos, goddess of the dawn. In dream, the morning wind is sharp as a whetted knife; a rosy-fingered dawn lights the way.

Dead at thirty-eight, he remains forever young: his hair pitch-dark like that of my sons, John and Daniel. In his silhouette I see the famed cut of the Symiot: square shoulders, strong jaw, and face of grace sculpted by noble forebears. He looks like King Nereus. His poetic eyes are set on the razor-sharp horizon.

"When power corrupts, poetry cleanses," President Kennedy reminded us at the dedication of the Robert Frost Library at Amherst College. It was October of 1963, a month before he was lost to the generation that admired and loved him and wanted to be like him. His loss was utterly Greek: an Adonis who died too young; athlete and friend Hyacinthus inexplicably gone.

The poet and sailor Metrophanes, my grandfather, knew in his Greek bones—the bones that his wife Anastasia would one day wash in wine—that when power corrupts, poetry cleanses. It is a lesson the Greeks taught us all.

John Masefield, poet laureate of the sea, surely speaks of my grandfather as he is now; and as I pray, I will one day find him, if only dream is prophecy.

> He has gone . . .
> Among the radiant
> ever venturing on somewhere,
> with morning,
> as such spirits will.

Telos.

THE END.

Bibliography

Alexakis, Effy, and Leonard Janiszewski. 1998. *In Their Own Image: Greek Australians.* Alexandria, New South Wales: Hale and Iremonger.

Alexiou, Margaret. 1974. *The Ritual Lament in Greek Tradition.* Cambridge: Cambridge University Press.

Ballard, Robert D. 2001. "Black Sea Mysteries." *National Geographic* (May).

Beavan, Colin. 1997. "Underwater Daredevils." *The Atlantic Monthly* (May).

Benedict, Ruth. 1934. *Patterns of Culture.* Boston: Houghton Mifflin.

Bernard, H. Russell. 1966. "The Fisherman and His Wife." Article presented at the Third Mediterranean Social Anthropological Conference, Athens.

———. 1967. "Kalymnian Sponge Diving." *Journal of Human Biology* 39, no. 2 (May).

———. 1976. "Sponge Markets of Kalymnos," Reprint Series 9, no. 14. Reprinted from *Anthropologica, N.S.* 18, no. 1 (1976). Regional Research Institute: Morgantown, W.Va.

Bernard, Harvey R. 1968. "Kalymnos: Economic and Cultural Change on a Greek Sponge Fishing Island." Ph.D. diss. University of Illinois.

———. 1987. "Sponge Fishing and Technological Change in Greece." In H. R. Bernard and P. J. Pelto, eds., *Technology and Social Change.* Prospect Heights, Ill.: Waveland Press.

Bradford, Ernle. 1963. *The Companion Guide to the Greek Islands.* London: Collins.

British Naval Intelligence Division. 1943. *Dodecanese.* Geographical Handbook Series. B.R. 500.

Broumas, Olga. 1999. *Rave: Poems 1975–1999.* Port Townsend, Wash.: Copper Canyon Press.

Buxbaum, Edwin Clarence. 1980. *The Greek-American Group of Tarpon Springs, Florida.* New York: Arno Press.

Carras, Andrew. 1996. "Ebb Tide: The Transformation of Tarpon Springs." *Odyssey: The World of Greece* (November–December).

Casson, Lionel. 1991. *The Ancient Mariners: Seafarers and Sea Fighters of the Mediterranean.* Princeton: Princeton University Press.

Clift, Charmian, and George Johnston. 1955. *The Sponge Divers.* London: Collins.

Constantinides, Elizabeth. 1983. "Andreiomeni: The Female Warrior in Greek Folk Songs." *Journal of Modern Greek Studies* 1, no. 1.

Croutier, Alev Lytle. 1989. *Harem: The World behind the Veil.* New York: Abbeville Press.

Danforth, Loring M. 1982. *The Death Rituals of Rural Greece.* Princeton: Princeton University Press.

Dean, Love. 1983. "Sponging." *Oceans* (March–April).

Detorakis, Yannis S. 1996. *O Kataktitis tou Aperantou Galaziou* (The Conqueror of the Deep Blue). Athens: Toubis.

Dickinson, Joan Younger. 1958. *The Book of Pearls.* New York: Bonanza Books.

Doumanis, Nicholas. 1997. *Myth and Memory in the Mediterranean.* New York: St. Martin's Press.

———, and Nicholas G. Pappas. 1997. "Grand History in Small Places: Social Protest on Castellorizo (1934). *Journal of Modern Greek Studies* 15.

Dubisch, Jill. 1986. *Gender and Power in Rural Greece.* Princeton: Princeton University Press.

Durrell, Lawrence. 1953. *Reflections on a Marine Venus: A Companion to the Landscape of Rhodes.* London: Faber & Faber.

Egan, Demetra. "Greek Australians: An Introduction." At the website ⟨www.topend.com.au/~konv/gr4.html.⟩

Facaros, Dana. 1994. *Greece: The Dodecanese.* London: Cadogan Books.

Fagles, Robert, trans. 1996. *The Odyssey.* New York: Penguin Group, Penguin Putnam.

Farmakidis, Kostas, and Agapi Karakatsani. 1975. *Symi: A Guide.* Alexandra Macfarlane Dumas, trans. Athens: K. Michalis.

Flegel, Karl. 1910. "Note on the Twelve Islands of the Dodecanese or the Southern Sporades." Unpublished monograph (May).

Frantzis, George Th. 1962. *Strangers at Ithaca: The Story of the Spongers of Tarpon Springs.* St. Petersburg, Fla.: Great Outdoors Publishing Company.

Goodwin, Jason. 1998. *Lords of the Horizon: A History of the Ottoman Empire.* New York: Henry Holt.

Grenald, Bethany Leigh. 1998. "Women Divers of Japan." At the "Michigan Today" website: ⟨www.umich.edu/~newsinfo/ MT/98/Sum 98/mt1sm98.html⟩.

Hadzidakis, Kyriacos. 1982. "O Agonas gia tin Katargisi ton Skafandron kai o Karolos Flegel" ("The Fight to Ban the Skafandra and Karl Flegel"). *Kalymniaka Chronika.* Tomos C.

Hamilton, Edith. 1940. *Mythology.* New York, Scarborough, Ontario, and London: Mentor.

Harris, Jennie E. 1947. "Sponge Fishermen of Tarpon Springs." *National Geographic* (January).

Haslip, Joan. 1958. *The Sultan.* New York: Holt, Rinehart and Winston.

Herzfeld, Michael. 1985. *The Poetics of Manhood.* Princeton: Princeton University Press.

Hines, Norman E. 1936. *Medical History of Contraception.* New York: Shocken Books.

Kasperson, Roger. 1966. *The Dodecanese: Diversity and Unity in Island Poli-*

tics. Department of Geography Research Paper no. 108, University of Chicago.

Keeley, Edmund. 1999. *Inventing Paradise*. New York: Farrar, Straus and Giroux.

Kontos, Kostas. 1999. "O Spoggalieutikos Stolos tis Symis: Statiski ton en Energia Spoggalieutikon Ploion ton Eton 1858–1900" (The Sponge Fleet of Symi: Statistics on Working Sponge Boats in the Years 1858–1900). *I Symi* (April–June).

Kunz, George Frederick, and Hugh Charles Stevenson. 1908. *The Book of the Pearl: The History, Science, and Industry of the Queen of Gems*. New York: Century Company.

Kurlansky, Mark. 1997. *Cod*. New York: Penguin Books.

Kyriakopoulos, Victoria. 1998. "The Oyster Is Their World." *Odyssey: The World of Greece* (September–October).

Lambert, Craig. 1998. *Mind Over Water*. Boston: Houghton Mifflin.

Loizos, Peter. 1994. "A Broken Mirror: Masculine Sexuality in Greek Ethnography." In Andrea Cornwall and Nancy Lindisfarne, eds., *Dislocating Masculinity: Comparative Ethnographies*. London: Routledge.

Manus, Willard. 1980. "The Last Days of the Sponge Divers." *Quest/80* (September).

McCullough, David. 1972. *The Great Bridge*. New York: Avon Books.

Nova. "The Perfect Pearl." Broadcast transcript, no. 2520. PBS air date December 29, 1998.

O'Dell, Scott. 1984. *Alexandra*. Boston: Houghton Mifflin.

Parker, Torrance R. 1997. *20,000 Jobs under the Sea: A History of Diving and Underwater Engineering*. Palos Verdes Peninsula, Calif.: Sub-Sea Archives.

Philbrick, Nathaniel. 2000. *In the Heart of the Sea: The Tragedy of the Whaleship Essex*. New York: Viking Penguin.

Rawlings, Charles. 1932. "The Dance of the Bends." *The Saturday Evening Post* (October).

Rozee, Lou and Eileen. 1994. *Sponge Docks: Tarpon Springs Florida*. Tarpon Springs, Fla.: Boys and Girls Clubs of the Suncoast.

Seferis, George. 1967. *Collected Poems (1924–1955)*. Edmund Keeley and Philip Sherrard, trans. Princeton: Princeton University Press.

Stewart, Charles. 2001. "Dreams of Treasure as Unconscious Historicizations" (in Greek). In C. Hadjitaki-Kapsomenou, ed., *Greek Traditional Culture: Folklore and History*. Thessaloniki: Paratiritis.

Stoughton, Gertrude K. 1975. *Tarpon Springs, Florida: The Early Years*. Tarpon Springs, Fla.: Tarpon Springs Historical Society.

Sutton, David E. 1998. *Memories Cast in Stone: The Relevance of the Past in Everyday Life*. Oxford, N.Y.: Berg.

Taussig, Michael. 1980. *The Devil and Commodity Fetishism in South America*. Chapel Hill: University of North Carolina Press.

Theodorakis, Mikis, and Yannis Ritsos. 1974. *Lianotragouda ths Pikris Patridas* (18 Thin Little Songs of the Bitter Homeland). Album. Lyra Records.

Travis, William. 1970. *Bus Stop Symi*. London: Rapp & Whiting Ltd.

Trypanis, C.A. 1981. *Greek Poetry: From Homer to Seferis*. Chicago: University of Chicago Press.

Ward, Fred. 1985. "The Pearl," *National Geographic* (August).

Wren, Faith. 2000. *Bitter Sea: The Real Story of Greek Sponge Diving.* South Woodham Ferrers, Great Britain: Guardian Angel Press.

Zervos, Skevos Georges. 1919. *The Dodecanese: The History of the Dodecanese Through the Ages, Its Services to Mankind and Its Rights.* London: A. Page and Company.

Acknowledgments

"Nothing happens unless first the dream," Carl Sandburg wrote. So it is with this book.

Without first my grandfather's "Winter Dream," there would be no book. There would be no book without first my uncle John's living out his dream of coming to America and seeing to it that the poem was published here in Greek in 1919. There would be no book without Olga Broumas who "inspired me" in the most literal sense: she breathed life into me when she told me that my grandfather's poem was "deeply beautiful and a national treasure of Greece." In so doing she sent me on a remarkable odyssey that became a book. Most important, Olga gave my grandfather new life in English; hers was an act of resurrection. She dug up my grandfather's bones from the black earth and brought them into the light of a new day.

A brilliant rendering of a piece of literature from one language into another occurs when the piece of literature appears to have been written originally in the new language. By her great gift, the poet Olga Broumas attained that lofty standard with "Winter Dream." I am honored that we will be joined together forever by my grandfather's poem, another of the many gifts given me by a grandfather I never knew.

At Brandeis I owe thanks to many: first and foremost to President Jehuda Reinharz who graciously granted me a six-week sabbatical to travel to Greece; to my boss and dear friend of a quarter century, David Gould, who supported the project from the get-go; and to Maureen Fessenden, chief of Human Resources, who strongly supported my sabbatical though it fit no model. In the Office of Admissions I want to thank Pat Erba and Bobbi Jacob, national treasures of Brandeis, as well as Susan Simon, Sherri Geller, Nicholas Senecal, and all of the Admissions staff who now know more about sponges than they ever cared to know.

On my first day back from Greece in 1997, John Hose, executive assistant to the President, and liaison to the University Press of New England, decided that I ought to meet with representatives from the Press. Amid my collection of anecdotes he saw the book; for that I owe him profound thanks.

There would be no book without Christos Stergiou, Brandeis '99, the student who became my teacher, inhabitant of my heart, and member of my family. I have also come to love his sweet parents, Costas and Petroula. Christos read everything I wrote, hunting down errors in my Greek transliterations and inadvertent affronts to the Greeks; wherever they now exist, they are in spite of Christos's vigorous objections.

I want to thank Ellen T. Delaney, dear friend and counselor at Boston Latin Academy, who passed to me pearls she fetched from deep in the Holy Script and enduring support as I made my way through the writing of the book. From Holy Script Eleni once offered, "And the spirit will blow where it will." Phyllis Deutsch, my editor at the University Press of New England, knew that truth in an innermost place and allowed my spirit to blow across four continents and to the uttermost parts of the sea. I am deeply grateful for her confidence, counsel, firm directive, and rapier wit, dispensed with virtuosity and apt timing. Also at UPNE I wish to thank Philip Pochoda who said to me, as I undertook the project, "You are the lens." I never forgot the words. I also want to thank copy editor Carol Sheehan whose suggestions made *The Bellstone* a better book.

Among others who took risks were Cliff Hauptman, editor of the *Brandeis Review*, who first published this story as a too-long article. Cliff urged me to write the book and offered sage advice at sundry Waltham pubs even though my book had nothing to do with fly-fishing. I want to thank him, Michal Regunberg, Vice President of Public Affairs at Brandeis, as well as designers Chuck Dunham and Kim Williams and writer Steve Anable of the Publications Office.

I owe thanks, too, to Michael Howard, Managing Editor, and Greg Maniatis, Publisher, of the magazine *Odyssey: The World of Greece*, for publishing a variation of the *Brandeis Review* article under the title "100 Years of Solitude." I am grateful to the intelligent and beautiful actress Melina Kanakaredes whose face appeared on the cover of the issue that contained my article; many people read my article simply because Melina was on the cover.

There is a tribe of anthropologists (I love terms of venery) to whom I owe special thanks. In a category by himself is Russ Bernard at the University of Florida who went to sea with the Greek sponge divers of the Aegean and wrote so brilliantly about them. Physical courage is not an attribute that leaps to mind when you think of scholars, but it is absolutely true of Russ. Because of his daring and intelligence, his work will forever be the definitive study of the divers. Anthropologists Michael Herzfeld, David Sutton, Charles Stewart, and Bob Hunt were all generous in shining light on dark places. Other academics were also extremely helpful: the geographer Roger Kasperson; the historian Nick Doumanis; the Classicist Lenny Muellner; and the physicist Bob Lange. At the Brandeis University Libaries, Ralph Szymczak was always swift, kind, and accurate. Others who supplied vital support, counsel, or information were Linda Nathanson, Jim Spurrell, George Chryssis, Ari Michopolous, Steve Wagner, Clement Wagner, Ira Farber, Avigdor Levy, Joy Playter, Nancy Steinberg, George Fullerton, Steve Whitfield, Dan O'Connor, Sylvia and Allan Furber, and all of the children of my uncle John Kalafatas—my first cousins of grace and beauty: Nicholas Kalafatas and his wife Helen, Ann Larouche, Bessie Papas, Peter King, and Demetra Bowers. My uncle and aunt, John and Ellie Tsicouleas, also gave critical information and support.

Among those in Greece who were magnanimous with their aid were the second-ranking officer in the Greek government, Minister of State Miltiades Papaioannou; on Kalymnos, Eparchos Georgios Roussos, Mayor Dimitris Diakomichalis, Nikos Papazoulou, Harilaos Billiris, Dimitiris Roditis, Manolis Makrillos, Constantine Tsangaris, Theophiles and Catherine Klonaris, George and Soula Karaiskos, and at the Anagnostirion, John Patellis and Kyriacos Hadzidakis, the person I met who was most like the poet Metrophanes himself; on Symi, Antonios Angelides, Mayor Miltiadis Sarris, the writers Irene Voyatzi-Charalambi and Yannis Hatzifotis, Kostas Kontos, Eleni Farmakidou, Eleni Kritikou, Theodoros Kapsalakis, Dimitris Antonoglou, and cousins Michael Foreys and Nikitas A. Kalafatas; on Rhodes, dear cousin Nikitas M. Kalafatas and his father Michael N. Kalafatas of beloved memory.

Louisa Velenza and George Syrimis did early translations of major portions of "Winter Dream" that were of great aid to Olga Broumas as she did her rendering of the entirety into English.

In Florida I had wonderful support from Congressman Michael Bilirakis and in Tarpon Springs, from Kathleen Monahan, Director of the Cultural and Civic Services Office and her assistant Hanni Najar, former Mayor Anita Protos and her late husband George Protos, and Phyllis Kolianos, Curator and Historical Society Manager of the Tarpon Springs Area Historical Society.

I must extend special thanks to four remarkable men in Tarpon Springs that I call "My Princes of Tarpon, my Kings of the Gulf." These are men of striking character who had long careers as international sponge merchants. Like Nicholas Vouvalis in the Old World of Kalymnos and London, these four men were "sponge princes" in the New World of America and Tarpon Springs: Michael Cantonis, Steve Katzaras, George Billiris, and Denis Cantonis. Beyond being business leaders, all have led lives of service. In 1998, for example, Michael Cantonis was awarded the Ellis Island Medal of Honor for his community leadership and visionary philanthropy. The four began as my informants and became my friends; all are full of stories, full of wisdom, and important to the Greeks, full of life. George Billiris is of Kalymnian lineage, born in the United States; all of the others were born on Symi. They are a generation older than I, men in their seventies and eighties—men, I am not abashed to say, that I love. As I wrote of Michael Foreys of Symi, so is it true of my relationship to them: "One who learns from the old is like one who eats ripe grapes and drinks old wine."

In Proust's *Remembrance of Things Past* a bite of a madeleine summons a sea of memory. These four men of Dodecanese origin love sponges: the touch of sponges, the feel of sponges, the fetching of sponges, the smell of the sea in sponges, the aroma of Sponge Rooms filled to the rafters with sponges, the scent in their nostrils and on their clothes, the scent of Mother Sea all around them, the scent of origin. That scent has borne them back ceaselessly into their Hellenic past—across the seaways, back beyond Byzantium, back to the forty-seven ships the Dodecanese sent to Troy. It has brought them to Eleni, to Helen, to the face that launched a thousand ships. It has brought them face-to-face with Sweet Mother Greece.

Walter Jaeger wrote, "We must always return to Greece because it fulfills some need of our own life. . . . Other nations made gods, kings, spirits. The Greeks alone made men." In the end we all return to Greece, and easily so, because, as Shelley said in his *Preface to Hellas* in 1821: "We are all Greek."

In the film "The Cider-House Rules," Michael Caine's character bids goodnight to the sweet children of his orphan school in Maine by saying, as he shuts off the light, "Good night, you princes of Maine, you kings of New England." Knowing that these four men—so like my father—are in the afterglow of well-led lives, my impulse is to say, "Good night, you Princes of Tarpon, you Kings of the Gulf." In writing those lines I realize too well that it is my way also of saying goodnight to my father, the beautiful little Greek boy of the Eleni Zannis Orphan School in Piraeus: "*Eleni loves you, Dad. Your mother loves you. And I do too.*"

For two years my wife Joan waved cheerily at The Man in the Window. Up early and writing while it was still dark, I could be seen backlit in my upstairs office as downstairs she threw back the drapes at first light. With kindness and care she read the whole manuscript, trying perseveringly to make it clearer. Where the book fails to be clear, it is because I failed to follow her advice.

I have never doubted that I was lucky to have been born in the United States, for the opportunities it afforded me, and to have had the loving parents that I did. Georgia and Nikitas Kalafatas, my parents, cheered me on at every turn, as did my brother Metro and my sister Roberta. Sadly, my brother Metro died as I was drawing the book to a close. Several months before his death, I read to him "The Purloined Letter," the letter I imagined our grandmother Anastasia wrote to him as a child on the night she died. I shall always thank God for allowing me to read that letter to my brother, my hero, before calling him too to the Eternal Shore. In further sadness, my sister Roberta, the Girl with the Pearl Earring, she who loved me always and unconditionally, died when the book was in production. I shall look forward to seeing Metro and Roberta again at some distant port-of-call. As we so often did as children, we shall once again sing rounds of

> Row, row, row your boat
> Gently down the stream.
> Merrily, merrily, merrily, merrily,
> Life is but a Dream.

I owe deepest thanks to my sons John and Dan, lights in my life from the instant I saw them, who offered unceasing love, support, and counsel, as did beautiful Joan, Dan's wife Hadley Mullin, and Marybeth Savicki.

And I wish to thank all of my informants in the Dodecanese and in Tarpon Springs, Florida. I am blessed to have the gifts of their stories. "Books are the carriers of civilization," I once read. The story of the Greek divers of the Aegean and of my grandfather has been carried forward because of these men and women.

Last, I wish to thank The Dead for their help, those so loved now gone and